DEPRESSION AND MANIA

From Neurobiology to Treatment

Advances in Biochemical Psychopharmacology
Volume 49

Advances in Biochemical Psychopharmacology

Series Editors

E. Costa, M.D.

Professor of Pharmacology,
Center for Neuropharmacology
Nathan S. Kline Institute for Psychiatric Research
140 Old Orangeburg Road
Orangeburg, NY 10962

Paul Greengard, Ph.D.

Professor of Molecular and Cellular Neuroscience
The Rockefeller University
1230 York Avenue
New York, NY 10021

DEPRESSION AND MANIA

From Neurobiology to Treatment

Advances in Biochemical Psychopharmacology

Volume 49

Volume Editors

Gian Luigi Gessa, M.D.
"Bernard B. Brodie" Department of Neuroscience
University of Cagliari
Cagliari, Italy

Walter Fratta, Ph.D.
"Bernard B. Brodie" Department of Neuroscience
University of Cagliari
Cagliari, Italy

Luca Pani, M.D.
"Bernard B. Brodie" Department of Neuroscience and
Center for Neuropharmacology
University of Cagliari
Cagliari, Italy

Gino Serra, M.D.
Institute of Biochemistry
School of Pharmacy
University of Sassari
Sassari, Italy

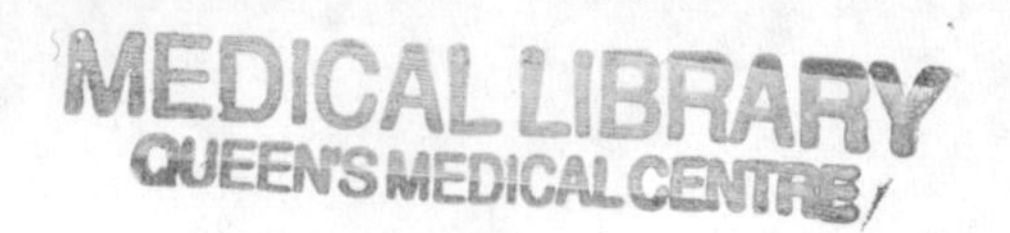

Lippincott–Raven Publishers, 227 East Washington Square, Philadelphia, Pennsylvania 19106

Made in the United States of America

ISBN: 0-7817-0307-7

Papers have been used as camera-ready copy as submitted by the authors. The views expressed are the responsibility of the authors. Great care has been taken to maintain the accuracy of the information contained in the volume. However, neither Lippincott–Raven Publishers nor the editors can be held responsible for errors or for any consequences arising from the use of information contained herein.

The use in this book of particular designations of countries or territories does not imply any judgment by the publisher or editors as to the legal status of such countries or territories, of their authorities or institutions, or of the delimitation of their boundaries.

Some of the names of products referred to in this book may be registered trademarks or proprietary names, although specific reference to this fact may not be made; however, the use of a name without designation is not to be construed as a representation by the publisher or editors that it is in the public domain. In addition, the mention of specific companies or of their products or proprietary names does not imply any endorsement or recommendation on the part of the publisher or editors.

Authors were themselves responsible for obtaining the necessary permission to reproduce copyright materials from other sources. With respect to the publisher's copyright, material appearing in this book prepared by individuals as part of their official duties as government employees is only covered by this copyright to the extent permitted by the appropriate national regulations.

9 8 7 6 5 4 3 2

This is a facsimile of the original edition. All material contained in the original is included in this edition.

Contents

Contributors

G. Agam
Division of Psychiatry
Beersheva Mental Health Center
Ben-Gurion University of the Negev
P.O. Box 4600
Beersheva 84105, Israel

Hagop S. Akiskal
Psychiatry Service (116A)
University of California San Diego School of Medicine
9500 Gilman Drive
San Diego, CA 92093-0603

Robert H. Belmaker
Division of Psychiatry
Beersheva Mental Health Center
Ben-Gurion University of the Negev
P.O. Box 4600
Beersheva 84105, Israel

J. Benjamin
Division of Psychiatry
Beersheva Mental Health Center
Ben-Gurion University of the Negev
P.O. Box 4600
Beersheva 84105, Israel

Y. Bersudsky
Division of Psychiatry
Beersheva Mental Health Center
Ben-Gurion University of the Negev
P.O. Box 4600
Beersheva 84105, Israel

Giovanni Battista Cassano
Institute of Psychiatry
School of Medicine
University of Pisa
Via Roma 37
I-56100 Pisa, Italy

H. Christian Fibiger
Division of Neurological Sciences
Department of Psychiatry
The University of British Columbia
2255 Wesbrook Mall
Vancouver, B.C., Canada, V6T 1Z3

Walter Fratta
"Bernard B. Brodie" Department of Neuroscience
University of Cagliari
Via Porcell 4
I-09124 Cagliari, Italy

Elliot S. Gershon
Clinical Neurogenetics Branch
National Institute of Mental Health
Intramural Research Program
Bldg 10 Room 3N218
10 CENTER DR MSC 1274
Bethesda, MD 20892-1274

Gian Luigi Gessa
"Bernard B. Brodie" Department of Neuroscience
University of Cagliari
Via Porcell 4
I-09124 Cagliari, Italy

F. Neil Johnson
Fylde College
University of Lancaster
Lancaster LA1 4YF, United Kingdom

O. Kofman
Division of Psychiatry
Beersheva Mental Health Center
Ben-Gurion University of the Negev
P.O. Box 4600
Beersheva 84105, Israel

Athanasio Koukopoulos
Centro "Lucio Bini"
Via Crescenzio 42
I-00193 Rome, Italy
and Clinica "Belvedere Montello"
Via Belvedere Montello 56
I-00166 Rome, Italy

J. Levine
Division of Psychiatry
Beersheva Mental Health Center
Ben-Gurion University of the Negev
P.O. Box 4600
Beersheva 84105, Israel

Stefano Michelini
Institute of Psychiatry
School of Medicine
University of Pisa
Via Roma 37
I-56100 Pisa, Italy

Giampaolo Minnai
Dipartimento di Salute Mentale
Azienda USL 5, Distretto di Ghilarza
Via Santa Lucia 39
I-09074 Ghilarza (OR), Italy

Luca Pani
"Bernard B. Brodie" Department of Neuroscience
University of Cagliari
Via Porcell 4
I-09124 Cagliari, Italy
and Center for Neuropharmacology, CNR
University of Cagliari, Italy

Daniela Reginaldi
Centro "Lucio Bini"
Via Crescenzio 42
I-00193 Rome, Italy
and Clinica "Belvedere Montello"
Via Belvedere Montello 56
I-00166 Rome, Italy

Gino Serra
Institute of Biochemistry
School of Pharmacy
University of Sassari
Via Muroni 23A
I-07100 Sassari, Italy

Paul Willner
Department of Psychology
University of Wales
Singleton Park
Swansea SA2 8PP, United Kingdom

Preface

Over the past decade, the field of affective disorders has exploded with new knowledge from behavioral studies to molecular biology and genetics; from preclinical and clinical pharmacology to prevention.

Animal models of mania and depression address the biological substrates of these psychiatric syndromes and, thus, help realize better therapeutic strategies. It is striking to notice that in laboratory animals some of the symptoms of mania are shared by depression and both are sensitive to the same pharmacological treatments. It is also interesting that the majority of animal models of these syndromes consist of paradigms based on the application of stress (i.e., footshock, restraint or water immersion with or without sleep deprivation, isolation). These procedures are characterized by a first phase of "behavioral arousal" (hypomania-like activation) followed by "despair reaction" (depression) reminiscent of a bipolar type of response.

At present, our understanding of the components and chemical anatomy of the circuitry constituting the neural correlates of mood swings is still rudimentary. In spite of the evidence that several neurotransmitter systems are targets for different antidepressant or antimanic drugs, little is known about the interaction between them and their relevant postsynaptic sites.

Another general issue with respect to the mechanisms by which antidepressant and antimanic drugs generate their therapeutic actions concerns the numerous attempts to explain all such effects via a single common neural mechanism (e.g., up or down regulation of adrenergic receptors, inhibition of 5-HT or NE re-uptake, enhanced or reduced 5-HT or DA neurotransmission, etc.). It is likely that there are, instead, various chemically distinct points at which the overall activity of these systems can be influenced. It should not be surprising, therefore, that manipulations of serotonergic, dopaminergic, noradrenergic, cholinergic or other neurochemically defined components have all been reported to generate clinically significant antidepressant or antimanic effects. According to this view it is held that none of the single, final common pathway hypotheses of antidepressant or antimanic action can encompass the known neurochemical profiles of all currently available psychotropic drugs.

There is little doubt that affective disorders fall into the genetic classification of diseases with a complex mode of inheritance, meaning that a single gene cannot account for the clinical manifestation of the same disorder, even within the same family. Progress toward identifying specific susceptibility genes has become possible with advances in DNA technology and analytic methodologies that are robust to this type of inheritance. Of particular importance is the emergence of a very dense and highly informative linkage map. However, in order to take full advantage of these technological assets, a profound and sharp diagnostic knowledge is needed. This crucial step should perhaps take into account a temperament-based approach so as to better grasp the origin of different affective subtypes. Temperamental instabilities might then represent the proximal behavioral phenotypes of the genetic diathesis underlying recurrent mood disorders. Indeed, family studies—among affective probands and their biologic kin—have revealed an uninterrupted series of transitions between near-normal temperaments and full-blown affective illness. Behavioral phenotypes in most mental disorders today are considered quantitatively distributed with no hint of discontinuity. This is a fundamental fact with which modern molecular genetics will have to come to terms.

Therefore cross-sectional and longitudinal analysis remain powerful diagnostic tools of modern descriptive psychiatry; in this perspective, soft mood signs, temperamental features and comorbidity become strong and consistent specifiers of depression and are crucial in the selection of medication. Far from being only a theoretical problem, physicians often face a complex array of depression-mania (mixed states) or depression-anxiety syndromes, which cannot be fully understood using only dimensional systems of classification.

The introduction of systematic prophylactic treatments in the management of affective disorders has advanced our knowledge and methodology and moreover has substantially improved the overall health of a large number of patients. The prophylactic value of these treatments, however, has proven with years to be less effective and the toll, in terms of side effects, greater than hitherto believed.

Recent "naturalistic" studies cast doubt upon the extent of prophylaxis in psychiatric clinical practice. Therapies are applied under the less formal circumstances of everyday practice; one should not, however, underestimate the strain of taking medications every day over a long period of time. The assessments of effectiveness under such circumstances are therefore of relevance to the exigencies of therapy.

There are general factors such as the overconsumption of alcohol, coffee, tea, and caffeine-containing beverages as well as the abuse of psychomotorstimulant drugs that are able to trigger affective episodes for the first time in predisposed people or precipitate new recurrences. Once again the interaction between temperament, life events and life style becomes crucial.

We hope that this book may contribute to a better understanding of the interaction between the neurobiology of human emotions, environmental stimuli and the genesis of the affective illness in order to recognize, treat, and prevent the disease from its first onset.

Acknowledgments

This book contains the papers of the Eight Plenary Lectures presented at the Symposium on Depression during the 8th Sardinian Conference on Neuroscience held in Villasimius (Cagliari), Italy in May 1995. The editors would like to express their wholehearted gratitude and appreciation to The Günther Foundation for sponsoring the initative and to Hugh Sugden for his assistance in editing the manuscripts.

DEPRESSION AND MANIA

From Neurobiology to Treatment

Advances in Biochemical Psychopharmacology
Volume 49

Depression and Mania: From Neurobiology to Treatment: edited by G. Gessa, W. Fratta, L. Pani, and G. Serra. Raven Press, New York © 1995.

Neurobiology of Depression: Focus on Dopamine

H.C. Fibiger

Division of Neurological Sciences, Department of Psychiatry, University of British Columbia, Vancouver, B.C., Canada, V6T 1Z3

Unlike the schizophrenias for which a case is beginning to be made, at present there is little reliable evidence to suggest that major depression is accompanied by significant structural abnormalities in the central nervous system (9,27,50). While it obviously remains possible that structural neuropathologies are associated with some types of major depression and have escaped detection for a variety of reasons, the responsiveness of major depression to pharmacological and electroconvulsive interventions, as well as the fluctuating natural history of these syndromes are suggestive of functional (i.e. neurochemical, neuroendocrinological) as opposed to structural neural bases for these disorders.

An understanding of the functional substrates of depression will depend critically on elucidating the neural substrates of mood. At present, knowledge regarding the components and chemical anatomy of this circuitry is rudimentary. For example, while there is evidence that noradrenergic, serotonergic and dopaminergic systems are targets for different antidepressant drugs, in most cases little is known about the relevant postsynaptic targets that mediate the therapeutic effects of altered monoaminergic transmission. This is a particularly difficult problem in view of the fact that each of these monoaminergic systems innervate nearly all (NE and 5-HT) or very diverse (DA) regions of the central nervous system. Furthermore, with regard to the pathochemistry of depression, it is worth noting that elucidation of the primary neurochemical mechanism by which an antidepressant drug produces its therapeutic effect may be of little relevance to the pathophysiological substrates of depression. For example, the growing evidence that many antidepressant treatments alter the function of serotonergic systems in the CNS (5), does not necessarily mean that the function of serotonergic systems is altered in depression. It is quite conceivable, for example, that in fluoxetine responsive depression the primary neurochemical dysregulation occurs in a non-serotonergic system whose normal function is antagonistic to that of the serotonergic neurons. In this case, fluoxetine based pharmacotherapy would be effective by virtue of restoring the appropriate balance between the serotonergic and the abnormal non-serotonergic systems.

Another general issue with respect to the mechanisms by which antidepressant drugs generate their therapeutic actions concerns the numerous past and present attempts to explain all such effects via a single common neural mechanism (e.g. down regulation of adrenergic receptors, inhibition of 5-HT or NE re-uptake, enhanced 5-HT or DA neurotransmission, etc.). Given the complex neural circuitry of affect, it is likely that there are numerous chemically distinct points at which the overall activity of the system can be influenced. It should not be surprising, therefore, that manipulations of serotonergic, dopaminergic, noradrenergic, cholinergic or other neurochemically defined components of this system have all been reported to generate clinically significant antidepressant effects. In a similar vein, according to this view it should not be surprising that none of the single, final common pathway hypotheses of antidepressant action can encompass the known neurochemical profiles of all of currently available antidepressant drugs. That is, for each such hypothesis, antidepressant compounds exist whose actions in the brain are not accommodated by that hypothesis.

THE DA HYPOTHESIS OF MOOD DISORDERS

Bearing the above caveats firmly in mind, this chapter reviews recent evidence which suggests that mesolimbic dopamine-containing neurons may be involved in the pathophysiology of some types of depression and may be a substrate for the therapeutic actions of some antidepressant drugs. The DA hypothesis of mood disorders is based on both clinical and preclinical findings. The core support for the hypothesis rests in the following observations: (1) the meso-accumbens DA projection is a component of the neural circuitry of reward and/or incentive motivation, and both of these processes are dysfunctional in mania and major depression; (2) some antidepressant treatments enhance the functional status of the mesolimbic DA system; (3) acute administration of drugs such as amphetamine produces, via a dopaminergic mechanism, effects in humans that are remarkably similar to the early phase of an idiopathic manic episode (16); (4) idiopathic mania can be treated with neuroleptic drugs; and (5) acute administration of DA receptor antagonists produces effects in normal volunteers that share important features with endogenous depression, including restlessness, paralysis of volition, lack of physical and psychic energy, and anxiety (3).

DOPAMINE AND REWARD

A substantial body of evidence indicates that the meso-accumbens DA projection is an important component of the neural circuitry of reward (19,20,34). For example, intracranial self-stimulation (ICSS) obtained from electrodes in the ventral tegmental area (VTA) is mediated to a large extent by activation of ascending DA fibres that course through the lateral hypothalamus (LH). Fibiger, LePiane, Jakubovic and Phillips (21) demonstrated that 6-hydroxydopamine (6-OHDA) lesions of DA axons coursing through the LH that caused extensive depletions of DA in the striatum, nucleus accumbens and olfactory tubercle resulted in large reductions in the rate of ICSS obtained from the VTA. Identical lesions contralateral to the VTA electrodes had no significant effects on this behavior, thus ruling out hemiparkinsonian-like motor deficits as being responsible for this effect. That the nucleus accumbens rather than other DA-rich structures is important for mediating the reinforcing properties of brain stimulation has been demonstrated by Mogenson et al. (47) who found that VTA-ICSS was significantly reduced by ipsilateral injections of the DA receptor antagonist spiroperidol into the nucleus accumbens. Similar injections into either the contralateral nucleus accumbens or the ipsi- or contralateral prefrontal cortex were without effect.

Neurochemical evidence is also consistent with the hypothesis that ICSS obtained from the VTA is largely mediated by activation of mesotelencephalic DA neurons. For example, several studies have demonstrated that DA synthesis, metabolism and release is increased during self-stimulation. Thus, under appropriate stimulation parameters and experimental conditions, both the synthesis (56) and metabolism (21,67) of DA in the nucleus accumbens and striatum are significantly increased during VTA self-stimulation. More recently, we have used *in vivo* brain microdialysis to study the effects of ICSS obtained from electrodes in the VTA on DA release in the nucleus accumbens (22). In one experiment both ICSS and yoked stimulation of the VTA produced significant increases in extracellular concentrations of DA and its metabolites in the nucleus accumbens. The fact that comparable increases were observed in the ICSS and yoked groups indicates that the enhanced DA release was associated with the electrical stimulation of the VTA and not the intense operant behavior in the ICSS group. In a second experiment, it was demonstrated that ICSS rate/intensity functions were positively correlated with the degree to which ICSS increased DA release. With regard to interpretation of the data from the yoked group in these experiments, it has commonly been assumed that exposure to non-contingent electrical brain stimulation is aversive (69). However, more recent data clearly show that brain stimulation can be rewarding when administered non-contingently to animals with a history of ICSS (12,13,71). In summary, the demonstrations that DA neurons are activated during VTA-ICSS and that VTA-ICSS is severely disrupted by 6-OHDA lesions of the mesotelencephalic DA projections provides strong evidence that these neurons are an important neural substrate for ICSS obtained from this part of the brain.

Other compelling evidence indicating that the mesolimbic DA projection is a reward-related system has been obtained from studies of intravenous drug self-administration. Since the classic work of Weeks (72), it has been known that animals will work for intravenous injections of various classes of psychoactive drugs, including stimulants and narcotics. Several studies indicate that the rewarding properties of stimulants such as cocaine and d-amphetamine are mediated by the effect of these compounds on DA release in the nucleus accumbens. In the first of these studies, Roberts et al. (59) trained rats to self-administer cocaine. After stable daily response rates had been achieved, the animals received bilateral 6-OHDA lesions of the nucleus accumbens. It was found that animals with extensive losses of DA in the nucleus accumbens showed large decreases in the rate at which they lever-pressed for intravenous injections of cocaine. In a similar study, Lyness et al. (37) observed that 6-OHDA lesions of the nucleus accumbens also disrupt intravenous self-administration of d-amphetamine. It is noteworthy that 6-OHDA lesions of the dorsal and ventral noradrenergic bundles, which caused large and widespread decreases in the concentration of NE in the forebrain, had no effect on the rate or pattern of cocaine self-administration (59). It appears, therefore, that central noradrenergic systems do not contribute significantly either to electrical brain stimulation (15) or to stimulant-induced reward.

In an informative series of experiments, Roberts et al. (60) analyzed the pattern of self-administration of cocaine after 6-OHDA lesions of the nucleus accumbens. After the 6-OHDA lesions, on the first day that they were given access to cocaine the animals responded rapidly for the drug early in the 3-hr session. However, as the session progressed, the rate of responding decreased gradually until there was little or no responding by the end of the session. Similar patterns were found on the following few days except that early responding was reduced and cessation of responding occurred more quickly. These data are important for several reasons. First, the high rate of responding for cocaine early in the first postlesion session indicated that the effects of the 6-OHDA lesions on cocaine self-administration could not be attributed to lesion-induced motor deficits. The fact that the lesions did not affect responding for the directly acting DA agonist apomorphine was consistent with this interpretation. Second, the pattern of cocaine self-administration after the 6-OHDA lesions resembled a classic extinction effect. Typically this has been characterized by high rates of responding when a reinforcer is first removed, which is followed by gradually decreasing rates of responding as the animal learns that the operant response no longer results in the delivery of a reward. The most parsimonious interpretation of this pattern of results is that extensive 6-OHDA lesions of the nucleus accumbens block the rewarding effects of intravenous cocaine.

The results of the experiments reviewed above suggest that DA terminals in the nucleus accumbens or a DA projection coursing through it are necessary for the normal expression of amphetamine and cocaine reinforcement. Martin-Iverson et al. (43) subsequently addressed the possibility that some of the effects of 6-OHDA lesions of the nucleus accumbens on cocaine self-administration may be due to damage of mesocortical DA axons that pass through this nucleus. This gained importance with the report of Goeders and Smith (24) that rats would not self-administer cocaine directly in the nucleus accumbens but would initiate and maintain responding for cocaine when infusion cannulae were placed in the medial prefrontal cortex. Martin-Iverson et al. (43) therefore trained rats to self-administer cocaine intravenously, and when stable rates of responding were obtained, bilateral 6-OHDA lesions were aimed at the medial prefrontal cortex. It was found that these lesions did not affect either the rate or pattern of cocaine self-administration, although substantial decreases in the concentration of DA in the medial prefrontal cortex were observed. In a similar experiment, Leccese and Lyness (37) found that 6-OHDA lesions of the medial prefrontal cortex also failed to influence either the acquisition or the maintenance of intravenous d-amphetamine self-administration. These results suggest that DA terminals in the medial prefrontal cortex are not a critical substrate for the rewarding properties of intravenous cocaine or d-amphetamine. The basis of the discrepancy between these results and those of Goeders and Smith (24) remains unclear. Nevertheless, the results of Martin-Iverson et al. (43) and Leccese and Lyness (37) are congruent with data of Mogenson et al. (47) who, it will be recalled, found that injections of spiroperidol into the nucleus accumbens but not into the prefrontal cortex reduced ICSS obtained from electrodes in the VTA.

The results of the ICSS and intravenous self-administration studies reviewed above provide strong support for the hypothesis that the meso-accumbens DA system is a key component in the neural circuitry of reward and/or incentive motivation. They do not, however, provide any information regarding the normal circumstances under which these neurons are activated or inhibited. Recent studies using *in vivo* brain microdialysis have been extremely useful in this regard. In two such studies, it was shown that DA release in the nucleus accumbens is enhanced in male rats during sexual behavior, with the peak increases being associated with the consummatory (copulation) as opposed to the anticipatory aspects of such behavior (10,55). Subsequent analyses indicated that these increases are innate, unconditioned neurochemical events and that copulation with intromission, but not mounting alone, is associated with the largest increases in DA release (74). Other studies have demonstrated that consumption of other primary rewards such as food or water are also associated with increased DA release in the nucleus accumbens (25,58,77). The results of this research are clearly compatible with the hypothesis that mesolimbic DA neurons are a component of the neural circuitry that mediates the rewarding and/or incentive motivational properties of natural rewards such as food, water and sex.

In complementary neurophysiological experiments, Schultz and his co-workers have recorded from midbrain DA neurons in monkeys during the performance of a variety of food reinforced behaviors (35,61,62,63,64). The results of these investigations indicate that dopaminergic neurons in the mesencephalon can be activated both by primary food and fluid rewards and by conditioned incentive stimuli predicting reward (35,61,62). Specifically, while midbrain DA neurons initially respond to primary rewards during learning, these responses gradually transfer to the conditioned stimuli that predict reward during the establishment of task performance. Furthermore, after overtraining even the responses to the conditioned stimuli become strongly reduced (35,64). From this series of experiments Schultz et al. (64) have concluded that midbrain "DA neurons respond phasically to alerting external stimuli with behavioral significance whose detection is crucial for learning ... and are involved with transient changes of impulse activity in basic attentional and motivational processes underlying learning and cognitive behavior" (p. 900). According to this formulation, the functions of mesotelencephalic DA neurons are not specifically related either to incentive motivation or reward; rather, they are part of an "alerting and attention-grabbing" mechanism that is activated by appetitive stimuli associated with the availability of an object of high interest, that is, "motivational arousal" (63,64).

DOPAMINE AND DEPRESSION

A core symptom of depressive illness in humans is an impaired ability to experience pleasure, there being a failure to react with enjoyment to events that are normally pleasurable. Incentive motivational processes also appear to be affected in that stimuli that normally serve to energize and direct behavior do so less efficaciously in depressed patients. Thus patients with major depression show a lack of interest in seeking out pleasurable events. Given that both reward and incentive motivation have been associated with mesolimbic DA function (4,20), it is reasonable to consider the extent to which the normal activity of this system may be impaired in depression, and if some antidepressant treatments produce their therapeutic effects by enhancing or restoring its normal function. It is interesting in this context that Belmaker and Wald (3) have provided the following description of their experience after receiving a moderate dose (5 mg) of the dopamine receptor antagonist haloperidol: "a marked slowing of thinking and movement developed, along with profound inner restlessness. Neither subject could continue to work, and each left work for over 36 hours. Each subject complained of a paralysis of volition, a lack of physical and psychic energy. The subjects felt unable to read, telephone or perform household tasks of their own will, but could perform these tasks if demanded to do so. There was no sleepiness or sedation; on the contrary both subjects complained of severe anxiety." Symptoms such as restlessness, paralysis of volition, lack of physical and psychic energy, inability to perform routine tasks, and anxiety are hallmarks of endogenous depression. Unfortunately, what is missing from this description is any mention of the subjects' mood state during this experience. In future investigations, it would be of considerable theoretical interest also to test specifically for the presence or absence of depressed mood (e.g. sad, discouraged, blue, down in the dumps, low, tearful, etc.) in normal volunteers given DA receptor antagonists. Nevertheless, that haloperidol can produce the above effects in normal individuals speaks strongly to the possible role of central dopaminergic systems in at least some aspects of the pathophysiology of major depression. The fact that mesolimbic DA neurons degenerate in Parkinson's disease and that this condition is characterized by a high incidence of depression is also entirely consistent with this hypothesis (17). There is other tantalizing evidence that is highly suggestive of a role for central DA systems in depression but space does not permit a review of this literature here. The interested reader is referred to Gessa and Serra (23) for reviews of this subject.

MESOLIMBIC DA NEURONS AND ANTIDEPRESSANT DRUGS

In view of the evidence that the meso-accumbens DA projection is a link in the neural circuitry of reward and/or incentive motivation, and that dysfunction of this system may contribute to some aspects of depression, it is reasonable to consider the possibility that meso-accumbens DA neurons are a target for the therapeutic actions of some antidepressant treatments. There is, in fact, a growing literature which is consistent with this hypothesis. For example, an early indication that the functional output of the mesolimbic DA system is enhanced by chronically administered desipramine, a prototypical tricyclic antidepressant, was obtained by Fibiger and Phillips (18) who found that the ICSS response rate - current intensity function was shifted significantly to the left in animals working for brain-stimulation reward from electrodes in the VTA. These findings were confirmed and extended by McCarter and Kokkinidis (44) who studied the effects of a number of antidepressants in animals with lateral hypothalamic electrodes that were responding for ICSS in a nose-poke task. While chronic desipramine shifted the rate-intensity function to the left, the other antidepressants (amitriptyline, nomifensine, bupropion and zimelidine) did not. In experiments using a different model (reversal of ICSS depression after chronic amphetamine withdrawal, an effect thought to be mediated by dopaminergic mechanisms), both amitriptyline and imipramine were effective in attenuating the decreased rates of responding for ICSS that occur after withdrawal from chronic amphetamine (32). It is possible that the post-amphetamine withdrawal test is a more sensitive measure of antidepressant drug effects on dopaminergic function. It should also be borne in mind, however, that unlike the VTA where dopaminergic substrates of ICSS have been documented (20), the neurochemical substrates of ICSS obtained from electrodes in the lateral hypothalamus are less clearly understood, probably heterogeneous, and only partly dopaminergic (46). Nevertheless, McCarter and Kokkinidis' (44) results are consistent with previous conclusions that not all antidepressant drugs enhance the functional status of the mesolimbic DA system (42,68). In this regard, it is perhaps worth re-emphasizing several points made earlier: given the enormous complexity of the neural substrates of affect, it would be naive to assume (1) that there is only one point at which the overall function of this circuitry can be influenced pharmacologically, and (2) that all antidepressant drugs must act on the same component of this circuitry. Unfortunately, there has been a tendency by many workers in this field to ignore these seemingly self-evident points and to attempt to explain both the neurobiology of depression and the neuropharmacology of all antidepressant drug action within single neurochemical constructs. It seems highly improbable that all depressions and their treatments will ever be explained by a single model approach.

Other data also suggest that the function of meso-accumbens dopaminergic neurons is enhanced by some antidepressant drugs. For example, d-amphetamine-induced locomotor activity, a behavior dependent on the integrity of meso-accumbens dopaminergic neurons, is enhanced in animals treated chronically with some antidepressants (1,40,42,68). Moreover, the locomotor stimulant effects of d-amphetamine administered directly into the nucleus accumbens are also enhanced after chronic administration of tricyclics such as desipramine, imipramine and amitriptyline (39,41). This could be due to antidepressant-induced down regulation of α_2 noradrenergic receptors which may normally serve to inhibit DA release in the nucleus accumbens (54). Recent microdialysis experiments in the author's laboratory have provided neurochemical support for the behavioral studies described above. Thus, 21 day treatment with desipramine significantly enhanced d-amphetamine-induced DA release in the nucleus accumbens (52). This effect was not seen after 2 days of desipramine administration and was regionally selective in that it was not observed in the dorsal striatum. Subsequently, Brown et al. (6) demonstrated that the effects of locally applied d-amphetamine (via "reverse dialysis") on DA release in nucleus accumbens were also greatly enhanced by chronic desipramine. These results exclude any possibility that the earlier results with systemically administered d-amphetamine were due to desipramine-induced changes in the pharmacokinetics of d-amphetamine. They also indicate that chronic desipramine may directly influence the functional status of dopaminergic terminals in the nucleus accumbens.

The effects of antidepressants on DA mediated behaviors are not restricted to enhanced d-amphetamine-induced locomotor activity. Thus, the motor stimulant effects of intra-accumbens injections of either apomorphine or dopamine are also increased in animals receiving chronic antidepressants (41,57). In addition, the motor stimulant effects of the D_2 receptor agonist quinpirole are greatly potentiated by chronic administration of imipramine, desipramine, mianserin or electroconvulsive shock (66). This suggests some of the effects of chronically administered antidepressant drugs on the mesolimbic DA system may be due to changes in postsynaptic DA receptor mechanisms. Receptor binding studies have provided some support for this hypothesis. Thus, while chronically administered antidepressant drugs do not affect the number (B_{max}) or affinity (K_d) of D_2 dopamine receptors for DA receptor antagonists in the nucleus accumbens (30,42), one study found an increase in the affinity of D_2 receptors for DA agonists in this structure (29). Furthermore, Klimek, Nielsen and Maj (31) and Klimek and Nielsen (30) have shown that a variety of chronically administered antidepressant drugs, as well as electroconvulsive shock, decrease the number of D_1 binding sites in both the striatum and what they termed the "limbic system" (composed of olfactory tubercle, preoptic area, nucleus accumbens, septum and amygdala). More recently, Nunes et al. (53) have shown that sleep deprivation, another procedure that can produce antidepressant effects, significantly increases the number of D_2 receptors in the nucleus accumbens. Although it is perhaps premature to attempt to relate the results of these receptor binding studies to the behavioral studies discussed above, these findings raise the possibility that functionally significant interactions between D_1 and D_2 dopamine receptors may be relevant to antidepressant mechanisms (8).

Another mechanism by which antidepressant treatments have been hypothesized to enhance the function of mesolimbic DA neurons is dopamine autoreceptor subsensitivity. Because these receptors are involved in negative feedback processes that decrease the firing of DA neurons and DA synthesis, subsensitivity of these receptors would have the effect of increasing the activity and output of these neurons. Although there are behavioral, physiological and neurochemical data that are consistent with antidepressant treatment-induced subsensitivity of DA autoreceptors, the literature on this subject contains many contradictory results. Thus, while some laboratories have reported significant decreases in apomorphine-induced hypomotility after chronic antidepressant treatments (1,65), others have not (68). Neurophysiological tests of DA autoreceptor sensitivity after antidepressant treatments have also generated inconsistent findings with some laboratories reporting subsensitivity(7) and others failing to observe such effects (38,73). Neurochemical studies have been equally inconsistent in their findings. Serra et al. (65) found that chronic treatment with imipramine, amitriptyline and mianserin blocked the ability of apomorphine to decrease DOPAC concentrations in rat striatum, but other investigators have not observed such effects after chronic desipramine, dothiepin, iprindole or nomifensine (11). Holcomb, Bannon and Roth (26) confirmed that imipramine and iprindole blocked apomorphine-induced decreases in striatal DOPAC concentrations but also found that these drug regimens substantially reduced basal DOPAC concentrations, thus complicating the interpretation of the apomorphine effects. Holcomb et al. (26) therefore used a second neurochemical measure of DA autoreceptor sensitivity in their studies, namely, the effect of apomorphine on DOPA accumulation in the striatum after blockade of impulse flow with gamma-hydroxybutyric acid lactone. The chronically administered antidepressants failed to attenuate apomorphine-induced decreases in DOPA accumulation. Using a similar approach Nielsen (51) also found that chronic imipramine, amitriptyline and bupropion failed to decrease apomorphine-induced DOPA accumulation in the nucleus accumbens or olfactory tubercle, although positive effects were observed in the striatum. Recent *in vivo* microdialysis experiments in the author's laboratory have directly tested the hypothesis that chronic treatment with antidepressants decrease DA autoreceptor sensitivity. In these experiments, it was found that neither acute (2 days) nor chronic (21 days) administration of desipramine influenced the ability of a low dose (25 μg/kg) of apomorphine to decrease extracellular concentrations of DA or its metabolites in the nucleus accumbens (52). It is noteworthy that in the same experiments, chronic desipramine significantly enhanced d-amphetamine-induced increases in DA release in this structure. At present, it seems appropriate to conclude that antidepressant treatments do not produce robust or reliable decreases in DA autoreceptor sensitivity.

Most of the experiments reviewed above involved treating normal, presumably non-depressed, laboratory rats with antidepressant drugs. This approach has been rightfully questioned in view of the fact that the effects of antidepressant drugs on mood in non-depressed humans have not been extensively studied. If it is the case that mood is not elevated by antidepressants in normal, non-depressed individuals, then the relevance of studying the behavioral and neurochemical effects of these compounds in normal, non-depressed animals is obviously open to question. In an attempt to address this potential problem Willner and colleagues have utilized a chronic mild stress (CMS) model of depression in rats (for reviews see Willner et al. (75,76)). As this model is reviewed in detail elsewhere in this volume (see chapter by Willner) it will not be dealt with extensively here. Suffice it to say, however, that there is accumulating evidence that CMS produces an anhedonic state in rats which may involve a downregulation of postsynaptic D_2 dopamine receptors in the nucleus accumbens. Furthermore, a broad range of chronically administered typical and atypical antidepressant drugs appear to reverse the stress-induced anhedonia via a dopaminergic mechanism (49,76). The results of these investigations are clearly compatible with the hypothesized role of mesolimbic dopaminergic neurons in some forms of depression, and again suggest that this system is either directly or indirectly targetted by many antidepressant drugs.

The preceding discussion has focussed on the effects of antidepressant treatments on various types of DA receptors. There are, of course, many other mechanisms by which antidepressant drugs could enhance the function of the mesolimbic DA system. These include changes in the afferent regulation of DA neurons in the VTA, alterations in second messenger systems in neurons postsynaptic to the DA terminals, and treatment-induced changes in the proportional release of co-transmitters such as cholecystokinin (CCK) and neurotensin (NT) from these dopaminergic neurons. To date, little work has been devoted to investigating the effects of antidepressant treatments on these other processes. With regard to the last point, however, it is noteworthy that Bartfai, Iverfeldt, Brodin and Ogren (2) have reported that chronic treatment with imipramine or zimelidine can increase substance P and decrease serotonin concentrations in the spinal cord where these neurotransmitters co-exist in the same neural elements. In addition, peptide transmitters are released in a frequency-dependent manner that is different from that of the classical co-transmitter (36). Antidepressant treatments which change the ratio of the peptide to the classical transmitter content in nerve terminals could, therefore, have substantial effects on information transfer across synapses formed by such terminals. It would be interesting in this regard to examine the effects of antidepressants on the content of CCK and NT in terminals of the meso-accumbens projection.

LIMITATIONS OF THE DA HYPOTHESIS OF MOOD DISORDERS

A number of observations seem incompatible with the DA hypothesis of mood disorders. First, despite extensive investigation there is no firm biochemical or physiological evidence that DA systems are dysfunctional during major depressive episodes. Thus, although there are numerous (but not invariant) reports of decreased DA metabolite concentrations in the CSF of depressed patients, it is uncertain whether this is simply a reflection of reduced motoric output in these patients or whether it is related to the affective disturbances *per se*. Despite the considerable effort that has been invested in this approach, it is at best a very crude test of the hypothesis because it is likely that only a small, perhaps insignificant, fraction of homovanillic acid and 3,4-dihydroxyphenylacetic acid in the CSF originates from the nucleus accumbens. Even if substantial abnormalities in DA release or metabolism in the nucleus accumbens of depressed or manic patients existed, it is quite conceivable that this would not be detected in CSF. It is worth mentioning here that there is strong evidence that the various components of the mesotelencephalic DA system can be regulated differentially (14,45,70). Abnormalities in meso-accumbens DA neurons need not, therefore, be accompanied by similar changes in nigrostriatal DA neurons.

Another potential problem for the hypothesis is that attempts to detect functional abnormalities in central DA systems on the basis of neuroendocrine measures of hypothalamic DA activity during mood disorders have produced inconsistent or negative results (28). However, because hypothalamic DA neurons have physiological, pharmacological and neurochemical characteristics that are distinct from mesotelencephalic DA neurons (48), inferences about the latter cannot be made on the basis of data obtained on the former. The absence of consistent abnormalities in hypothalamic-pituitary DA function in psychiatric disease is irrelevant, therefore, to hypotheses concerning the role(s) of mesotelencephalic DA systems in such conditions.

The third, and perhaps most serious potential problem with the DA hypothesis of mood disorders is that major depressive episodes with psychotic features (delusions or hallucinations) are often treated successfully with neuroleptic drugs. If a major depressive episode is associated with reduced dopaminergic tone in the nucleus accumbens, how then could DA receptor antagonists be of therapeutic value to such patients? While space does not permit an extensive discussion of this important issue here, an understanding of the symptoms in psychotic depression that respond to neuroleptics may hold the key to this apparent paradox (16).

REFERENCES

1. Arnt J, Overo KF, Hyttel J, Olson R. Changes in rat dopamine- and serotonin function *in vivo* after prolonged administration of the specific 5-HT uptake inhibitor, citalopram. *Psychopharmacology* 1984;84:457-465.
2. Bartfai T, Iverfeldt K, Brodin E, Ogren S. Functional consequences of coexistence of classical and peptide neurotransmitters. In: Hokfelt T, Fuxe K, Pernow B, eds. *Coexistence of Neuronal Messengers: A New Principle in Chemical Transmission. Progress in Brain Research, Vol. IV.* Amsterdam: Elsevier, 1986:321-330.
3. Belmaker RH, Wald D. Haloperidol in normals. *Br J Psychiatry* 1977;131:222-223.
4. Blackburn JR, Phillips AG, Jakubovic A, Fibiger HC. Dopamine and preparatory behavior. II: A neurochemical analysis. *Behav Neurosci* 1989;103:15-23.
5. Blier P, de Montigny C. Current advances and trends in the treatment of depression. *TIPS* 1994;15:220-226.
6. Brown EE, Nomikos GG, Wilson C, Fibiger HC. Chronic desipramine enhances the effect of locally applied amphetamine on interstitial concentrations of dopamine in the nucleus accumbens. *Eur J Pharmacol* 1991;202:125-127.
7. Chiodo LA, Antelman SM. Repeated tricyclics induce a progressive dopamine autoreceptor subsensitivity independent of daily drug treatment. *Nature* 1980;287:451-454.
8. Clark D, White FJ. D_1 dopamine receptor - the search for a function: a critical evaluation of the D_1/D_2 dopamine receptor classification and its functional implications. *Synapse* 1987;1:347-388.
9. Coffey CE, Wilkinson WE, Weiner RD, et al. Quantitative cerebral anatomy in depression. *Arch Gen Psychiatry* 1993;50:7-16.
10. Damsma G, Pfaus JG, Wenkstern D, Phillips AG, Fibiger HC. Sexual behavior increases dopamine transmission in the nucleus accumbens and striatum of male rats: comparison with novelty and locomotion. *Behav Neurosci* 1992;106:181-191.
11. Diggory GL, Buckett WR. Chronic antidepressant administration fails to attenuate apomorphine-induced decreases in rat striatal dopamine metabolites. *Eur J Pharmacol* 1984;105:257-263.
12. Ettenberg A, Duvauchelle CL. Haloperidol blocks the conditioned place preferences induced by rewarding brain stimulation. *Behav Neurosci* 1988;102:687-691.
13. Ettenberg A, Laferriere A, Milner PM, White N. Response involvement in brain stimulation reward. *Physiol Behav* 1981;27:641-647.
14. Fadda F, Argiolas A, Melis MR, Tissaari AH, Onali PL, Gessa GL. Stress-induced increase in 3,4-dihydroxyphenylacetic acid (DOPAC) levels

in cerebral cortex and in N. accumbens: reversal by diazepam. *Life Sci* 1978;23:2219-2224.
15. Fibiger HC. Drugs and reinforcement: a critical review of the catecholamine theory. *Annu Rev Pharmacol Toxicol* 1978;18:37-56.
16. Fibiger HC. The dopamine hypotheses of schizophrenia and mood disorders: contradictions and speculations. In: Willner P, Scheel-Kruger J, eds. *The Mesolimbic Dopamine System: From Motivation to Action.* Chichester: John Wiley & Sons, 1991:615-637.
17. Fibiger HC. The neurobiological substrates of depression in Parkinson's disease: a hypothesis. *Can J Neurol Sci* 1984;11:105-107.
18. Fibiger HC, Phillips AG. Increased intracranial self-stimulation in rats after long-term administration of desipramine. *Science* 1981;214:683-685.
19. Fibiger HC, Phillips AG. Reward, motivation and cognition: Psychobiology of meso-telencephalic dopamine systems. In: Bloom FE, Geiger SR, eds. *Handbook of Physiology: The Nervous System: Intrinsic Regulatory Systems of the Brain, Vol. IV.* Bethesda: American Physiological Society, 1986:647-675.
20. Fibiger HC, Phillips AG. Role of catecholamine transmitters in brain reward systems: implications for the neurobiology of affect. In: Engel J, Oreland L, eds. *Brain Reward Systems and Abuse.* New York: Raven Press, 1987:61-74.
21. Fibiger HC, LePiane FG, Jakubovic A, Phillips AG. The role of dopamine in intracranial self-stimulation of the ventral tegmental area. *J Neurosci* 1987;7:3888-3896.
22. Fiorino DF, Coury A, Fibiger HC, Phillips AG. Electrical stimulation of reward sites in the ventral tegmental area increases dopamine transmission in the nucleus accumbens of the rat. *Behav Brain Res* 1993;55:131-141.
23. Gessa GL, Serra G. *Advances in the Biosciences. Dopamine and Mental Depression, Vol. 77.* Oxford: Pergamon Press, 1990.
24. Goeders NE, Smith JE. Cortical dopaminergic involvement in cocaine reinforcement. *Science* 1983;221:773-775.
25. Hernandez L, Hoebel BG. Feeding and hypothalamic stimulation increase dopamine turnover in the accumbens. *Physiol Behav* 1988;44:599-606.
26. Holcomb HH, Bannon MJ, Roth RH. Striatal dopamine autoreceptors uninfluenced by chronic administration of antidepressants. *Eur J Pharmacol* 1982;82:173-178.
27. Jeste DV, Lohr JB, Goodwin FK. Neuroanatomical studies of major affective disorders: a review and suggestions for further research. *Br J Psychiatry* 1988;153:444-459.
28. Jimerson DC. Role of dopamine mechanisms in the affective disorders. In: Meltzer HY, ed. *Psychopharmacology The Third Generation of Progress.* New York: Raven Press, 1987:505-511.

29. Klimek V, Maj J. Repeated administration of antidepressant drug enhanced agonist affinity for mesolimbic D-2 receptors. *J Pharm Pharmacol* 1989;41:555-558.
30. Klimek V, Nielsen M. Chronic treatment with antidepressants decreases the number of [3H]SCH 23390 binding sites in the rat striatum and limbic system. *Eur J Pharmacol* 1987;139:163-169.
31. Klimek V, Nielsen M, Maj J. Repeated treatment with imipramine decreased the number of [3]piflutixol binding sites in the rat striatum. *Eur J Pharmacol* 1985;109:131-132.
32. Kokkinidis L, Zacharko RM, Predy PA. Post-amphetamine depression of self-stimulation responding from the substantia nigra: reversal by tricyclic antidepressants. *Pharmacol Biochem Behav* 1980;13:279-383.
33. Leccese AP, Lyness WH. Lesions of dopamine neurons in the medial prefrontal cortex: effects of self-administration of amphetamine and dopamine synthesis in the brain of the rat. *Neuropharmacology* 1987;26:1303-1308.
34. Liebman JM, Cooper SJ. *The Neuropharmacological Basis of Reward.* Oxford: Clarendon Press, 1989.
35. Ljungberg T, Apicella P, Schultz W. Responses of monkey dopamine neurons during learning of behavioral reactions. *J Neurophysiol* 1992;67:145-163.
36. Lundberg JM, Hokfelt T. Multiple co-existence of peptides and classical transmitters in peripheral autonomic and sensory neurons - functional and pharmacological implications. In: Hokfelt T, Fuxe K, Pernow B, eds. *Coexistence of Neuronal Messengers: A New Principle in Chemical Transmission. Progress in Brain Research, Vol. IV.* Amsterdam: Elsevier, 1986;241-262.
37. Lyness WH, Friedle NM, Moore KE. Destruction of dopaminergic nerve terminals in nucleus accumbens: Effect of *d*-amphetamine self-administration. *Pharmacol Biochem Behav* 1979;11:553-556.
38. MacNiel DA, Gower M. Do antidepressants induce dopamine autoreceptor subsensitivity? *Nature* 1982;298:302.
39. Maj J, Wedzony K. Repeated treatment with imipramine or amitriptyline increases the locomotor response of rats to (+)-amphetamine given into the nucleus accumbens. *J Pharm Pharmacol* 1985;37:362-364.
40. Maj J, Rogoz Z, Skuza G, Sowinska H. Repeated treatment with antidepressant drugs potentiates the locomotor response to (+)-amphetamine. *J Pharm Pharmacol* 1984;36:127-130.
41. Maj J, Wedzony K, Klimek V. Desipramine given repeatedly enhances behavioural effects of dopamine and d-amphetamine injected into the nucleus accumbens. *Eur J Pharmacol* 1987;140:179-185.
42. Martin-Iverson MT, Leclere J-F, Fibiger HC. Cholinergic-dopaminergic interactions and the mechanisms of action of antidepressants. *Eur J Pharmacol* 1983;94:193-201.

43. Martin-Iverson MT, Szostak C, Fibiger HC. 6-Hydroxydopamine lesions of the medial prefrontal cortex fail to influence intravenous self-administration of cocaine. *Psychopharmacology* 1986;88:310-314.
44. McCarter BD, Kokkinidis L. The effects of long-term administration of antidepressant drugs on intracranial self-stimulation responding in rats. *Pharmacol Biochem Behav* 1988;31:243-247.
45. Miller JD, Speciale SG, McMillen BA, German DC. Naloxone antagonism of stress-induced augmentation of frontal cortex dopamine metabolism. *Eur J Pharmacol* 1984;98:437-439.
46. Mitchell MJ, Nicolaou NM, Arbuthnott GW, Yates CM. Increases in dopamine metabolism are not a general feature of intracranial self-stimulation. *Life Sci* 1982;30:1081-1085.
47. Mogenson GJ, Takigawa M, Robertson A, Wu M. Self-stimulation of the nucleus accumbens and ventral tegmental area of Tsai attenuated by microinjections of spiroperidol into the nucleus accumbens. *Brain Res* 1979;171:247-259.
48. Moore KE. Hypothalamic dopaminergic neuronal systems. In: Meltzer HY, ed. *Psychopharmacology The Third Generation of Progress*. New York: Raven Press, 1987:127-139.
49. Muscat R, Papp M, Willner P. Reversal of stress-induced anhedonia by the atypical antidepressants, fluoxetine and maprotiline. *Psychopharmacology* 1992;109:433-438.
50. Nasrallah HA, Coffman JA, Olson SC. Structural brain-imaging findings in affective disorders: an overview. *J Neuropsychiatry Clin Neurosci* 1989;1:21-26.
51. Nielsen JA. Effects of chronic antidepressant treatment on nigrostriatal and mesolimbic dopamine autoreceptors in the rat. *Neurochem Int* 1986;9:61-67.
52. Nomikos GG, Damsma G, Wenkstern D, Fibiger HC. Chronic desipramine enhances amphetamine-induced increases in interstitial concentrations of dopamine in the nucleus accumbens. *Eur J Pharmacol* 1991;195:63-73.
53. Nunes GP, Tufik S, Nobrega JN. Autoradiography analysis of D1 and D2 dopaminergic receptors in rat brain after paradoxical sleep deprivation. *Brain Res Bull* 1994;34:453-456.
54. Nurse B, Russell VA, Taljaard JJF. Effect of chronic desipramine treatment on adrenoceptor modulation of [^{3}H]dopamine release from rat nucleus accumbens slices. *Brain Res* 1985;334:235-242.
55. Pfaus JG, Damsma G, Nomikos GG, et al. Sexual behavior enhances central dopamine transmission in the male rat. *Brain Res* 1990;530:345-348.
56. Phillips AG, Jakubovic A, Fibiger HC. Increased *in vivo* tyrosine hydroxylase activity in rat telencephalon produced by self-stimulation of the ventral tegmental area. *Brain Res* 1987;402:109-116.

57. Plaznik A, Kostowski W. The effects of antidepressants and electroconvulsive shocks on the functioning of the mesolimbic dopaminergic system: a behavioral study. *Eur J Pharmacol* 1987;135:389-396.
58. Radhakishun FS, Van Ree JM, Westerink BHC. Scheduled eating increases dopamine release in the nucleus accumbens of food-deprived rats as assessed with on-line brain microdialysis. *Neurosci Lett* 1988;85:351-356.
59. Roberts DCS, Corcoran ME, Fibiger HC. On the role of ascending catecholaminergic systems in intravenous self-administration of cocaine. *Pharmacol Biochem Behav* 1977;6:615-620.
60. Roberts DCS, Koob GF, Klonoff P, Fibiger HC. Extinction and recovery of cocaine self-administration following 6-hydroxydopamine lesions of the nucleus accumbens. *Pharmacol Biochem Behav* 1980;12:781-787.
61. Romo R, Schultz W. Dopamine neurons of the monkey midbrain: contingencies of responses to active touch during self-initiated arm movements. *J Neurophysiol* 1990;63:592-606.
62. Schultz W. Responses of midbrain dopamine neurons to behavioral trigger stimuli in the monkey. *J Neurophysiol* 1986;56:1439-1461.
63. Schultz W, Romo R. Dopamine neurons of the monkey midbrain: contingencies of response to stimuli eliciting immediate behavioral reactions. *J Neurophysiol* 1990;63:607-624.
64. Schultz W, Apicella P, Ljungberg T. Responses of monkey dopamine neurons to reward and conditioned stimuli during successive steps of learning a delayed response task. *J Neurosci* 1993;13:900-913.
65. Serra G, Argiolas A, Klimek V, Fadda F, Gessa GL. Chronic treatment with antidepressants prevents the inhibitory effect of small doses of apomorphine on dopamine synthesis and motor activity. *Life Sci* 1979;25:415-424.
66. Serra G, Collu M, D'Aquila PS, De Montis GM, Gessa GL. Possible role of dopamine D1 receptor in the behavioural supersensitivity to dopamine agonists induced by chronic treatment with antidepressants. *Brain Res* 1990;527:234-243.
67. Simon H, Stinus L, Tassin JP, et al. Is the dopaminergic mesocorticolimbic system necessary for intracranial self-stimulation? *Behav Neurol Biol* 1979;27:125-145.
68. Spyraki C, Fibiger HC. Behavioural evidence for supersensitivity of postsynaptic dopamine receptors in the mesolimbic system after chronic administration of desipramine. *Eur J Pharmacol* 1981;74:195-206.
69. Steiner SS, Beer B, Shaffer MM. Escape from self-produced rates of brain stimulation. *Science* 1969;163:90-91.
70. Thierry AM, Tassin J-P, Blanc G, Glowinski J. Selective activation of the mesocortical DA system by stress. *Nature* 1976;263:242-244.

71. Tsang W-K, Stutz RM. Subject control as a determinant of the reinforcing properties of intracranial stimulation. *Physiol Behav* 1984;32:795-802.
72. Weeks JF. Experimental morphine addiction: Method for automatic intravenous injections in unrestrained rats. *Science* 1962;138:143-144.
73. Welch J, Kim H, Fallon S, Liebman J. Do antidepressants induce dopamine autoreceptor subsensitivity? *Nature* 1982;298:301-302.
74. Wenkstern D, Pfaus JG, Fibiger HC. Dopamine transmission increases in the nucleus accumbens of male rats during their first exposure to sexually receptive female rats. *Brain Res* 1993;618:41-46.
75. Willner P, Muscat R, Papp M, Sampson D. Dopamine, depression and anti-depressant drugs. In: Willner P, Scheel-Kruger J, eds. *The Mesolimbic Dopamine System From Motivation to Action.* Chichester: John Wiley & Sons, 1991:387-410.
76. Willner P, Muscat R, Papp M. Chronic mild stress-induced anhedonia: a realistic animal model of depression. *Neuroscience and Behavioral Reviews* 1992;16:525-534.
77. Young AMJ, Joseph MJ, Gray JA. Increased dopamine release in vivo in nucleus accumbens and caudate nucleus of the rat during drinking; a microdialysis study. *Neuroscience* 1992;48:871-876.

Depression and Mania: From Neurobiology to Treatment: edited by G. Gessa, W. Fratta, L. Pani, and G. Serra. Raven Press, New York © 1995.

Animal Models of Depression: Validity and Applications

Paul Willner

Department of Psychology, University of Wales, Swansea, SA2 8PP, U.K.

From its early beginnings in the reserpine reversal, amphetamine potentiation and muricide (mouse killing) tests, the list of animal models of depression has grown to include upwards of twenty experimental procedures in current use. Their common feature is that behavioural abnormalities are reversed by antidepressant drugs. In other respects, animal models of depression vary widely in the means of inducing abnormal behaviour, in the aspects of behaviour chosen for study, and in the time course of antidepressant action.

The largest group of animal models of depression consists of paradigms based on the application of stress: it tends to be the case that the behavioural sequelae of stress are usually reversible by antidepressants. These paradigms include the acute application of a variety of moderate to severe stressors (footshock, restraint or water immersion); the chronic application of collections of mild or severe stressors; and certain other manipulations that are most conveniently thought of as stressors, such as social defeat or the administration of high doses of psychostimulant drugs. These procedures lead to decreases in locomotor activity and/or rewarded behaviours, which are reversed in whole or in part by antidepressants, administered acutely or chronically depending upon the model. A second group of models is based on social separation or isolation. The most familiar of these models involve non-human primates, either infants isolated from their parents or juveniles isolated from their peer group; separation models have also been developed in other species, including rats. These procedures are characterized by successive phases of 'protest' followed by 'despair'. In contrast to these two groups of models, in which antidepressants by-and-large increase the target behaviour from an abnormally low baseline, in a third group, antidepressants decrease the target behaviour; these effects involve in part an inhibition of impulsive behaviours. The two most familiar models in this group are the hyperactivity that follows lesions to the olfactory bulb and the operant differential-reinforcement-of-low-rate (DRL) procedure. Finally, there are a miscellany of other models, which include selective breeding procedures, manipulations of circadian rhythms, and a variety of procedures involving interactions between antidepressants and other drug classes.

The literature on animal models of depression has been summarized recently in a number of comprehensive reviews (31,34,55,73,78,80,81). Rather than digging over this well-trodden ground, the present chapter will examine two specific aspects of animal models of depression: the steps needed to evaluate their validity, and the types of information that a well-validated model can provide.

VALIDATION OF ANIMAL MODELS OF DEPRESSION

Although an animal model of depression must respond appropriately to antidepressant drugs, the converse does not apply: the fact that a behaviour is sensitive to antidepressants is not in itself sufficient to define the procedure as an animal model of depression. Antidepressant drugs have side effects irrelevant to their clinical action that may have irrelevant behavioural consequences. Antidepressants also have clinical actions outside depression, including a spectrum of anxiolytic effects (36); and they are active in at least some animal models of anxiety, following chronic treatment (10,25). For these and other reasons, it is important at the outset to consider what criteria a valid animal model of depression should meet. These are most conveniently described under the three general headings of predictive validity (the extent to which the model responds appropriately to drugs that are clinically effective and those that are not), face validity (the degree of similarity between the behaviours modelled and the symptoms of depression), and construct validity (the theoretical rationale underlying the model) (73,73,79).

Predictive Validity

The concept of predictive validity implies that manipulations known to influence the pathological state should have similar effects in the model. In practice, the predictive validity of animal models of depression is determined largely by their response to antidepressant drugs. A valid test should be sensitive and specific: it should respond to effective antidepressants but not to ineffective agents. Positive responses should occur at sensible doses, and should be demonstrable with a range of structurally diverse compounds.

Although the basic requirement for predictive validity is that a putative animal model of depression should respond to antidepressant drugs, in fact, some 30% of depressed patients fail to do so. Nevertheless, a model that did not respond to tricyclics would not at present be taken seriously, and this situation is unlikely to change in the absence of well-established therapies for tricyclic-resistant depressions. The position in relation to the older monoamine oxidase inhibitors (MAOIs) is more forgiving, as the older MAOIs tend to be less effective than tricyclics (41), though they have good anxiolytic activity and so may be clinically useful in mixed anxiety/depression states (61). Therefore, a failure to respond to MAOIs is not usually considered to invalidate an animal model of depression (provided that it does respond to tricyclics). However, the newer reversible inhibitors of MAO-A (RIMAs) do appear to be as efficacious as tricyclics (68,87), so the validity of an animal model of depression would be called into question by a failure to respond to these drugs.

Beyond the classical antidepressants (tricyclics and MAOIs) are a wide range of newer compounds for which antidepressant activity has been claimed, ranging from reasonably well-established antidepressants (eg. selective 5HT or NA uptake inhibitors), through compounds that are probably effective (eg. alpha2 antagonists; 5HT1 agonists), to compounds of uncertain status (eg. phosphodiesterase inhibitors; calcium antagonists; anticonvulsants). Even in the case of the specific 5HT uptake inhibitors, whose antidepressant efficacy is beyond doubt, it is still uncertain whether their spectrum of activity is identical to that of the tricyclics. Therefore, while a well-rounded description of an animal model of depression should include an account of its pharmacological profile broader than that provided by the response to traditional antidepressants, the contribution of these newer compounds to validation is limited.

To some extent, similar uncertainties exist in relation to drugs that are ineffective as antidepressants. The 'false negatives' most commonly encountered in animal models of depression are psychomotor stimulants, anticholinergics and opiates. However, prior to the development of antidepressants, drugs from all three of these classes were regularly prescribed for the relief of depression (74). Some recent studies have confirmed that certain opiates (eg. buprenorphine) have antidepressant activity (24) but anticholinergics and stimulants have never been properly assessed, as their use was discontinued prior to the introduction of blind clinical trials. Again, the uncertain status of these compounds to some extent undermines their value as definitive standards.

Finally, as noted above, it has recently become clear that the response to antidepressant drugs is insufficient to define an animal model of depression, since antidepressants are active in at least some animal models of anxiety, following chronic treatment (10,25), and indeed, are increasingly seen as the drugs of choice in many forms of anxiety (36). It is therefore crucial for establishing the predictive validity of an animal model of depression to demonstrate that the model does not respond to benzodiazepines.

Face Validity

Face validity refers to a phenomenological similarity between the model and the disorder modelled. In the paper that first considered the problem of validating animal models, and so formed a starting point for subsequent research, McKinney and Bunney (40) proposed that an animal model should resemble the condition modelled in terms of its etiology, symptomatology, treatment and biological basis. However, in a second important theoretical contribution, Abramson and Seligman (1) pointed out that not all symptoms carry equal weight: a valid animal model should demonstrate a resemblance to the clinically defined core symptoms of the disorder, rather than the subsidiary symptoms. Furthermore, not all of the symptoms of depression can be modelled in animals; symptoms that can only be known by subjective verbal report (such as excessive guilt, feelings of worthlessness, or thoughts of suicide) are in principle excluded (74,78). A DSM-III-R diagnosis of major depression requires the presence of a least one of two core symptoms: loss of interest or pleasure (anhedonia) and depressed mood. Of these two core symptoms, anhedonia can be modelled in animals, but depressed mood cannot. In assessing the face validity of animal models of depression, anhedonia therefore assumes a central position.

The subsidiary symptoms of depression that are amenable to modelling in animals include psychomotor change, decreased persistence, decreased sexual activity, and disturbances of sleep or food intake. However, psychomotor, sleep and appetite changes may be in either direction, so that, for example, both decreases and increases in locomotor activity may be claimed as support for the validity of a model. This lack of precision, together with the fact that the clinical phenomena of psychomotor retardation and agitation are considerably more complex than gross changes in locomotor activity, and indeed, may co-exist (53), suggests that simulations in which a change in locomotor activity is the major, or only, behavioural feature should not be taken too seriously. Unfortunately, it is precisely these behaviours that feature most prominently in the majority of animal models of depression (80).

Little attention has been paid to the question of sub-types of depression in the development of animal models, which have tended to focus either on an undifferentiated depressive state or on the principal subtype of major depression, melancholia. Some other well defined subtypes of depression have been largely ignored: for example, delusional depression. This condition is difficult to translate into behavioural terms, being differentiated from non-delusional depression only by a greater association with psychomotor agitation (53). However, delusional depressions are pharmacologically distinct, being unresponsive to tricyclic antidepressants, but responsive to electroconvulsive therapy (ECT) or to tricyclic/neuroleptic combinations (52). The challenge of developing an animal model that responds to ECT but not to tricyclics remains to be met. Bipolar disorder is another well defined diagnostic category for which there are no animal models. In this case, the depressive episodes appear to be identical to those of unipolar endogenous depression, but episodes of mania are interspersed. While there are a number of animal models of mania (39), the alternation of depressive-like and manic-like behaviours in an animal model has not yet been systematically addressed. Indeed, the episodic nature of unipolar depression is itself another area that has not been explored in animal models.

In DSM-III (though not in DSM-III-R or DSM-IV), the defining symptom of melancholia was anhedonia, which is readily modelled as a decrease in sensitivity to rewards. In many empirical studies, psychomotor retardation has emerged as the symptom most characteristic of melancholia, while psychomotor agitation tends to be more closely associated with psychotic features such as delusions of guilt (53). Nevertheless, there is considerable overlap between these two groups of symptoms, and agitated melancholias are not uncommon. Unlike non-melancholic depressions, melancholia is characterized by a decrease in the latency to enter the first period of rapid eye movement (REM) sleep (35) and an increased secretion of cortisol, usually detected by the dexamethasone suppression test (DST) (16). In a valid simulation of melancholia, these biological markers might be expected to coexist alongside a decreased sensitivity to reward.

It is widely believed that because the pharmacotherapy of depression requires chronic drug treatment, the validity of an animal model is called into question by an acute antidepressant response. In fact, the clinical requirement for chronic treatment may be more apparent than real: there is some evidence of very early antidepressant responses in clinical studies designed explicitly to detect them (eg. 26; see also 76). The real test for a simulation of depression is that tolerance must not develop to the antidepressant response: irrespective of how it responds to acute antidepressant treatment, the model must respond to chronic treatment. This test has not been universally applied to animal models of depression, but in general, those models to which the test has been applied have passed it. Indeed, it is usually found that if a test does respond acutely to antidepressants, the response is potentiated by chronic treatment (76), though tolerance to antidepressant effects has been reported in some behavioural paradigms (20,54). However, a chronic time course becomes a critical feature if the model is to be used to investigate the physiological mechanisms of antidepressant action, and even longer durations are necessary if the focus of the investigation is the reversal of behavioural abnormalities by antidepressants, rather than simply their prophylaxis.

Construct Validity

In order to evaluate the theoretical rationale of an animal model, we require a theoretical account of the disordered behaviour in the model, a theoretical account of the disorder itself, and a means of bringing the two theories into alignment. This can only be done if the clinical theory occupies an appropriate framework, which uses terms and concepts applicable also to subhuman species. However, the evaluation of animal models of depression is intrinsically limited by the rudimentary state of biologically oriented theories of depression. While there is an extensive literature describing neurochemical abnormalities or biochemical markers associated with depression, there is little in this literature that can be used to provide theoretical standards against which to validate animal models. For example, even the most basic questions of whether the level of activity in monoaminergic systems is elevated or decreased in depression remain controversial (74). As a result, the construct validity of the reserpine model, which is based upon the assumption that monoaminergic transmission is decreased, is difficult to assess (11). [The fact that this model has minimal predictive validity or face validity (73) is beside the point!].

Similar problems arise in relation to modelling the etiology of depression. It is now clear that variety of different factors are implicated in the etiology of depression: 'psychological' factors include undesirable life events, chronic mild stress, adverse childhood experiences, and personality traits such as introversion and impulsiveness; 'biological' factors include genetic influences, and a variety of physical illnesses and medications (see 4,5,74 for reviews). However, there is little theoretical understanding of the processes by which these factors influence the physiological processes underlying mood. In certain cases, the immediate precipitant of a depression may be clearly identified: for example, seasonal affective disorder or post-partum depression. More usually, the pathogenesis of depression is better understood as the result of an accumulation of a number of different risk factors (see eg. 4,7,14). This point has been largely overlooked in the construction of animal models of depression, which in general have assumed a single causal factor. This may be counterproductive, since few of the identified etiological factors appear sufficiently potent to precipitate depression in an otherwise risk-free individual.

Although attempts to assess the theoretical rationale of animal models are limited by this lack of theoretical structure at the clinical level, a number of generalizations are possible. The major group of animal models of depression are based on responses to stressors of various kinds, and are usually justified by reference to role of stressful life events in the etiology of depression (14,15,38). However, if very severe acute stress is used (eg. 71) there is a clear onus on the user to justify the relevance of these procedures to depression, rather than, for example, to post-traumatic stress disorder. Furthermore, the adverse consequences of life events endure for a prolonged period of six to twelve months, in part by exacerbating ongoing life difficulties (13,15). Thus, life events should not be viewed as acute stressors (indeed, in the case of bereavement, a diagnosis of depression is explicitly excluded during the period of acute loss); from this perspective, it may be more appropriate to use chronic stress regimes, rather than acute stressors, to model the etiological role of life events. Other factors have been identified that confer a long-lasting vulnerability to depression, in particular, an inadequate level of social support, which to a large extent arises from inadequate socialization (7,13-15,77). From these starting points, a number of animal models of depression have been developed that are based on the adverse effects of social isolation. However, with the exception of some of the primate studies (65,70), these models have largely ignored both the complexity of childhood social deprivation phenomena and the mediation of their effects through later social relationships.

Although assessment of the theoretical rationale of animal models of depression is limited by the paucity of theory, construct validity can also be evaluated at the level of constructs. This approach is exemplified by the extensive experimental analysis of whether 'learned helplessness' is an appropriate term to describe the impairments of escape learning that follow exposure to inescapable electric shock (66). The 'learned helplessness' hypothesis proposed that this learning impairment occurs because exposure to uncontrollable stress provides the basis, in animals as in people, for learning that stress is uncontrollable (helplessness); and that this learning has a number of debilitating consequences, including depression (66). In contrast to the proposal that animals perform poorly because they have learned that their responses are ineffective in controlling their environment, a number of alternative accounts of the learning impairment have been suggested, which take as their starting point the observation that, inescapable shock has a variety of other, simpler effects, that could also explain many of the behavioural impairments, such as decreased locomotor activity (8,28) and analgesia (37). In order to demonstrate that inescapable shock does, additionally, cause 'cognitive' impairments, Jackson et al. (33) assessed performance accuracy using a maze task, in which performance would be independent of factors influencing motor speed. Under these circumstances, stress did impair learning ability, but subsequent work demonstrated that this effect was secondary to an impairment of attention: stressed animals are more fearful and therefore more easily distracted (42). So inescapable shock does cause 'cognitive' impairment, but at the level of attentional processes rather than 'helplessness'. The attentional impairment is mediated by a functional incapacitation of noradrenergic transmission in the forebrain (43,71), and may indicate some functional correlates of the disorders of noradrenergic transmission in depressedpatients, which have frequently been observed but have proved extremely difficult to interpret (see 74 for review). An additional problem for the learned helplessness model is that the behavioural impairments appear to owe rather more to the unpredictability of stress than to its uncontrollability (32). Together with the importance of fear in generating the learning impairments, this implies that the conventional 'learned helplessness' paradigm may actually be of greater relevance to anxiety than to depression. It is perhaps worth adding that the clinical hypothesis implicating perceptions of helplessness in the etiology of depression has passed through a number of incarnations (2,3), and now takes a form so complex that it is doubtful whether animal studies can make any further direct contribution. Thus, while the learned helplessness paradigm has undoubtedly had a major impact on clinical thinking, this is now largely of historical importance.

This example of successful experimental analysis of construct validity (albeit that the analysis takes off in an unexpected and disconcerting direction) contrasts sharply with a second stress model, the 'behavioural despair' test (60). This term was introduced to describe the immobility seen in rats or mice forced to swim in a confined space; it was assumed that when the animals adopted an immobile posture, they had 'despaired' of escaping. Unfortunately, this interpretation is not susceptible to experimental analysis. Consequently, although the test continues to be very widely used, the name 'behavioural despair' has been largely abandoned, and replaced instead by the theoretically neutral term 'the forced swim test'.

A Case Study: The Chronic Mild Stress Procedure

The chronic mild stress (CMS) model, which was developed with the explicit objectives of using relatively realistic inducing conditions to model a core symptom of depression that would be reversed by chronic administration of effective antidepressants, provides an example of the systematic application of the three sets of validating criteria.

In the CMS model, rats or mice are exposed sequentially to a variety of extremely mild stressors (eg. overnight illumination; cage tilt; change of cage mate), which change every few hours over a period of weeks or months. This

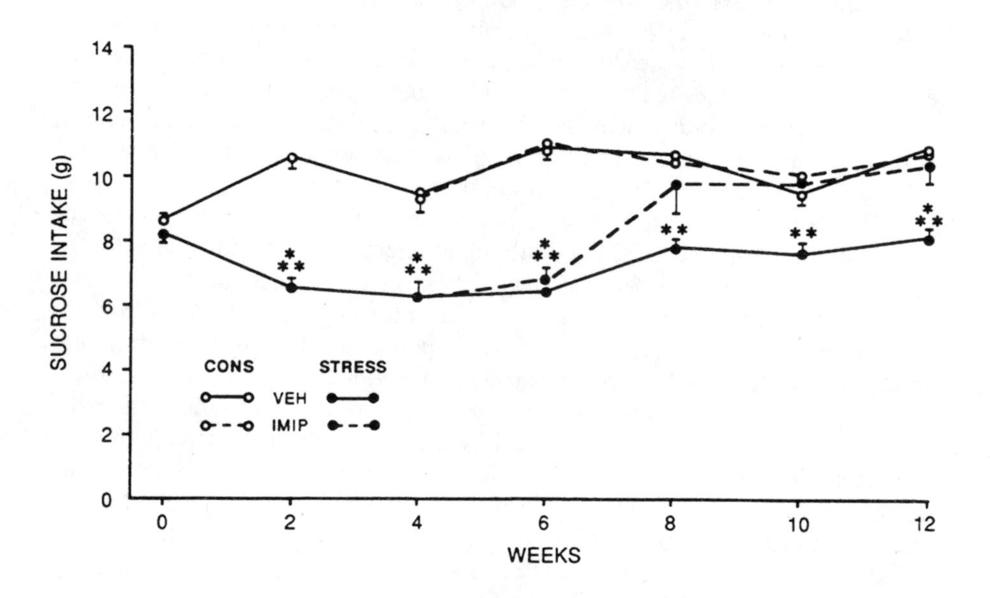

FIG. 1 Reduction of sucrose consumption by chronic mild stress and its restoration by imipramine (IMIP). Stress (closed circles) was administered for a total of 12 weeks; imipramine treatment (5 mg/kg/day) commenced after 4 weeks of stress (dotted lines). Imipramine restored normal behaviour after 4 weeks of treatment in the stressed animals, but had no effect in non-stressed controls.

procedure causes a decrease in sensitivity to rewards, which is usually monitored by a substantial decrease in the consumption of and/or preference for a palatable weak sucrose solution (44,83,86). No single element of the chronic mild stress (CMS) schedule is either necessary or sufficient for these effects; variety is essential (49). CMS-induced behavioural deficits may be maintained for several months; however, normal behaviour is restored, during continued application of CMS, by chronic treatment with tricyclic or atypical antidepressants (Fig. 1).

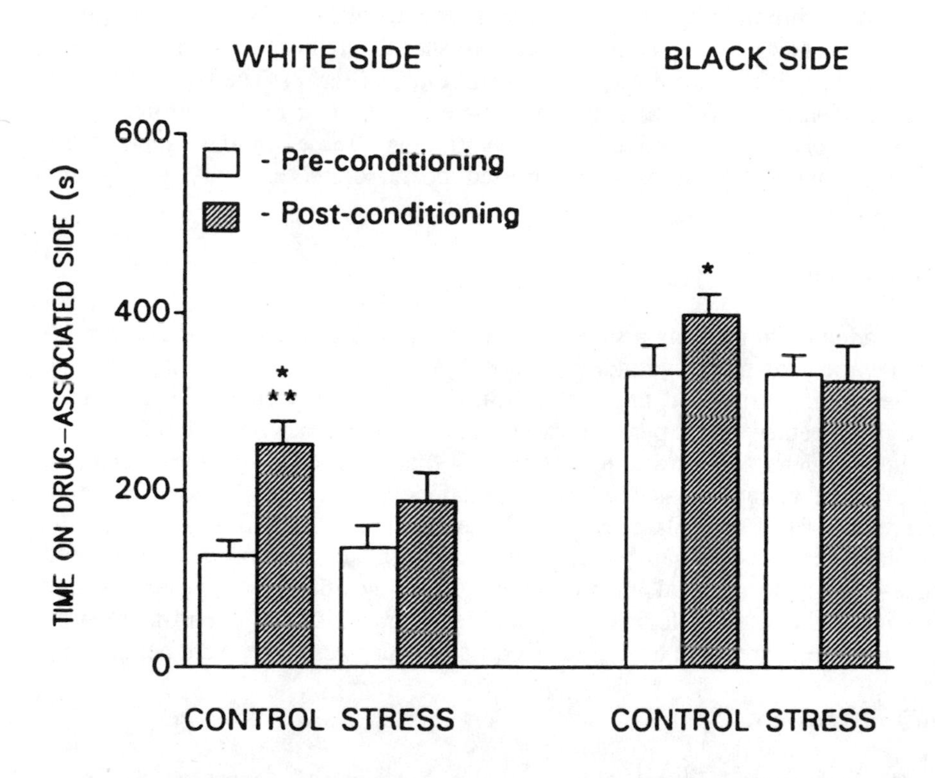

FIG. 2 Effects of chronic mild stress on morphine-induced place preference conditioning. Animals were first allowed to explore freely in an apparatus containing two distinctive compartments (white and black). In conditioning trials, morphine was administered prior to confining the animal in either the white (left) or the black (right) compartment. The data are time spent in the drug-associated side before (open bars) and after (hatched bars) conditioning. Irrespective of whether morphine was paired with the initially preferred (black) or initially nonpreferred (white) side, control animals showed an increase in preference for the drug-associated side: this effect was abolished in stressed animals (57). Similar effects of stress are seen using a variety of other drug or natural reinforcers.

The predictive, face and construct validity of the CMS model are illustrated by the following findings:

(i) Construct validity

Decreases in sucrose drinking cannot be explained by nonspecific changes (eg. decreased thirst), since the intake of plain water is unaffected by CMS (49). Furthermore, behavioural deficits are apparent in rewarded paradigms that do not depend on consummatory behaviour. Thus, CMS causes an increase in the threshold current required to support intracranial self-stimulation (brain stimulation reward), and attenuates or abolishes the ability to associate rewards with a distinctive environment (place conditioning) (Fig. 2). The latter effect has been demonstrated with a variety of different natural or drug reinforcers, but does not extend to aversive place conditioning. These findings support the concept that CMS causes a generalized decrease in sensitivity to rewards (45,46,56,57).

(ii) Face validity

In addition to inducing a state of anhedonia, CMS also causes the appearance of a variety of other symptoms of major depressive disorder. These include decreases in sexual and aggressive behaviour (21); a decrease in locomotor activity together with a phase advance in the circadian activity cycle (29); loss of body weight (49); adrenal hypertrophy (49) and corticosterone hypersecretion (9); and a variety of sleep disorders characteristic of depression, including decreased REM sleep latency (19,48). In contrast, CMS did not cause the appearance of an 'anxious' profile in two animal models of anxiety, the elevated plus-maze and the social interaction test (21). Thus the model generates both behavioural and physiological abnormalities characteristic of major depression, and the effects appear to have some specificity to depression-relevant behaviours.

(iii) Predictive validity

Antidepressants do not alter rewarded behaviour in nonstressed control animals. Drugs shown to be effective in reversing CMS-induced anhedonia include tricyclics (50,83), the specific monoamine uptake inhibitors fluoxetine and maprotiline (51), the monoamine oxidase inhibitors moclobemide (46) and brofaromine (M. Papp, pers. comm), and the atypical antidepressant mianserin (18,47). Electroconvulsive shock (48), lithium (69) and buspirone (M. Papp, pers. comm) have also recently been shown to be effective in this model. The reversal of CMS-induced anhedonia typically requires 3-4 weeks of treatment, which closely resembles the clinical time course of antidepressant action. Ineffective agents include chlordiazepoxide (51), the neuroleptics haloperidol and chlorprothixene, d-amphetamine, and morphine (M. Papp, pers. comm). The model thus appears to be both specific and selective in responding to a wide range of antidepressants (including all of the clinically effective agents so far tested), and failing to respond to non-antidepressants.

APPLICATIONS OF ANIMAL MODELS OF DEPRESSION

Of the various animal models of depression in current use, the CMS model is probably the best validated, when all three dimensions (predictive, face and construct validity) are taken into account. The following discussion of the applications of animal models of depression therefore relies heavily on findings derived from the CMS model. However, it is important to keep the full spectrum of models in mind, since the data derived from different models show both convergence and divergence. Where data diverge it may well be the case that a more valid model is providing correct information and a less valid model is not. However, it is also possible that both are correct, and the differences between them reflect the chaotic heterogeneity of depressive disorders.

Etiology of depression

Animal models can potentially provide important insights into the factors that lead some individuals to succumb to stress while others are resistant. A variety of factors have been identified that cause individuals to vary in their susceptibility to depression. For example, there is strong evidence of a major genetic contribution to bipolar (manic-depressive) disorder (6), unipolar depressions are up to three times more prevalent in women than in men (72), and adverse early childhood experiences are known to increase greatly the risk of depression in later life (14). Current studies demonstrate the feasibility of using animal models to investigate these risk factors. For example, the effects of CMS are potentiated by adverse rearing conditions: rats reared in isolation from weaning were more susceptible than group-reared animals to the suppressive effects of CMS on rewarded behaviour (sucrose drinking) and sexual behaviour (21). In contrast, preliminary studies failed to demonstrate sex differences in the CMS model (21); nevertheless, sex differences in behavioural and biochemical responses to stress are well established in other paradigms (30).

A number of selective breeding programmes have resulted in strains of rodent that to some extent bear behavioural and physiological resemblances to depressed humans (see 55 for review). Depressed patients are known to be hypersensitive to drugs that stimulate central acetylcholine receptors, and some physiological abnormalities characteristic of depression are consistent with a state of cholinergic hyperfunction (55). One selected rat strain, the Flinders Sensitive Line (FSL), which were bred for their sensitivity to a cholinergic agonist, show abnormalities in a number of behavioural tests, including an increased susceptibility to CMS-induced anhedonia, as assessed by the suppression of saccharin drinking (63).

A related experimental strategy has been to screen a variety of available inbred mouse strains in behavioural tests responsive to the effects of acute stress. Despite the reservations expressed above concerning the validity of the 'learned helplessness' paradigm, an attractive feature of this model is the breadth of symptomatic parallels to severe depression (71). In addition to the impairment of shock-escape learning, uncontrollable stress has many other consequences, including impairments of rewarded behaviour. One manifestation of this effect is a long-lasting decrease in responding for brain stimulation reward, which is specific to certain electrode placements, and therefore suggests a subsensitivity within part of the brain mechanism of reward (anhedonia), rather than, for example, a motor impairment (88). Significantly, inescapable foot-shock has variable behavioural effects (most of which are antidepressant-reversible) in different mouse strains. To take an extreme example, in the C57BL/67 strain, uncontrollable shock severely impaired subsequent learning to escape shock, but had no effect on responding for brain stimulation reward, while the DBA/2J strain showed exactly the opposite pattern of deficits (67,89). These genetic studies provide a starting point for future investigation of the physiological mechanisms underlying individual differences in responses to stress.

Neurobiological mechanisms underlying depressive symptomatology

The most obvious questions to ask of a valid animal model of psychopathology concerns the neurobiological mechanisms underlying the behavioural disturbances. Although depression has traditionally been viewed as a disorder of noradrenergic and, increasingly, serotonergic function, the most obvious starting point for investigation of the mechanisms underlying changes in sensitivity to reward is the mesolimbic dopamine (DA) system, which is known to play a crucial role in the performance of rewarded behaviours (82).

Both behavioural and biochemical data suggest that the anhedonia elicited by the CMS procedure reflects a decrease in the sensitivity of D2/D3 DA receptors in the ventral striatum. Anhedonic stressed animals are subsensitive to the locomotor stimulant effects of directly (quinpirole) and indirectly (d-amphetamine) acting DA agonists, and are also subsensitive to the rewarding effects of these agents as assessed using the place conditioning paradigm. In particular, stressed animals were subsensitive to the rewarding effect of the D2/D3 agonist quinpirole administered directly within the nucleus accumbens (56,58). Receptor binding studies (Fig. 3) concur with the behavioural data in showing a decrease in the number of D2/D3 receptors in the ventral striatum of chronically stressed animals, with no effect in dorsal striatum (59). Other data suggest that these changes in postsynaptic receptor function may be secondary to a stress-induced activation of the mesolimbic DA system, causing a chronically increased level of DA release (86).

While there are strong theoretical grounds for predicting a dopaminergic substrate for anhedonia, other symptoms of depression are likely to involve

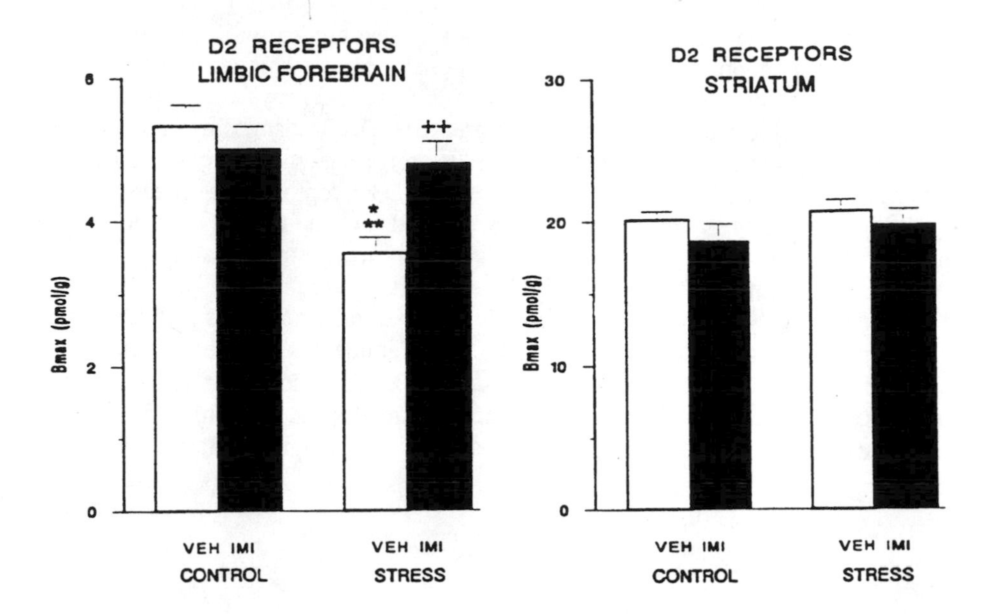

FIG. 3 B_{max} values for D2 receptor binding in limbic forebrain (left) and dorsal striatum (right) of animals receiving chronic mild stress for 8 weeks and/or imipramine (10 mg/kg b.i.d.) for 5 weeks. Stress reduced D2 receptor binding in limbic forebrain (primarily, nucleus accumbens) only, and the effect was completely reversed by imipramine (59).

different brain mechanisms. The noradrenergic basis of the attentional deficit caused by acute exposure to uncontrollable stress has already been mentioned; other animal models of depression, for example the olfactory bulbectomized rat, display symptoms that are attributable to disturbances of serotonergic function (see 76,77 for review). These findings provide strong support for the view that the analysis of the neurobiological mechanisms underlying psychopathology is more readily addressed at the level of symptoms rather than syndromes.

Mechanisms of antidepressant action

Chronic administration of antidepressant drugs to normal animals causes multiple changes in the functioning of a variety of neuronal systems (see 76 for review). However, the functional relevance of these findings is called into question by the fact that antidepressants only elevate mood in people who are depressed. This problem can most readily be addressed using models that maintain abnormal behaviour over long periods of time in order to simulate the conditions under which antidepressant drugs are used clinically.

Although antidepressant drugs have traditionally been assumed to exert their clinical effects through an interaction with NA or 5HT systems, following chronic treatment, antidepressants also potentiate DA transmission at D2/D3 receptors in the nucleus accumbens (see 76 for review). Current evidence suggests that this sensitization of postsynaptic D2/D3 receptors is the mechanism by which antidepressants reverse CMS-induced anhedonia. The decreased number of D2/D3 receptors seen in anhedonic chronically stressed animals (Fig. 3) was reversed in animals chronically treated with imipramine (59). Evidence that sensitized D2/D3 receptors mediate the behavioural recovery is provided by studies in which the increase in sucrose intake in antidepressant-treated animals was in turn reversed by acute administration of D2/D3 receptor antagonists, at low doses that were without effect in control animals (Fig. 4). This effect has been observed with tricyclic antidepressants, the atypical antidepressant

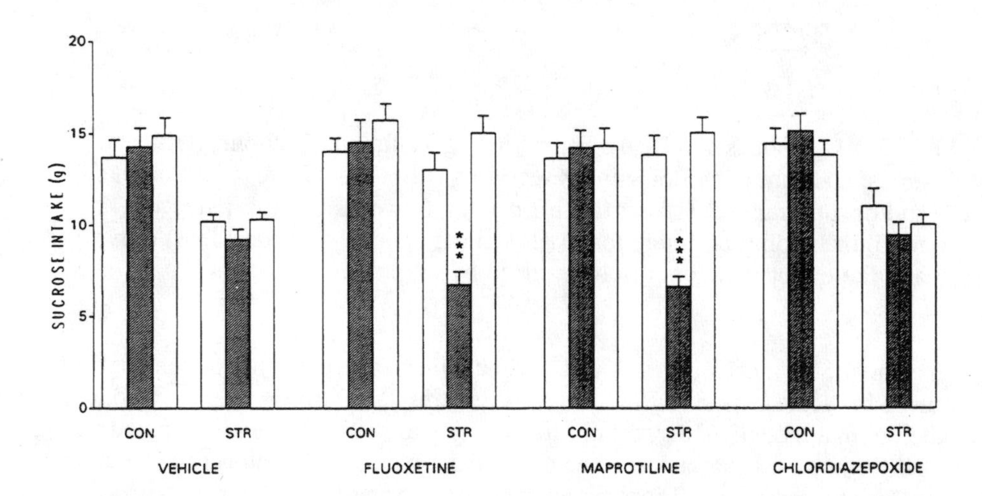

FIG. 4 Reversal of antidepressant effects in the chronic mild stress model by a DA antagonist. Data are sucrose intakes from control (CON) or stressed (STR) animals treated for 9 weeks with vehicle, the antidepressants fluoxetine and maprotiline, or the anxiolytic chlordiazepoxide (5 mg/kg/day). Each block of data shows two tests under normal conditions (white bars) and a third test (hatched bars) that was preceded by a single injection of the D2/D3 receptor antagonist raclopride, administered at a low dose (0.1 mg/kg) that was without effect in control animals. Sucrose intake was decreased by stress and restored by antidepressant treatment. However, the effects of fluoxetine and maprotiline were abolished by raclopride, which was without effect in all other groups (51).

mianserin, and significantly, the specific noradrenaline and serotonin reuptake inhibitors maprotiline and fluoxetine (18,51,86). These data suggest that sensitization of D2/D3 receptors in the ventral striatum may represent a final common pathway for the reversal of stress-induced anhedonia, irrespective of the primary site and mechanism of antidepressant drug action.

A predominant role of DA mechanisms in antidepressant action is supported by studies in another, less valid model, the forced swim test (17,64). Again, however, the generality of this conclusion must be tempered by the observation that in other models, antidepressants may act through different mechanisms. In the CMS model the prototypical tricyclic antidepressant imipramine and the SSRI fluoxetine appear equally sensitive to reversal by DA receptor blockade. In the learned helplessness model, however, while the effect of imipramine was completely reversed by the D1 antagonist SCH-23390, this drug antagonized fluoxetine to a much lesser extent (27). In the olfactory bulbectomized rat (12) and in a social isolation model (84), the action of imipramine was reversed by the 5HT receptor antagonist metergoline, which is ineffective in reversing imipramine in the CMS model. These results raise the interesting possibility that the same drug may act simultaneously through different neural mechanisms to alleviate different symptoms of depression.

Drug development: models as windows and mirrors

Animal models of depression are used for a variety of purposes. This discussion has been concerned primarily with the use of animal models as simulations for investigating aspects of the neurobiology of depression, and as experimental models within which to study the mechanisms of action of antidepressant drugs. However, animal models of depression are most frequently encountered within the pharmaceutical industry, where they are used as screening tests in antidepressant discovery and development programmes, and many of them were developed explicitly for this purpose. These different functions have different, and to some extent, conflicting requirements. Although the only essential requirement for antidepressant screening tests is that they make accurate predictions of antidepressant activity, they should also be cheap, robust, reliable and easy to use (23,79); for all of these subsidiary reasons, it is usually assumed that a screening test should be as simple as possible and should respond acutely to antidepressant treatment. However, a simulation of depression aims to mimic aspects of the clinical situation, and from this perspective should embody a degree of complexity, to permit investigation of the validity of the model. In addition, as discussed earlier, if a model is to be used to investigate antidepressant actions, a slow onset over several weeks of chronic treatment, comparable to the clinical time course, is highly desirable.

For these reasons, questions of face validity and construct validity have not been emphasized in the design of antidepressant screening tests, which by their nature focus on the narrow question of how well the test predicts clinical efficacy; as a result, the models used routinely as antidepressant screening tests are of limited or minimal validity as simulations of depression (cf. 73). However, the traditional requirement for screening tests to be quick and easy is predicated on an increasingly obsolete model of the drug development process. In the past, chemists produced new compounds in great profusion and behavioural models were used to predict what if any the clinical indications might be. However, most pharmaceutical companies have now abandoned the high volume, random-screening approach in favour of the development of a small number of compounds specifically designed to meet predetermined pharmacological criteria. An antidepressant development programme, for example, might aim to produce a specific serotonin reuptake inhibitor, or a receptor-subtype specific agonist, or a compound that desensitizes cortical beta-adrenergic receptors. Animal models aligned to this development strategy frequently serve as little more than a test for bioavailability of the compound at the appropriate receptor sites. (For example, subsensitivity to the inhibition of drinking behaviour by the beta-adrenergic agonist salbutamol, following chronic antidepressant treatment (62), serves to confirm that beta receptors are indeed subsensitive.)

An animal model serves as a window into the brain, through which aspects of neuronal functioning can be viewed that by reason of ethical and technical limitations are inaccessible to direct investigation in human subjects. The clarity of the view through a window depends largely on two factors: the cleanness of the glass and the intensity of the ambient illumination. In this regard, developments in both the techniques for neurobehavioural investigation and the accumulated knowledge of brain structure and function provide a clarity of vision in neurobiology that was until recently unimaginable. However, a more troublesome issue is whether the objects viewed through a window are those we wish to see. Irrespective of the clarity and quality of information it provides, the value of the insights derived from a model depends crucially on its validity: if the model is not valid it answers questions different from those asked. Conversely, the more valid the model, the higher the probability that inferences drawn from investigations using the model will be reliable.

If a valid model provides a window into the brain, then tests for the presence of predetermined functional characteristics act more like mirrors, reflecting back only what is presented to them. This analogy applies also to another feature of traditional screening tests, their time course. The major consideration in the design of antidepressant screening procedures has traditionally been that they respond to acute or subacute drug administration. A direct consequence of this strategy is that these tests are incapable, by virtue of their design, of discovering new antidepressants that have a shorter onset of action. As this represents the major current challenge in antidepressant drug development, the inability of traditional screening tests to respond to it represents a fundamental limitation on their continued usefulness. This provides a powerful argument for the use of chronic procedures in antidepressant screening programmes; and once this step is taken than it makes sense to go the whole way and use models that have been well validated. Although this approach has traditionally been avoided on grounds of convenience and cost, when we leave the old world of chemical roulette for the modern world of designer molecules, behavioural screening methods are located more within the drug development than drug discovery stage, and the logistical disadvantages of using complex, chronic models appear in much smaller perspective, relative to the costs of testing an ineffective drug in the clinic.

An example of this approach is illustrated in Fig. 5, which shows the effects in the chronic mild stress procedure (in mice) of a novel serotonergic compound, BIMT-17. In contrast to fluoxetine, which acts slowly to reverse the stress-induced suppression of sucrose drinking, BIMT-17 appears to exert its full effect after a single administration (22). Only time will tell whether the prediction of a rapid onset of antidepressant action will be borne out in the clinic.

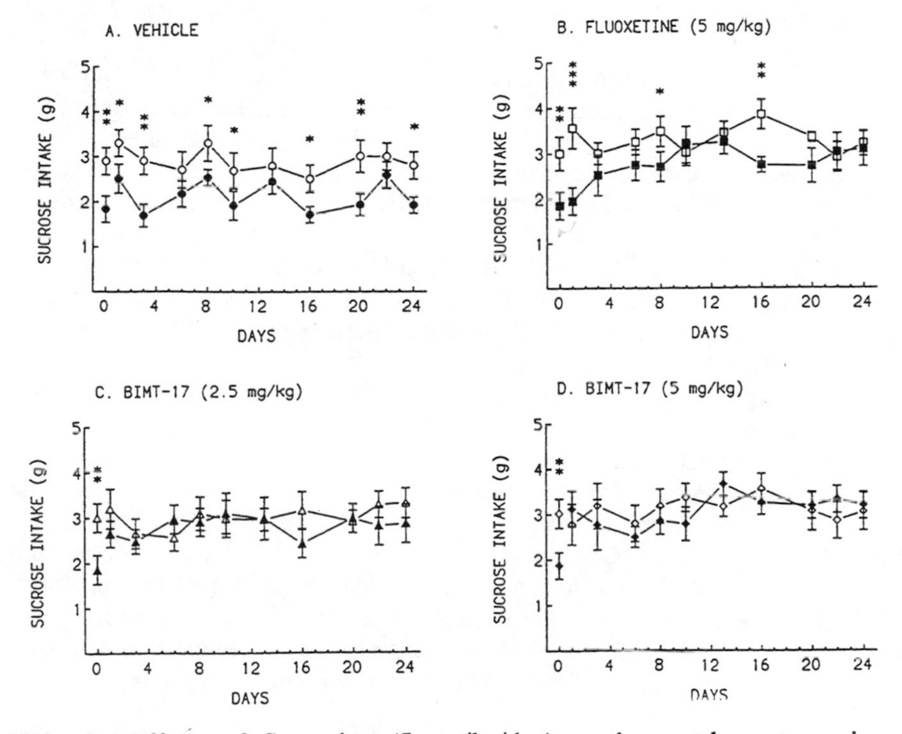

FIG. 5 Effects of fluoxetine (5 mg/kg/day) or the novel serotonergic compound BIMT-17 (2.5 or 5 mg/kg/day) on sucrose intake in stressed mice. The values shown over 'Day 0' represent intakes on the final test prior to the start of drug treatment, which commenced after 2 weeks of stress. In contrast to the gradual recovery seen in fluoxetine-treated animals (and the absence of recovery in vehicle-treated animals), BIMT-17 appeared to exert its full effect after a single injection, particularly at the higher dose (22).

REFERENCES

1. Abramson LY, Seligman MEP. Modeling psychopathology in the laboratory: History and rationale. In: Maser JD, Seligman MEP. eds. *Psychopathology: Experimental Models*. San Francisco: Freeman, 1989:1-26.
2. Abramson LY, Seligman MEP, Teasdale JD. Learned helplessness in humans: Critique and reformulation. *J Abnorm Psychol* 1978;87:49-74.
3. Abramson LY, Metalsky G, Alloy LB. Hopelessness depression: A theory-based subtype of depression. *Psychol Rev* 1989;96:358-372.
4. Akiskal HS. Interaction of biologic and psychologic factors in the origin of depressive disorders. *Acta Psychiatr Scand* 1985;71:131-139.
5. Akiskal HS. A developmental perspective on recurrent mood disorders: A review of studies in man. *Psychopharmacol Bull* 1986;22:579-586.
6. Allen MG. Twin studies of affective illness. *Arch Gen Psychiatr* 1976;33:1476-1478.
7. Aneshensel CS, Stone JD. Stress and depression: A test of the buffering model of social support. *Arch Gen Psychiatr* 1982;39:1392-1396.
8. Anisman HA, Remington G, Sklar LS. Effects of inescapable shock on subsequent escape performance: Catecholaminergic and cholinergic mediation of response initiation and maintenance. *Psychopharmacology* 1979;61:107-124.
9. Ayensu WT, Pucilowski O, Mason GA, Overstreet DH, Rezvani AH, Janowsky DS. Effects of chronic mild stress on serum complement activity, saccharin preference and corticosterone levels in Flinders lines of rats. *Physiol Behav* : in press.
10. Bodnoff SR, Suranyi-Codotte B, Aitken DH, Quirion R, Meaney MY. The effects of chronic antidepressant treatment in an animal model of anxiety. *Psychopharmacology* 1988;95:298-302.
11. Bourin M, Poncelet M, Chermat R, Simon P. The value of the reserpine test in psychopharmacology. *Arneim-Forsch* 1983;33:1173-1176.
12. Broekkamp CL, Garrigou D, Lloyd KG. Serotonin-mimetic and antidepressant drugs on passive avoidance learning by olfactory bulbectomized rats. *Pharmacol Biochem Behav* 1980;13:643-646.
13. Brown GW. A psychosocial view of depression. In: Bennett DH, Freeman H. eds. *Community Psychiatry*. London: Churchill-Livingstone, 1989:71-114.
14. Brown GW, Harris T. *Social Origins of Depression*. London: Tavistock, 1978.
15. Brown GW, Harris T. eds. *Life Events and Illness*. New York: Guilford Press, 1988.
16. Carroll BJ. The dexamethasone suppression test for melancholia. *Brit J Psychiatr* 1982;140:292-304.
17. Cervo L, Samanin R. Evidence that dopamine mechanisms in the nucleus

accumbens are selectively involved in the effect of desipramine in the forced swim test. *Neuropharmacology* 1987;26:1469-1472.

18. Cheeta S, Broekkamp C, Willner P. Stereospecific reversal of stress-induced anhedonia by mianserin and its (+)-enantiomer. *Psychopharmacology* : in press.
19. Cheeta S, Ruigt G, van Proosdij J, Willner P. Changes in sleep architecture following chronic mild stress. Submitted for publication.
20. Cuomo V, Cagiano R, Brunello N, Fumagalli R, Racagni G. Behavioural changes after acute and chronic administration of typical and atypical antidepressants in rat: Interactions with reserpine. *Neurosci Lett* 1983;40:315-319.
21. D'Aquila P, Brain PF, Willner P. Effects of chronic mild stress in behavioural tests relevant to anxiety and depression. *Physiol Behav* 1994;56:861-867.
22. D'Aquila P, Monleon S, Borsini F, Brain P, Willner P. Anti-anhedonic actions of the novel serotonergic agent BIMT-17, a potential rapidly-acting antidepressant. Submitted for publication.
23. Danysz W, Archer T, Fowler CJ. Screening for new antidepressant compounds. In: Willner P. ed. *Behavioural Models in Psychopharmacology: Theoretical, Industrial and Clinical Perspectives*. Cambridge: Cambridge University Press, 1991:126-156.
24. Emrich HM, Vogt P, Herz A. Possible antidepressant effects of opioids: Action of buprenorphine. *Ann NY Acad Sci* 1983;398:108-112.
25. Fontana DJ, Carbary TJ, Commisaris RL. Effects of acute and chronic anti-panic drug administration on conflict behavior in the rat. *Psychopharmacology* 1989;98:157-162.
26. Frazer A, Lucki I, Sills M. Alterations in monoamine-containing neuronal function due to administration of antidepressants repeatedly to rats. *Acta Pharmacol Toxicol* 1985;56:Suppl.1,21-34.
27. Gambarana C, Ghiglieri O, Taddei I, Tagliamonte A, De Montis MG. Imipramine and fluoxetine prevent the learned helplessness behavior acquisition in rats through a distinct mechanism of action. *Behav Pharmacol* 1995;5:66-73.
28. Glazer HI, Weiss JM. Long-term interference effect: an alternative to "learned helplessness". *J Exp Psychol: Anim Behav Proc* 1976;2:201-213.
29. Gorka Z, Moryl E, Papp M. Chronic mild stress influences the diurnal activity rhythms in rats. *Behav Pharmacol* 1994;5:Suppl.1,88.
30. Heinsbroek R. Sex difference in behavioral and biochemical consequences of aversive stimulation in rats. *PhD thesis*, University of Amsterdam, 1990.
31. Henn FA, McKinney WT. Animal models in psychiatry. In: Meltzer HY. ed. *Psychopharmacology: The Third Generation of Progress*. New York: Raven, 1987:697-704.
32. Jackson RL, Minor TR. Effects of signaling inescapable shock on

subsequent escape learning: Implications for theories of coping and "learned helplessness". *J Exp Psychol: Anim Behav Proc* 1988;14:390-400.

33. Jackson RL, Maier SF, Rapoport PM. Exposure to inescapable shock produces both activity and associative deficits in rats. *Learn Motiv* 1978;9:69-98.
34. Jesberger JA, Richardson JS. Animal models of depression: Parallels and correlates to severe depression in humans. *Biol Psychiatr* 1985;20:764-784.
35. Kupfer DJ, Thase ME. The use of the sleep laboratory in the diagnosis of affective disorders. *Psychiatr Clin North Am* 1983;6:3-25.
36. Lader M Animal models of anxiety: A clinical perspective. In: Willner P. ed. *Behavioural Models in Psychopharmacology: Theoretical, Industrial and Clinical Perspectives*. Cambridge: Cambridge University Press, 1991:76-88.
37. Lewis JW, Cannon JT, Liebeskind JC. Opioid and non-opioid mechanisms of stress-induced analgesia. *Science* 1980;208:623-625.
38. Lloyd C. Life events and depressive disorder reviewed. *Arch Gen Psychiatr* 1980;37:529-548.
39. Lyon M. Animal models of mania and schizophrenia. In: Willner P. ed. *Behavioural Models in Psychopharmacology: Theoretical, Industrial and Clinical Perspectives*. Cambridge: Cambridge University, 1991:253-310.
40. McKinney WT, Bunney WE. Animal model of depression: Review of evidence and implications for research. *Arch Gen Psychiatr* 1969;21:240-248.
41. Medical Research Council. Clinical trials of the treatment of depressive illness. *Brit Med J* 1965;1:881-886.
42. Minor TR, Jackson RL, Maier SF. Effects of task-irrelevant cues and reinforcement delay on choice-escape learning following inescapable shock: Evidence for a deficit in selective attention. *J Exp Psychol: Anim Behav Proc* 1984;10:543-556.
43. Minor TR, Pelleymounter MA, Maier SF. Uncontrollable shock, forebrain norepinephrine, and stimulus selection during choice escape learning. *Psychobiology* 1988;16:135-145.
44. Monleon S, D'Aquila P, Parra A, Simon VM, Brain PF, Willner P Attenuation of sucrose consumption in mice by chronic mild stress and its restoration by imipramine. *Psychopharmacology* : in press.
45. Moreau J-L, Jenck F, Martin JR, Mortas P, Haefely WE. Antidepressant treatment prevents chronic mild stress-induced anhedonia as assessed by ventral tegmentum self-stimulation behaviour in rats. *Europ Neuropsychopharmacol* 1992;2:43-49.
46. Moreau J-L, Jenck F, Martin JR,, Mortas P, Haefely WE. Effects of moclobemide, a new generation reversible MAO-A inhibitor, in a novel animal model of depression. *Pharmacopsychiatry* 1993;26:30-33.

47. Moreau J-L, Jenck F, Martin JR, Mortas P. Curative effects of the atypical antidepressant mianserin in the chronic mild stress-induced anhedonia model of depression. *J Psychiatr Neurosci* 19:51-56.
48. Moreau J-L, Jenck F, Martin JR, Scherschlicht R. The chronic mild stress-induced anhedonia model of depression: REM sleep abnormalities and curative effects of electroshock treatment. *Behav Pharmacol* 1994;5:Suppl.1,32.
49. Muscat R, Willner P. Suppression of sucrose drinking by chronic mild unpredictable stress: a methodological analysis. *Neurosci Biobehav Rev* 1992;16:507-517.
50. Muscat R, Sampson D, Willner P. Dopaminergic mechanisms of imipramine action in an animal model of depression. *Biol Psychiatr* 1990;28:223-230.
51. Muscat R, Papp M, Willner P. Reversal of stress-induced anhedonia by the atypical antidepressants, fluoxetine and maprotoline. *Psychopharmacology* 1992;109:433-438.
52. Nelson JC. The use of antipsychotic drugs in the treatment of depression. In: Zohar J, Belmaker RH. eds. *Treating Resistant Depression*. New York: PMA Corp, 1987:131-146.
53. Nelson JC, Charney DS. The symptoms of major depression. *Am J Psychiatr* 1981;138:1-13.
54. Niesink RJM, van Ree JM. Antidepressant drugs normalize the increased social behaviour of pairs of male rats induced by short term isolation. *Neuropharmacology* 1982;21:1343-1348.
55. Overstreet DH, Russell RW, Crocker AD, Gillin JC, Janowsky DS. Genetic and pharmacological models of cholinergic supersensitivity and affective disorders. *Experientia* 1988;44:465-472.
56. Papp M, Willner P, Muscat R. An animal model of anhedonia: attenuation of sucrose consumption and place preference conditioning by chronic unpredictable mild stress. *Psychopharmacology* 1991;104:255-259.
57. Papp M, Lappas S, Muscat R, Willner P. Attenuation of place preference conditioning but not place aversion conditioning by chronic mild stress. *J Psychopharmacol* 1992;6:352-356.
58. Papp M, Muscat R, Willner P. Subsensitivity to rewarding and locomotor stimulant effects of a dopamine agonist following chronic mild stress. *Psychopharmacology* 1993;110:152-158.
59. Papp M, Klimek V, Willner P. Parallel changes in dopamine D2 receptor binding in limbic forebrain associated with chronic mild stress-induced anhedonia and its reversal by imipramine. *Psychopharmacology* 1994;115:441-446.
60. Porsolt RD. Behavioural despair. In: Enna SJ, Malick JB, Richelson E. eds. *Antidepressants: Neurochemical, Behavioural and Clinical Perspectives*. New York: Raven Press, 1981:121-139.
61. Przegalinski E, Baran L, Siwanowicz J. The effect of chronic treatment

with antidepressant drugs on salbutamol-induced hypoactivity in rats. *Psychopharmacology* 1983;80:355-359.

62. Potter WZ, Rudorfer MV, Manji H. The pharmacologic treatment of depression. *New Engl Med J* 1991;325:633-642.
63. Pucilowski O, Overstreet DS, Rezvani A, Janowsky DS. Effects of acute and chronic stressors on saccharin preference in hypercholinergic rats. *Behav Pharmacol* 1992;3:Suppl.1,50.
64. Pulvirenti L, Samanin R. Antagonism by dopamine, but not noradrenaline receptor blockers of the anti-immobility activity of desipramine after different treatment schedules in the rat. *Pharmacol Res Comm* 1986;18:73-80.
65. Reite M, Short R, Seiler C, Pauley JD. Attachment, loss and depression. *J Child Psychol Psychiatr* 1981;22:141-169.
66. Seligman MEP. *Helplessness: On Depression, Development and Death.* San Francisco: Freeman, 1975.
67. Shanks N, Anisman H. Stressor-provoked behavioral changes in six strains of mice. *Behav Neurosci* 1988;102:894-905.
68. Silverstone T. Moclobemide: Placebo-controlled trials. *Int Clin Psychopharmacol* 1993;7:133-136.
69. Sluzewska A, Nowakowska E. The effects of carbamazepine, lithium and ketoconazole in chronic mild stress model of depression in rats. *Behav Pharmacol* 1994;5:Suppl.1,86.
70. Suomi SJ. Factors affecting responses to social separation in rhesus monkeys. In: Serban G, Kling A. eds. *Animal Models in Human Psychobiology*. New York: Plenum, 1976:9-46.
71. Weiss JM, Bailey WH, Goodman PA, Hoffman LJ, Ambrose MJ, Salman S, Charry JM. A model for neurochemical study of depression. In: Spiegelstein MY, Levy A. eds. *Behavioural Models and the Analysis of Drug Action*. Amsterdam: Elsevier, 1982:195-223.
72. Weissman MS, Paykel ES. *The Depressed Woman: A Study of Social Relationships*. Chicago: Univ. Chicago Press, 1974.
73. Willner P. The validity of animal models of depression. *Psychopharmacology* 1984;83:1-16.
74. Willner P. *Depression: A Psychobiological Synthesis*. New York: Wiley, 1985.
75. Willner P. Validation criteria for animal models of human mental disorders: Learned helplessness as a paradigm case. *Prog Neuro-Psychopharmacol* 1986;10,677-690.
76. Willner P. Sensitization to the actions of antidepressant drugs. In: Emmett-Oglesby MV, Goudie AJ. eds. *Psychoactive drugs: Tolerance and Sensitization*. Clifton, NJ: Humana, 1989:407-459.
77. Willner P. Towards a theory of serotonergic dysfunction in depression. In: Bevan P, Cools A, Archer T. eds. *Behavioural Pharmacology of 5-HT*. Hillsdale, N.J: Erlbaum, 1989:157-178.

78. Willner P. Animal models of depression: An overview. *Pharm Ther* 1990;45,425-455.
79. Willner P. Behavioural models in psychopharmacology. In: Willner P. ed. *Behavioural Models in Psychopharmacology: Theoretical, Industrial and Clinical Perspectives*. Cambridge: Cambridge University Press, 1991:3-18.
80. Willner P. Animal models as simulations of depression. *Trends Pharmacol Sci* 1991;12:131-136.
81. Willner P. Animal models of depression. In: Den Boer JA, Sitsen A. eds. *Handbook on Depression and Anxiety: A Biological Approach*. New York: Dekker, 1994:291-316.
82. Willner P, Scheel-Kruger J. eds. *The Mesolimbic Dopamine System: From Motivation to Action*. Chichester: Wiley, 1991.
83. Willner P, Towell A, Sampson D, Sophokleous S, Muscat R. Reduction of sucrose preference by chronic mild unpredictable stress, and its restoration by a tricyclic antidepressant. *Psychopharmacology* 1987;93:358-364.
84. Willner P, Sampson D, Phillips G, Fichera R, Foxlow P, Muscat R. Effects of isolated housing and chronic antidepressant treatment on cooperative social behaviour in rats. *Behav Pharmacol* 1989;1:85-90.
85. Willner P, Muscat R, Papp M, Sampson D. Dopamine, depression and antidepressant drugs. In: Willner P, Scheel-Kruger J. eds. *The Mesolimbic Dopamine System: From Motivation to Action*. Chichester: Wiley, 1991:387-410.
86. Willner P, Muscat R, Papp M. Chronic mild stress-induced anhedonia: A realistic animal model of depression. *Neurosci Biobehav Rev* 1992;16:525-534.
87. Woggon B. The role of moclobemide in endogenous depression: A survey of recent data. *Int Clin Psychopharmacol* 1993;7:137-139.
88. Zacharko RM, Bowers WJ, Kokkinidis L, Anisman H. Region-specific reductions of intracranial self-stimulation after uncontrollable stress: Possible effects on reward processes. *Behav Brain Res* 1983;9:129-141.
89. Zacharko RM, Lalonde GT, Kasian M, Anisman H. Strain specific effects of inescapable shock on intracranial self-stimulation from the nucleus accumbens. *Brain Res* 1987;426:164-168.

Depression and Mania: From Neurobiology to Treatment: edited by G. Gessa, W. Fratta, L. Pani, and G. Serra. Raven Press, New York © 1995.

Animal Models of Mania

Gian Luigi Gessa, Luca Pani *, Gino Serra §, Walter Fratta

"Bernard B. Brodie" Department of Neuroscience, University of Cagliari, Italy.
** Center for Neuropharmacology, CNR, Cagliari, Italy.*
§ Institute of Biochemistry, School of Pharmacy, University of Sassari, Italy.

Animal models of psychoses are addressed at determining the biological substrates of psychiatric syndromes. This, in turn, is aimed at generating strategies for treatment and prevention. To clarify the biological substrates of brain dysfunctions should also inevitably increase our knowledge of the physiology of the normal brain. The discovery of the neural substrate of Parkinson's disease is the classical example of the far-reaching returns that animal models may offer to progress in neuroscience.

Mania is a psychiatric syndrome characterized by affective, cognitive and behavioral symptoms that usually occur in clusters. However, there is considerable variability with respect to the clusters of symptoms displayed by manic patients depending on individual case, stage and history of the illness, environmental conditions, etc. Moreover, some of the symptoms of mania are shared by schizophrenia and depression, and are sensitive to the same pharmacological treatments, regardless of whether they occur in schizophrenia or in affective disorders.

Indeed, no symptom of schizophrenia and mood disorder is so peculiar to or pathognomonic of these conditions, as to allow their clear-cut distinction as separate disease entities (56). Therefore, a more appropriate title for this review would read "Models of symptoms of mania", since, rather than to address the neurobiological substrates of this psychiatric syndrome as a whole, it is focused on specific symptoms or cluster of symptoms, regardless of whether they are peculiar to idiopathic mania or whether they are present in schizophrenia or depression as well.

Many models of mania have been described in detail in different reviews (see 61,72,75). Here, we have chosen only a few time-honored models, that have been validated by progress in neuroscience, are clinically relevant, present clear homologies with the symptoms of idiopathic mania, are interpretable in terms of neurochemical correlates, and are sensitive to the same pharmacological treatments as the clinical condition. Two of these models, the antidepressant and sleep deprivation models of mania, have been developed and extensively studied in our laboratory; they not only possess the above-listed requirements, but may offer a possible indication of etiological mechanisms for the onset of manic episodes.

The models of mania to be described here are:
- Psychomotorstimulant model in humans,
- Psychomotorstimulant-induced behavioral sensitization model,
- Antidepressant-induced behavioral sensitization model,
- Sleep deprivation model,
- Morphine model.

PSYCHOMOTORSTIMULANT MODEL IN HUMANS

The Model

Psychomotorstimulants, like d-amphetamine, metamphetamine, methylphenidate and cocaine are capable of producing a syndrome that mirrors quite faithfully the manic syndrome. This observation has remarkable heuristic relevance because these drugs share the common ability of increasing dopamine (DA) output, and of producing a similar syndrome in animals. Moreover, their effect is suppressed both in animals and in humans by DA receptor antagonists which are also able to suppress symptoms of idiopathic mania (4, see 28).

Historically psychmotorstimulant-induced psychosis has been viewed as a model of paranoid schizophrenia (84). Indeed, the symptomatology produced by chronic administration of high doses of these drugs resembles very closely those of paranoid schizophrenia (3,70). However, as stated above, paranoid schizophrenia and dysphoric or psychotic mania share so many common features as to render their diagnostic differentiation extremely difficult. Leading psychiatrists have convincingly argued that many patients diagnosed as schizophrenics are in fact suffering from manic-depressive psychosis (69). On the other hand, the similarities of psychomotorstimulant-induced psychoses with idiopathic mania are more striking if one considers the initial symptomatology produced by the acute administration of high or even low doses of these drugs to non-psychiatric individuals. These treatments produce the same symptoms present in euphoric mania, also termed hypomania; namely, euphoria, overconfidence, expansiveness, heightened sensory awareness, alertness, insomnia and their functional consequences, such as logorrhea, psychomotor activity, curiosity, increased social contacts and enhanced sexual drive (13). With high doses of psychomotorstimulants, paranoid trends may also be present (9).

Following chronic exposure to high doses of psychomotorstimulants, the above symptomatology may progress into a syndrome that mirrors the symptoms of dysphoric and psychotic mania which, as mentioned, closely resemble those of paranoid schizophrenia (3,70). Some of the symptoms of the dysphoric and psychotic stage of the manic syndrome induced by psychomotorstimulants may be considered an exacerbation of the symptoms of the euphoric phase, and may be sustained by the same neuronal circuits. Namely, curiosity, suspiciousness and paranoid delusions may constitute a continuum sustained by a progressively greater stimulation of the same DA receptors. The same applies to the sequence self-confidence, grandiosity, omnipotence delusion; to the progress from decreased need for sleep to total insomnia; and to the sequence psychomotor activity, restlessness, stereotypy. Interestingly, a continuum from alertness to increased motor activity and stereotypy is produced in rats by the administration of progressively higher doses of psychomotorstimulants.

On the other hand, additional symptoms of the early phase of the syndrome undergo qualitative changes in its evolution. Namely, euphoria evolves into dysphoria and, possibly, agitated depression. Positive social interactions are replaced by loss of interest, irritability, anger and hostility. Energy gives way to apathy, self-confidence to fear and panic. Delusions, hallucinations and flattening of affect may also appear, which makes it almost impossible to distinguish this stage of psychomotorstimulant-induced psychosis from either an idiopathic psychotic manic or paranoid schizophrenic episode.

The only difference between the psychomotorstimulant-induced psychosis and idiopathic manic syndrome is that the evolution of the idiopathic manic episode takes weeks to progress from the initial to final phase, whereas in the psychomotorstimulant-induced psychosis the sequential progression of the symptoms occurs in a few days (see 28). Moreover, the symptomatology of the psychomotorstimulant-induced psychosis often readily recedes after interruption of intoxication (2,52).

Dopaminergic Correlate

Most of the symptoms present in the different phases of psychomotorstimulant-induced psychosis are sensitive to neuroleptics, which indicates that they are mediated by endogenously released DA. When symptoms in the late phase appear to be an exaggeration of the corresponding symptoms occurring in the early phase of the syndrome, they may be the expression of a stronger stimulation of the same DA receptors, in the same neural circuitry. The appearance of additional symptoms may reflect the recruitment of different dopaminergic circuitries in other brain areas. For instance, it has been suggested that the amygdala, particularly its central nucleus, may mediate paranoid delusions. Indeed. the central nucleus of the amygdala, which is heavily innervated by DA (32), is considered to play an important role in fear-motivated behavior (17), and it has been suggested that manic psychosis may be the result of neuronal dysfunction in the amygdaloid complex (91).

A problem arises in interpreting those symptoms in the late phase of the syndrome that appear to be antithetical of early symptoms in the syndrome, such as dysphoria and depression with respect to euphoria, panic versus over-self-confidence. If these antithetical symptoms are mediated by the same dopaminergic neural circuitry, a possible reason for the shift in the psychological correlate might be a change in the pattern of DA output.

Recent results seem to offer solid support to this possibility. DA output in the nucleus accumbens has been continuously monitored by microdialysis in freely moving rats over 15 consecutive days of chronic administration of cocaine (10 mg/kg twice daily) (43) or amphetamine (5 and 10 mg/kg twice daily) (Imperato et al., in preparation). Both treatments produced a progressively greater increase in DA release during the first 3-5 days; afterwards, both basal and cocaine- or amphetamine-stimulated DA output fell to less than 20% of control values.

While the mechanism underlying the dramatic shift in DA output is still unexplained, a fall in DA release following an excessive and prolonged exposure to psychomotorstimulants might well explain the switch from euphoria to dysphoria and depression. A reduction of DA output is consistent with the fact that neuroleptics are not effective in alleviating depression, anhedonia and lack of energy when they occur either after chronic psychomotorstimulants or during idiopathic psychoses (68).

PSYCHOMOTORSTIMULANT-INDUCED BEHAVIORAL SENSITIZATION MODEL

Acute Psychomotorstimulant Model

The term "psychomotorstimulant" is used to distinguish the class of behavioral activating stimulants from that of CNS stimulants (e.g. strychnine, picrotoxin) essentially devoid of behavioral consequences other than convulsions. (99).

Psychomotorstimulants may be divided into three categories; one category, such as cocaine, amphetamine and methylphenydate, produces its central effects by releasing DA from nerve terminals in the limbic areas and basal ganglia (22). Accordingly, their behavioral effects are suppressed by depletion of endogenous

DA stores combined with inhibition of DA synthesis (14,99). A second category of psychomotorstimulants, such as apomorphine and quinpirole, acts by directly stimulating DA receptors (7,74). A third category, like nicotine and morphine, acts by activating the firing rate of DA neurons in the mesolimbic system (62,65).

The behavioral responses to all categories of psychomotorstimulants is suppressed by the inhibition of DA receptors with either D_1 or D_2 DA receptor antagonists (7,36,94). The behavioral syndrome produced by the acute administration of psychomotorstimulants has been proposed as a model both for mania and schizophrenia (see 28).

The acute administration of psychomotorstimulants produces many symptoms of mania including hyperactivity, elation (e.g. measured as lower threshold for intracrania self-stimulation, or increase in secondary reinforcement values, self administration, etc.), increased irritability and aggressiveness, sexual hyperactivity, and insomnia. This model will not be discussed here because it has been described in detail elsewhere in different reviews to which the reader may refer (see 61,67).

Behavioral Sensitization Model

On the other hand, more recently a new conceptual issue originated from the psychomotorstimulant model; the psychomotorstimulant sensitization (51,52,54,72,76,89,100). It consists of a progressive increase in behavioral responses to the repeated administrations of psychomotorstimulants, such as amphetamine or cocaine. Sensitization develops not only to the locomotor stimulant responses, but also to other effects of these drugs, including the rewarding effect (40,41,59). Sensitization to amphetamine or cocaine can be obtained even with a single high dose, and such sensitization may be long-lasting. For instance, a single high dose of cocaine (40 mg/kg) has been shown to produce a behavioral sensitization to a low dose of the drug (10 mg/kg) which lasts for one week (97), while sensitization produced by repeated administration of amphetamine or cocaine may even be a permanent phenomenon (71,100).

Besides its clinical implications, to clarify the mechanism of sensitization to psychomotorstimulants may be useful in understanding the molecular mechanisms of learning and memory, conditioned reflexes, kindling-induced epilepsy, and even Pavlovian conditioning. Indeed, an important component of the development of psychomotorstimulant sensitization is conditioned (77,97), in the sense that the animals are more sensitive to the test dose, if this is readministered in the same cage where sensitization has developed. However, when sensitization has been obtained with high repeated doses of a psychomotorstimulant, such as cocaine, the behavioral sensitization is largely context-independent (12,73).

Sensitization to the effect of a psychomotorstimulant may be crossed with the effect of another psychmotorstimulant, e.g. animals sensitized to cocaine, by repeated treatments, are also sensitive to amphetamine, and vice versa (100). Most relevant with respect to psychoses, repeated, or prolonged stress (see sleep deprivation) sensitizes to psychomotorstimulants, while sensitization to stress and to psychomotorstimulants may be crossed (6,60). The above data indicate which potential role sensitization and cross-sensitization may play not only in drug addiction, but, and most important for the purpose of this review, in the precipitation or development of manic psychosis. In fact, it has been shown that repeated psychomotorstimulants can precipitate manic states and increase the probability of relapses in psychotic patients who are in remission (47,84). Moreover, repeated stress, similarly to repeated cocaine or amphetamine, can precipitate a psychotic reaction to a subsequent stressor (5,6,73). With regard to the clinical relevance of psychomotorstimulant sensitization for idiopathic mania, it is of great interest that sensitization to cocaine and amphetamine is extended to different behavioral and physiological effects of the drugs, besides motor activity, such as euphoria, aggressiveness, stereotypies, etc. (72,102).

Mechanisms of Behavioral Sensitization

To cover the overwhelming and conflicting literature on the neurochemical and molecular mechanisms underlying induction and expression of behavioral sensitization is beyond the scope of this review (see 52,87). Here, only a brief outline of the matter will be presented. Behavioral sensitization can be induced by endogenously released DA, acting on both D_1 and D_2 receptors, by mixed D_1/D_2 agonists, and by selective D_2 agonists (39,63). Development of behavioral sensitization induced not only by D_1/D_2 but also by D_2 agonists may be prevented by the concomitant administration of the D_1 receptor antagonist SCH 23390, suggesting that activation of D_1 receptors or their occupancy by endogenous DA, in the case of D_2 agonists, is a condition *sine qua non* for development of behavioral sensitization, irrespective of whether it is initiated by D_1/D_2 or D_2 agonists (64,89).

On the other hand, the location of DA receptors, the dopaminergic circuits, and the neurochemical changes responsible for development and expression of behavioral sensitization are not clear. Kalivas et al. (52) have proposed an intriguing hypothesis to explain the neural mechanisms of development and expression of behavioral sensitization to amphetamine, which might be considered a paradigm for other psychomotorstimulant-induced behavioral sensitizations. According to a semplified version of this theory, recurrent amphetamine-induced DA outputs within the somatodendritic region of DA neurons would cause desensitization of DA autoreceptors. This, in turn, would result in a reduced self inhibition of DA neuronal activity and, therefore, in a greater DA output from nerve terminals. This hypothesis is mainly based on results obtained with intra VTA microinjection of amphetamine; such a repeated treatment producing behavioral sensitization to systemically administered amphetamine (92). Not only have the pitfalls of this technique been convincingly criticized by Di Chiara (21), but a more relevant weakness of the above hypothesis stands on the conflicting results obtained with microdialysis on DA output in the nucleus accumbens and in the basal ganglia. Namely, there are results in the literature reporting increases, decreases and no change in DA release in the nucleus accumbens and striatum in behaviorally sensitized animals (42,43,78,79,102, Imperato et al., in preparation).

Finally, there is no consensus in the literature supporting the desensitization of D_2 autoreceptors, the second main pillar of the above hypothesis. Again, the literature reveals a great divergence in the effects of repeated psychostimulants on D_2 autoreceptor function. Some laboratories have reported a decrease in autoreceptor function (53,98,103), others an increase (24), while one laboratory found no change (29). Since behavioral sensitization to amphetamine and morphine is crossed, it is possible that the mechanisms discussed for the latter might apply to amphetamine behavioral sensitization as well (see morphine model). Further experiments are needed to define this matter.

ANTIDEPRESSANT-INDUCED BEHAVIORAL SENSITIZATION MODEL

Chronic treatment with different classes of antidepressants (ADs) has been shown to potentiate the psychomotorstimulant effect of direct and indirect DA agonists, such as apomorphine, amphetamine, cocaine, etc. This potentiation is produced after chronic but not acute treatment, takes place during the course of treatment and persists long after treatment withdrawal. The potentiation is selective for D_2 receptor-mediated behavioral responses, and for those responses mediated by the mesolimbic dopaminergic system (see 82). Accordingly, chronic imipramine potentiates the behavioral responses to quinpirole, a specific D_2 receptor agonist, but not to SKF 38393, a specific D_1 receptor agonist. Conversely, the behavioral activation to DA agonists in chronic AD-treated rats is suppressed by the D_2 antagonist sulpiride, but only weakly by the specific D_1 antagonist SCH 23390 (81). Moreover, chronic ADs potentiate the motorstimulant responses that are considered to be mediated by the mesolimbic DA system such as motoractivity and rearing, but not stereotypies, which are thought to be mediated by the activation of the nigro striatal DA system (86). These observations have led to the conclusion that chronic ADs produce a selective supersensitivity of postsynaptic D_2 receptors in the limbic system.

However, in spite of the above negative evidence, further investigations have suggested the possibility that D_1 receptors might play a permissive role in the development of D_2 receptor supersensitivity (80,81). Thus, in spite of the functional evidence of D_2 receptor supersensitivity, binding studies have failed to detect changes in D_2 receptors after chronic ADs (57). On the other hand, a significant reduction in the number of D_1 receptors has been observed, particularly in the limbic areas (18,57). To reconcile the apparent contradiction of a down regulation of D_1 receptors with their permissive role in the development of D_2 supersensitivity, we suggested that down regulation might be a compensatory adaptation to overstimulation of these receptors or to enhanced DA neurotransmission via a mechanism downstream with respect to the D_1 receptor itself (81). This hypothesis seems to be supported by the finding that down regulation of D_1 receptors is associated with a significant increase in the V_{max} of adenylate cyclase. This change, like down regulation of D_1 receptors, is restricted to the limbic areas (19). The possibility that dopaminergic neurotransmission is enhanced via a mechanism downstream with respect to D_1 receptors may explain the relative ineffectiveness of SCH 23390 in antagonizing the behavioral responses to quinpirole (81).

Clinical Relevance

A number of depressed patients, and in particular those suffering from bipolar type of mood disorders, treated with ADs, switch from depression to mania (11,37,90). Thus, it may be suggested that the increased sensitivity of D_2 receptors in the mesolimbic system might be responsible not only for the therapeutic effect of ADs, but also for the switch from depression to mania observed during AD treatments in susceptible patients.

Whatever the mechanism involved, the observation that after chronic imipramine the stimulant effect of quinpirole becomes resistant to the D_1 receptor blockade suggests that "mania" induced by ADs might be associated with modifications of D_1 receptors so that they resist the blockade by selective D_1 antagonists. This hypothesis is in apparent contrast with the observation that SCH 23390 is extremely effective in reducing the behavioral syndrome in sleep-deprived rats. A possible explanation for this apparent paradox is that the latter behavioral syndrome might mimic the euphoric mania or hypomania, while the behavioral response to DA agonists after chronic ADs might represent a model of severe manic syndrome (as the psychomotorstimulant sensitization model) in which the efficacy of D_1 receptor blockers has not yet been proved (33,34).

SLEEP DEPRIVATION MODEL

The Model

The platform method, or watertank, is the technique originally designed by Jouvet et al. in 1964 for paradoxical sleep (PS) deprivation in animals (48). For sleep studies it is still widely used because it is effective, economic, and does not include any invasive manipulation of the animal brain. It consists of keeping the rat on a small platform (about 7 cm in diameter) surrounded by water for a prolonged time (usually 72 hours). As mentioned, the method was originally designed to selectively deprive the animal of paradoxical sleep (PS). In fact, muscle relaxation, a peculiar feature of PS, is precluded by the consequent falling into the water. However, it has been shown that this method deprives the rat not only of 100% of PS, as predicted, but also of a considerable percentage of slow wave sleep. Besides its action on sleep, the platform method causes heavy stress to the rat, due to isolation, immobilization, falling into the water, soaking, etc. Therefore, this experimental model is a chronic stressful condition of which sleep deprivation is only one component of a much more generalized stress (15,58).

However, while sleep studies must pay careful attention to separating the specific effects of sleep deprivation, or even PS-deprivation from the effects due to unspecific stress, the presence of multiple stresses poses no problem to the present model, but actually, it may even add to the model an etiological relevance for the human condition. At the end of the period of sleep deprivation, the rat does not readily fall asleep as soon as it is returned to its home cage, as could be expected by the prolonged sleep deprivation, but shows a period of wakefulness of about 30 minutes, during which the animal presents a cohort of symptoms that appear to mimic those present in idiopathic mania (1). Namely, during this half-hour or so the animal displays insomnia, a high degree of hyperactivity, irritability (defined as stimulation-induced aggressivity), aggressiveness (38) (spontaneous both against another rat and mouse), hypersexuality (66) (homosexual mounting behavior) and stereotypy (rearing, sniffing). A peculiarity of the syndrome is the decreased need for sleep (30,31), in spite of the prolonged sleep deprivation. This feature suggests that the model may be used to investigate mechanisms of stress-induced insomnia.

Pharmacology

A pharmacological characterization of the manic-like syndrome induced by sleep deprivation has been carried out in our laboratory. A quick estimate of the effects of treatments on this syndrome can be obtained by measuring the latency to sleep onset. If a drug puts the animal to sleep after a shorter or longer interval than the sleep-deprived control, this may be considered an anti-manic and pro-manic effect, respectively.

i) Dopamine

Two D_2 DA receptor antagonists, haloperidol and L-sulpiride, have been tested for their ability to modify the latency to sleep. These drugs were given acutely prior to the end of the sleep deprivation period, in time to obtain peak action during the testing session. Haloperidol (0.2 mg/kg) was highly effective and potent in reducing latency to sleep, while L-sulpiride was much weaker (>50 mg/kg) (31), the difference reflecting that in their clinical potency.

However, the most striking results obtained were that the D_1 DA receptor antagonist, SCH 23390, exhibited an extremely high potency and efficacy in reducing sleep latency, a significant effect being observed with 3 μg/kg (31). Vice versa, the administration of the D_2 DA receptor agonist, quinpirole, produced a biphasic effect. Doses of quinpirole small enough (10-50 μg/kg) to selectively activate DA autoreceptors, reduced sleep latency, while "post-synaptic" doses (above 200 μg/kg) prolonged sleep latency in a dose-related manner. During the quinpirole-induced additional period of insomnia, the animals continued to display the full-blown "manic" symptomatology as described above. Also the administration of the specific D_1 DA receptor agonist SKF 38393 markedly prolonged the period of insomnia with the correlated behavioral syndrome (31). These data indicate that the behavioral syndrome induced by sleep deprivation is critically dependent on dopaminergic activity. The results also indicate a cooperativity between D_1 and D_2 DA receptors; namely, D_1 receptor activation seems to be essential for expression of D_2 receptor stimulation. The data obtained with presynaptic doses of quinpirole suggest that sleep deprivation fails to modify DA autoreceptor sensitivity.

ii) Sensitivity to Lithium

An important validation for the sleep deprivation-induced manic-like syndrome as a model for the human condition stands on its sensitivity to lithium. The latter was added to the diet and consumed during the sleep deprivation period in adequate amounts to produce serum lithium levels of 0.7 to 1.0 mEq/l at the time of the test. This treatment significantly reduced sleep latency. Moreover, during the reduced period of wakefulness, rats showed reduced hyperactivity, aggressiveness and irritability (35).

iii) Opioids

In order to clarify the possible role of endogenous opioids in the sleep deprivation-induced syndrome, the effect of naloxone and various opioid agonists and antagonists was tested. As shown in the table, the administration of naloxone (1 to 10 mg/kg) reduced the latency to sleep in a dose-related manner. On the contrary, morphine (1 and 5 mg/kg, intraperitoneally), ß-endorphine and [D-Ala^2,D-Leu^5] enkephalin (DADLE), intraventricularly, (2 and 1 μg, respectively) markedly prolonged the insomnia with the connected psychomotor activation, following sleep deprivation (31). Morphine-induced prolongation of the insomnia and behavioral stimulation in sleep deprived animals could be antagonized not only, as expected, by naloxone, but also by SCH 23390. This suggests that the activation of dopaminergic transmission is downstream to stimulation of opioid receptors. The exact definition by which opioid receptor types might be involved in the above model of mania is still under investigation (see below).

Neurochemical Correlates

Since sleep deprivation is an effective antidepressant treatment, several studies have been published concerning the effect of sleep deprivation, performed with the small platform technique on noradrenergic receptors in brain. Unlike that which has been observed after chronic treatment with tricyclic antidepressants, changes in adrenergic and serotoninergic receptors after sleep deprivation were modest and contradictory (83).

On the other hand, more relevant changes have been observed in D_1 and opioid receptors. In fact, the number of D_1 receptors, as well as the connected DA-stimulated adenylate cyclase activity, were found to be increased in the limbic areas, such as olfactory tubercle, nucleus accumbens and the septum, whereas no changes were observed in the striatum (20).

On the contrary, sleep deprivation produced a significant (about 30%) decrease in the B_{max} both of μ (measured by [^{3}H] DADLE binding) and delta receptors (measured by [^{3}H] DAGO binding). As for D_1 receptors also these changes in opioid receptors were found to be localized in limbic areas, while they were absent in the striatum and in the mesencephalon. No changes in kappa receptors were observed after sleep deprivation (26,27).

The up regulation of D_1 receptors associated with the down regulation of opioid receptors in the limbic areas may play an important role in the behavioral syndrome produced by sleep deprivation. Indeed, enhanced dopaminergic transmission may result from the up regulation of D_1 receptors in limbic areas combined with the desensitization of those opioid receptors localized on DA nerve terminals, which tonically inhibit DA release (85). Desensitization of these receptors should result in disinhibition of DA nerve terminals from opioid inhibitory control. However, if this hypothesis is correct, why then is naloxone so effective in suppressing the behavioral syndrome? One might postulate that opioid receptors, whose activation produces enhanced dopaminergic firing, do not desensitize, unlike those receptors localized presynaptically on DA neurons. This possibility is supported by the finding that the number of opioid receptors in the mesencephalon remains unaltered after sleep deprivation (26,27), and that no tolerance to the stimulant effect of morphine on the firing of mesolimbic DA neurons has been demonstrated after chronic treatment.

The important question remains as to how the behavioral syndrome ends in a relatively short time. Does DA release suddenly cease? Is the sensitivity of the opioid receptors controlling DA release back to normal? To clarify why the "manic syndrome" gives way to deep sleep, after about 30 minutes, might provide important information for biphasic mood changes, such as the switch from mania to depression.

Clinical Relevance

Many of the factors believed to play a role in inducing mania interfere with sleep. Disruptions of routine connected with travel or various types of emergencies may preclude sleep. Emotional reactions to people and events, such as excitement, anxiety, fear, grief, and despair, commonly cause insomnia. Sleep is often disrupted in the postpartum period by the demands of feeding and caring for a newborn infant. Drugs, such as amphetamines and monoamine oxidase inhibitors, and hormones, such as thyroxine, reduce sleep. Sleep is also disrupted during withdrawal from alcohol and from various drugs used to treat bipolar patients, including antidepressants, neuroleptics, lithium, minor tranquilizers, and sedatives (23,50).

Wehr et al. (95) have proposed that many of the diverse psychological, interpersonal, environmental, and pharmacological factors that appear to trigger the onset of mania could do so through their capacity to cause sleep deprivation. Accordingly, in experiments in which sleep has been manipulated as an independent variable, partial or total sleep deprivation for one night has been shown to induce transient or sustained switches into mania or hypomania in bipolar patients. Although sleep reduction causes mania, mania also causes sleep reduction. In fact, the onset of mania is sometimes accompanied by alternate nights of total insomnia (96). The results of the sleep deprivation experiments strongly suggest that the insomnia caused by mania in turn exacerbates or sustains the mania. Thus the causal relationship between sleep loss and mania is bidirectional and results in a vicious circle that could spiral out of control because of its self-reinforcing properties. In this way, sleep loss arising from a variety of causes could set in motion a manic process that is capable of becoming autonomous.

To date the most reliable correlates of sleep deprivation in humans regard the neuroendocrine system. Sleep deprivation stimulates thyrotrophin and cortisol secretion while reducing that of prolactin and growth hormone (8). Obtaining meaningful biochemical or physiological evidence for altered dopaminergic activity after sleep deprivation in humans is a difficult problem. In fact only a small fraction of DA metabolites in the CSF originates in the limbic system. Even if sleep deprivation were to produce substantial abnormalities in DA release and metabolism in the limbic system, this would not be detectable in the CSF. At the present, neither is positron emission tomography sufficiently sensitive to detect changes in brain metabolism in selected limbic areas, nor is single photon emission tomography adequate to measure changes in DA receptors in the same areas (25).

Does Naloxone Work in Mania?

If the manic symptoms in idiopathic mania are produced by the activation of the limbic dopaminergic system by endogenous opioids, then the opioid antagonist naloxone should be capable of producing a temporary reduction in manic symptoms.

However, the effects of naloxone on mania are equivocal, with some positive but, more frequently, also negative responses (10). A study by Judd et al. (49) might offer an explanation for these discrepancies. These authors found that an intravenous infusion of 20 mg of naloxone significantly reduced the manic symptomatology in 4 out of 12 "carefully diagnosed affective disorder patients". The authors suggest the possibility "that naloxone may have singled out a subpopulation of manics who may be unique in ways that are not completely apparent other than in their response to naloxone". To verify the validity of this important hypothesis should be a relatively simple task.

MORPHINE MODEL

The Model

The acute administration of morphine to mice and rats produces a number of effects, such as analgesia, euphoria, catalepsy, sedation, hyperactivity, stereotypy, etc. depending on the animal strains, dose administered, administration route, time after treatment, etc.

The validity of this morphine model of mania stands on the fact that:

a) morphine may produce under appropriate experimental conditions euphoria, motor stimulation and stereotypy (16,55),
b) these effects are suppressed (only partially in the case of euphoria) by neuroleptics and by α-methyltyrosine, a classic inhibitor of tyrosine hydroxylase (16),
c) morphine activates the firing of mesolimbic DA neurons (62),
d) morphine rather selectively increases DA release in the nucleus accumbens, as measured by microdialysis (22),
e) morphine-induced activation of DA firing and DA release is antagonized by naloxone indicating that it is mediated by opioid receptors (22,62),
d) chronic administration of morphine produces a behavioral sensitization that is identical to that produced by cocaine or amphetamine (101),
e) morphine-induced behavioral sensitization is crossed with that produced by cocaine or amphetamine and is similarly sensitive to neuroleptic blockade (44,87,88,89,93).

The data indicate that dopaminergic and opioidergic substrates are critically important for the symptomatology produced by morphine. The two models, chronic morphine-induced behavioral sensitization and cocaine-induced behavioral sensitization, appear to be equivalent. However, an important feature that makes the morphine model heuristically more relevant is that it indicates a possible role of opioids and opiate receptors in the excessive activation of dopaminergic systems in mania.

Mechanism of Behavioral Sensitization to Morphine

While investigating the effect of morphine on acetylcholine (ACh) release in the hippocampus we obtained possible indications of the mechanisms sustaining morphine-induced behavioral sensitization. We found that while acute morphine administration does not modify ACh release, after chronic treatment the drug acquires the capability of stimulating ACh output. The onset of this effect coincides with the onset of behavioral sensitization, moreover, morphine-induced release seems to be mediated by endogenously released DA, as it is suppressed by α-MT and by SCH 23390 (44).

However, a problem arises since morphine is capable of releasing DA not only after chronic treatment, but even more after acute treatment. As a possible explanation for this apparent contradiction of morphine failure to acutely release ACh in spite of stimulating DA output, we suggested that morphine might counteract its own effect by a direct inhibitory action on cholinergic neurons (44), but that tolerance to the latter action might develop after chronic treatment. In an attempt to verify this hypothesis we studied whether acute morphine was able to suppress hippocampal ACh release induced by a direct stimulation of DA receptors. Indeed, morphine suppressed amphetamine-induced ACh release in normal rats but failed to do so in rats that had been chronically treated with morphine (44). This finding suggests that, after chronic treatment, morphine maintains its capability of stimulating DA release, but loses that of inhibiting ACh release. It is possible that acute morphine counteracts other DA-mediated responses, such as behavioral stimulation, and that these responses may become apparent only after tolerance to the inhibitory action has developed.

Since behavioral sensitization to morphine is crossed with that to cocaine and amphetamine (87,88,89,93), it is possible that the above-mentioned mechanism may be responsible for the behavioral sensitization to these drugs as well. This hypothesis implies that endogenous opioids normally dampen the effects of excessive stimulation of DA receptors, but that tolerance to this action takes place after chronic stimulation. This important conclusion seems to be supported by recent results from our laboratory showing that the ACh releasing effect of amphetaminc (a DA-mediated effect) is potentiated by naloxone (Imperato et al., in preparation). Further experiments should clarify whether endogenous opioids are normally counterbalancing the expression of the overstimulation of DA receptors besides those controlling ACh release in the hippocampus. These findings raise the important issue of the interaction between opioids and the mesolimbic dopaminergic system in the genesis of mania. It may be noticed in passing that the enhancement in ACh output is a common feature in those models of mania based on the administration of morphine, cocaine or amphetamine (44,45,46). This observation contradicts the old hypothesis that idiopathic mania is sustained by a reduced cholinergic activation (see 61).

Clinical Relevance

Two problematic features in the morphine model are that heroin addicts exhibit few of the manic symptoms that are produced by chronic cocaine or amphetamine, and that the evidence for the anti-manic effect of opioid antagonists is conflicting (10), but see Judd et al. (49).

CONCLUSIONS

Models of mania such as sleep deprivation, chronic antidepressant (AD) and behavioral sensitization models reproduce in rats what is known to occur in humans, supporting the validity of the animal model as a mirror of the human condition. However, these models represent something that goes beyond the mere confirmation in the rat of what we already know for man, i.e. there is a liaison dangereuse between vice (drug abuse) and madness, and that sleep deprivation may precede and cause a manic episode; these models indicate possible etiological and pathogenetic mechanisms involved in the development and expression of the manic syndrome, which would be otherwise impossible to obtain in man. Indeed, models of mania both in man and animals provide convincing evidence that hyperactivity of the mesolimbic DA system plays a central role in mediating the symptomatology of idiopathic mania.

For instance, the sleep deprivation model not only represents a confirmation in the rat that sleep loss often precedes and may trigger a manic episode in man, but suggests that an opioid-DA interaction may play a pathogenetic role in mania. Moreover, this animal model suggests possible therapeutic interventions in the clinic, such as re-examining the efficacy of opioid antagonists in the treatment of mania with greater confidence than in previous trials when the rationale for these experiments was not clearly defined.

The fact that SCH 23390 is very effective in suppressing the symptomatology in the sleep deprivation model, but is almost ineffective in the chronic AD model, raises the question of whether D_1 receptor antagonists may be ineffective in manic patients with a history of AD-treatment; vice versa, the sleep deprivation model suggests that this treatment may be effective in manic patients not previously treated with ADs. The development of behavioral changes produced by chronic ADs, sleep deprivation and repeated psychomotorstimulants is prevented by the concomitant administration of NMDA-receptor blockers, suggesting that NMDA-receptor stimulation is required for the development of the adaptive changes in dopaminergic transmission underlying the symptomatology in the above manic models. These results also predict that NMDA-receptor antagonists will have great clinical validity in the prevention of mania. This is a very hot area of research at the present time.

REFERENCES

1. Albert I, Cicala GA, Siegel J. The behavioral effects of REM sleep deprivation in rats. *Psychophysiology* 1970:7:552-560.
2. Angrist BM, Gershon S. Psychiatric sequelae of amphetamine use. In: Shader RI, ed. *Psychiatric Complications of Medical Drugs*. New York: Raven Press, 1972;175-199.
3. Angrist BM, Gershon S. The phenomenology of experimentally induced amphetamine psychosis - preliminary observations. *Biol Psychiatry* 1970;2:95-107.
4. Angrist B, Lee HK, Gershon S. The antagonism of amphetamine-induced symptomatology by a neuroleptic. *Am J Psychiatry* 1974;131:817-819.
5. Antelman SM. Stressor-induced sensitization to subsequent stress: implications for the development and treatment of clinical disorders. In:

Kalivas PW, Barnes CD, eds. *Sensitization in the Nervous System.* Caldwell, NJ: Telford Press, 1988;227-256.

6. Antelman SM, Eichler AJ. Black CA, Kocan D. Interchangeability of stress and amphetamine in sensitization. *Science* 1980;207:329-331.
7. Arnt J, Hyttel J, Perregaard. Dopamine D-1 receptor agonists combined with the selective D-2 agonist quinpirole facilitate the expression of oral stereotyped behaviour in rats. *Eur J Pharmacol* 1987;133:137-145.
8. Baumgartner A, Riemann D, Berger M. Neuroendocrinological investigations during sleep deprivation in depression. II. Longitudinal measurement of thyrotropin, TH, cortisol, prolactin, GH, and LH during sleep and sleep deprivation. *Biol Psychiatry* 1990;28:569-587.
9. Bell DS. Comparison of amphetamine psychosis and schizophrenia. *Br J Psychiatry* 1965;3:701-707.
10. Berger PA, Barchas JD. Studies of beta-endorphin in psychiatric patients. In: Verebey K, ed. *Opioids in Mental Illness: Theories, Clinical Observations, and Treatment Possibilities.* New York: Ann NY Acad Sci, 1982;398:448-459.
11. Bunney Jr. WE. Psychopharmacology of the switch process in affective illness. In: Lipton M, Di Mascio A, Killam K, eds. *Psychopharmacology - A Generation of Progress.* New York: Raven Press, 1978;1249-1259.
12. Camp DM, Robinson TE. Susceptibility to sensitization. II. The influence of gonadal hormones on enduring changes in brain monoamines and behavior produced by the repeated administration of D-amphetamine or restraint stress. *Behav Brain Res* 1988;30:69-88.
13. Carlson GA, Goodwin FK. The stages of mania. A longitudinal analysis of the manic episode. *Arch Gen Psychiatry* 1973;28:221-228.
14. Clarke PBS, Jakubovic A, Fibiger HC. Anatomical analysis of the involvement of mesolimbocortical dopamine in the locomotor stimulant actions of *d*-amphetamine and apomorphine. *Psychopharmacology* 1988;96:511-520.
15. Coll-Andreu M, Ayora-Mascarell L, Trullas-Oliva R, Morgado-Bernal I. Behavioral evaluation of the stress induced by the platform method for short-term paradoxical sleep deprivation in rats. *Brain Res Bull* 1989;22:825-828.
16. Cooper SJ. Interactions between endogenous opioids and dopamine: implications for reward and aversion. In: Willner P, Scheel-Kruger J, eds. *The Mesolimbic Dopamine System: From Motivation to Action.* Chichester: John Wiley & Sons Ltd, 1991;331-366.
17. Davis M, Rainnie D, Cassell M. Neurotransmission in the rat amygdala related to fear and anxiety. *TINS* 1994;17(N° 5):208-214.
18. De Montis GM, Devoto P, Gessa GL et al. Chronic imipramine reduces [^{3}H]SCH 23390 binding and DA-sensitive adenylate cyclase in the limbic

system. *Eur J Pharmacol* 1989;167:299-303.

19. De Montis GM, Devoto P, Gessa GL, Porcella A, Serra G, Tagliamonte A. Selective adenylate cyclase increase in the limbic area of long-term imipramine-treated rsts. *Eur J Pharmacol* 1990;180:169-174.
20. Demontis MG, Fadda P, Devoto P, Martellotta MC, Fratta W. Sleep deprivation increases dopamine D_1 receptor antagonist [^{3}H]SCH 23390 binding and dopamine-stimulated adenylate cyclase in the rat limbic system. *Neurosci Lett* 1990;117:224-227.
21. Di Chiara G. Searching for the hidden order in chaos. Commentary on Kalivas *et al.* "The pharmacology and neural circuitry of sensitization to psychostimulants". *Behav Pharmacol* 1993;4:335-337.
22. Di Chiara G, Imperato A. Drugs abused by humans preferentially increase synaptic dopamine concentrations in the mesolimbic system of freely moving rats. *Proc Natl Acad Sci* 1988;85:5274-5278.
23. Dilsaver SC, Greden JF. Antidepressant withdrawal-induced activation (hypomania and mania): mechanism and theoretical significance. *Brain Res* 1984;7:29-48.
24. Dwoskin LP, Peris J, Yasuda RP, Philpott K, Zahniser NR. Repeated cocaine administration results in supersensitivity of striatal D-2 dopamine autoreceptors to pergolide. *Life Sci* 1988;42:255-262.
25. Ebert D, Feistel H, Kaschka W, Barocka A, Pirner A. Single photon emission computerized tomography assessment of cerebral dopamine D2 receptor blockade in depression before and after sleep deprivation - preliminary results. *Biol Psychiatry* 1994;35:880-885.
26. Fadda P, Martellotta MC, De Montis MG, Gessa GL, Fratta W. Dopamine D_1 and opioid receptor binding changes in the limbic system of sleep deprived rats. *Neurochem Int* 1992;20(Suppl):153S-156S.
27. Fadda P, Tortorella A, Fratta W. Sleep deprivation decreases μ and δ opioid receptor binding in the rat limbic system. *Neurosci Lett* 1991;129:315-317.
28. Fibiger HC. The dopamine hypotheses of schizophrenia and mood disorders: contradictions and speculations. In: Willner P, Scheel-Kruger J, eds. *The Mesolimbic Dopamine System: From Motivation to Action.* Chichester: John Wiley & Sons Ltd, 1991;615-637.
29. Fitzgerald JL, Reid JJ. Chronic cocaine treatment does not alter rat striatal D2 autoreceptor sensitivity to pergolide. *Brain Res* 1991;541:327-333.
30. Fratta W, Collu M, Martellotta MC, Pichiri M, Gessa GL. Opioid dopamine interactions in stress induced insomnia. In: Spano PF, Biggio G, Toffano G, Gessa GL, eds. *Central and Peripheral Dopamine Receptors: Biochemistry and Pharmacology*. Berlin: Springer, 1988;197-204.
31. Fratta W, Collu M, Martellotta MC, Pichiri M, Muntoni F, Gessa GL. Stress-induced insomnia: opioid-dopamine interactions. *Eur J Pharmacol*

1987;142:437-440.

32. Freedman LJ, Cassell MD. Distribution of dopaminergic fibres in the central division of the extended amygdala of the rat. *Brain Res* 1994;633:243-252.
33. Gessa GL, Canu A, Del Zompo M, Burrai C, Serra G. Lack of acute antipsychotic effect of Sch 23390, a selective dopamine D_1 receptor antagonist. *Lancet* 1991;337:854-855.
34. Gessa GL, Canu A, Del Zompo M, Burrai C, Serra G. SCH 23390 and psychosis. *Lancet (Letter)* 1991;338:185-186.
35. Gessa GL, Fadda P, Serra G, Fratta W. Modelli animali di patologia psichiatrica e loro utilità nella sperimentazione dei nuovi psicofarmaci. In: Maj M, Racagni G, eds. *La Sperimentazione dei Nuovi Farmaci in Psichiatria.* Milano: Masson, 1994;17-28.
36. Gessa GL, Porceddu ML, Collu M, Mereu G, Serra M, Ongini E, Biggio G. Sedation and sleep induced by high doses of apomorphine after blockade of D-1 receptors by SCH 23390. *Eur J Pharmacol* 1985;109:269-274.
37. Goodwin FK, Jamison KR. In: *Manic-depressive illness.* New York: Oxford University Press, 1990;642-647.
38. Hicks RA, Moore JD, Hayes C, Phillips N, Hawkins J. REM sleep deprivation increases aggressiveness in male rats. *Physiol Behav* 1979;22:1097-1100.
39. Hoffman DC, Wise RA. Locomotor-activating effects of the D2 agonist bromocriptine show environment-specific sensitization following repeated injections. *Psychopharmacology* 1992;107:277-284.
40. Horger BA, Giles MK, Schenk S. Preexposure to amphetamine and nicotine predisposes rats to self-administer a low dose of cocaine. *Psychopharmacology* 1992;107:271-276.
41. Horger BA, Wellman PJ, Morien A, Davies BT, Schenk S. Caffeine exposure sensitizes rats to the reinforcing effects of cocaine. *NeuroReport* 1991;2:53-56.
42. Hurd YL, Weiss F, Koob GF, Anden N-E, Ungerstedt U. Cocaine reinforcement and extracellular dopamine overflow in rat nucleus accumbens: an *in vivo* microdialysis study. *Brain Res* 1989;498:199-203.
43. Imperato A, Mele A, Scrocco MG, Puglisi-Allegra S. Chronic cocaine alters limbic extracellular dopamine. Neurochemical basis for addiction. *Eur J Pharmacol* 1992;212:299-300.
44. Imperato A, Obinu MC, Casu MA, Mascia MS, Carta G, Gessa GL. Chronic morphine increases hippocampal acetylcholine release. Possible relevance in drug dependence. *Eur J Pharmacol* 1995 : in press.
45. Imperato A, Obinu MC, Demontis MV, Gessa GL. Cocaine releases limbic acetylcholine through endogenous dopamine action on D_1 receptors.

Eur J Pharmacol 1992;229:265-267.

46. Imperato A, Obinu MC, Gessa GL. Effects of cocaine and amphetamine on acetylcholine release in the hippocampus and caudate nucleus. *Eur J Pharmacol* 1993;238:377-381.
47. Janowsky DS, El-Yousef MK, Davis JM, Sekerke JH. Provocation of schizophrenic symptoms by intravenous administration of methylphenidate. *Arch Gen Psychiatry* 1973;28:185-191.
48. Jouvet D, Vimont P, Delorme F, Jouvet M. Etude de la privation selective de la phase paradoxale de sommeil chez le Chat. *C. R. Soc Biol* 1964;158:756-759.
49. Judd LJ, Janowsky DS, Segal DS, Huey LY. Naloxone-induced behavioral and physiological effects in normal and manic subjects. *Arch Gen Psychiatry* 1980;37:583-586.
50. Kales A, Scharf MB, Kales JD. Rebound insomnia: a new clinical syndrome. *Science* 1978;201:1039-1041.
51. Kalivas PW, Stewart J. Dopamine transmission in the initiation and expression of drug- and stress-induced sensitization of motor activity. *Brain Res Rev* 1991;16:223-244.
52. Kalivas PW, Sorg BA, Hooks MS. The pharmacology and neural circuitry of sensitization to psychostimulants. *Behav Pharmacol* 1993;4:315-334.
53. Kamata K, Rebec GV. Long-term amphetamine treatment attenuates or reverses the depression of neuronal activity produced by dopamine agonists in the ventral tegmental area. *Life Sci* 1984;34:2419-2427.
54. Karler R, Calder LD, Bedingfield JB. Cocaine behavioral sensitization and the excitatory amino acids. *Psychopharmacology* 1994;115:305-310.
55. Katz RJ. Morphine- and endorphin-induced behavioral activation in the mouse: implications for mania and some recent pharmacogenetic studies. In: Verebey K, ed. *Opioids in Mental Illness*. New York: Ann NY Acad Sci, 1982;398:291-300.
56. Kendell RE. Diagnosis and classification of functional psychoses. *Br Med Bull* 1987;43:499-513.
57. Klimek V, Nielsen M. Chronic treatment with antidepressants decreases the number of $[^3$H]SCH 23390 binding sites in the rat striatum and limbic system. *Eur J Pharmacol* 1987:139:163-169.
58. Kovalzon VM, Tsibulsky VL. REM-sleep deprivation, stress and emotional behavior in rats. *Behav Brain Res* 1984;14:235-245.
59. Lett BT. Repeated exposures intensify rather than diminish the rewarding effects of amphetamine, morphine, and cocaine. *Psychopharmacology* 1989;98:357-362.
60. Leyton M, Stewart J. Preexposure to foot-shock sensitizes the locomotor response to subsequent systemic morphine and intra-accumbens amphetamine. *Pharmacol Biochem Behav* 1990;37:303-310.

61. Lyon M. Animal models for the symptoms of mania. In: Boulton A, Baker G, Martin-Iverson M, eds. *Neuromethods, Vol. 18: Animal Models in Psychiatry I.* Clifton, NJ: The Humana Press Inc, 1991;197-244.
62. Matthews RT, German DC. Electrophysiological evidence for excitation of rat ventral tegmental area dopamine neurons by morphine. *Neuroscience* 1984;11:617-625.
63. Mattingly BA, Gotsick JE, Marin C. Locomotor activity and stereotypy in rats following repeated apomorphine treatments at 1-, 3- or 7-day intervals. *Pharmacol Biochem Behav* 1989;31:871-875.
64. Mattingly BA, Rowlett JK, Graff JT, Hatton BJ. Effects of selective D1 and D2 dopamine antagonists on the development of behavioral sensitization to apomorphine. *Psychopharmacology* 1991;105:501-507.
65. Mereu G, Kong-Woo PY, Boi V, Gessa GL, Naes L, Westfall TC. Preferential stimulation of ventral tegmental area dopaminergic neurons by nicotine. *Eur J Pharmacol* 1987;141:395-399.
66. Morden B, Mullins R, Levine S. Effects of REMs deprivation on the mating behavior of male rats. *Psychophysiology* 1968;5:241-242.
67. Murphy DL. Animal models for mania. In: Hanin I, Usdin E, eds. *Animal Models in Psychiatry and Neurology.* New York: Pergamon, 1977;211-222.
68. Nelson JC. The use of antipsychotic drugs in the treatment of depression. In: Zohar J, Belmaker RH, eds. *Treating Resistant Depression.* New York: PMA Publishing Corporation, 1987;131-146.
69. Ollerenshaw DP. The classification of the functional psychoses. *Br J Psychiatry* 1973;122:517-530.
70. Post RM. Cocaine psychoses: a continuum model. *Am J Psychiatry* 1975;132:225-231.
71. Post RM, Contel NR. Human and animal studies of cocaine: implications for development of behavioral pathology. In: Creese I, ed. *Stimulants: Neurochemical, Behavioral, and Clinical Perspective.* New York: Raven Press, 1983;169-203.
72. Post RM, Weiss SRB, Pert A. Animal models of mania. In: Willner P, Scheel-Kruger J, eds. *The Mesolimbic Dopamine System: From Motivation to Action.* Chichester: John Wiley & Sons Ltd, 1991;443-472.
73. Post RM, Weiss SRB. Sensitization and kindling: implications for the evolution of psychiatric symptomatology. In: Kalivas PM, Barnes CD, eds. *Sensitization in the Nervous System.* Caldwell, NJ: Telford Press, 1988;257-291.
74. Riffee WH, Wilcox RE, Vaughn DM, Smith RV. Dopamine receptor sensitivity after chronic dopamine agonists. *Psychopharmacology* 1982;77:146-149.
75. Robbins TW, Sahakian BJ. Animal models of mania. In: Belmaker R, van

Praag H, eds. *Mania: An Evolving Concept*. New York: Spectrum, 1980;143-216.
76. Robinson TE, Becker JB. Enduring changes in brain and behavior produced by chronic amphetamine administration: a review and evaluation of animal models of amphetamine psychosis. *Brain Res Rev* 1986;11:157-198.
77. Schiff SR. Conditioned dopaminergic activity. *Biol Psychiatry* 1982;17:135-154.
78. Segal DS, Kuczenski R. *In vivo* micordialysis reveals a diminished amphetamine-induced dopamine response corresponding to behavioral sensitization produced by repeated amphetamine pretreatment. *Brain Res* 1992;521:330-332.
79. Segal DS, Kuczenski R. Repeated cocaine administration induces behavioral sensitization and corresponding decreased extracellular dopamine responses in caudate and accumbens. *Brain Res* 1992:577:351-355.
80. Serra G, Collu M, D'Aquila PS, De Montis GM, Gessa GL. Chronic imipramine "reverses" B-HT 920-induced hypomotility in rats. *J Neural Transm [GenSect]* 1991;84:237-240.
81. Serra G, Collu M, D'Aquila PS, De Montis GM, Gessa GL. Possible role of dopamine D_1 receptor in the behavioural supersensitivity to dopamine agonists induced by chronic treatment with antidepressants. *Brain Res* 1990;527:234-243.
82. Serra G, Collu M, D'Aquila PS, Gessa GL. Role of the mesolimbic dopamine system in the mechanism of action of antidepressants. In: Proceedings of XVIIIth C.I.N.P. Congress Satellite Symposium "The Biology and Pharmacology of Manic-Depressive Disorders: From Molecular Theories to Clinical Practice". Copenhagen, June 24-26, 1992 *Pharmacol Toxicol* 1992;71(Suppl I):72-85.
83. Siegel JM, Rogawski MA. A function for REM sleep: regulation of noradrenergic receptor sensitivity. *Brain Res Rev* 1988;13:213-233.
84. Snyder SH. Amphetamine psychosis: a "model" schizophrenia mediated by catecholamines. *Am J Psychiatry* 1973;130:61-67.
85. Spanagel R, Herz A, Shippenberg TS. Opposing tonically active endogenous opioid systems modulate the mesolimbic dopaminergic pathway. *Proc Natl Acad Sci* 1992;89:2046-2050.
86. Spyraki C, Fibiger HC. Behavioral evidence of supersensitivity of postsynaptic dopamine receptors in the mesolimbic system after chronic administration of desimipramine. *Eur J Pharmacol* 1981;74:131-135.
87. Stewart J, Badiani A. Tolerance and sensitization to the behavioral effects of drugs. *Behav Pharmacol* 1993;4:289-312.
88. Stewart J, Vezina P. Environment-specific enhancement of the

hyperactivity induced by systemic or intra-VTA morphine injections of rats pre-exposed to amphetamine. *Psychobiology* 1987;15:144-153.

89. Stewart J, Vezina P. Microinjections of SCH-23390 into the ventral tegmental area and substantia nigra pars reticulata attenuate the development of sensitization to the locomotor activating effects of systemic amphetamine. *Brain Res* 1989;495:401-406.
90. Stoll AL, Mayer PV, Kolbrener M, Goldstein E, Suplit B, Lucier J, Cohen BM, Tohen M. Antidepressant-associated mania: a controlled comparison with spontaneous mania. *Am J Psychiatry* 1994;151:1642-1645.
91. Swerdlow NR, Koob GF. Dopamine, schizophrenia, mania, and depression: toward a unified hypothesis of cortico-striato-pallido-thalamic function. *Behav Brain Sciences* 1987;10:197-245.
92. Vezina P. Amphetamine injected into the ventral tegmental area sensitizes the nucleus accumbens dopaminergic response to systemic amphetamine: an *in vivo* microdialysis study in the rat. *Brain Res* 1993;605:332-337.
93. Vezina P, Stewart J. Amphetamine administered to the ventral tegmental area but not to the nucleus accumbens sensitizes rats to systemic morphine: lack of conditioned effects. *Brain Res* 1990;516:99-106.
94. Waddington JL, O'Boyle KM. Drugs acting on brain dopamine receptors: a conceptual re-evaluation five years after the first selective D-1 antagonist. *Pharmacol Ther* 1989;43:1-52.
95. Wehr TA, Sack DA, Rosenthal NE. Sleep reduction as a final common pathway in the genesis of mania. *Am J Psychiatry* 1987;144(2):201-204.
96. Wehr TA, Wirz-Justice A, Goodwin FK, et al. 48-Hour sleep-wake cycles in manic-depressive illness: naturalistic observations and sleep deprivation experiments. *Arch Gen Psychiatry* 1982;39:559-565.
97. Weiss SRB, Post RM, Pert A, Woodward R, Murman D. Role of conditioning in cocaine-induced behavioral sensitization: differential effect of haloperidol. *Pharmacol Biochem Behav* 1989;34:655-661.
98. White FJ, Wang RY. Electrophysiological evidence for A10 dopamine autoreceptor subsensitivity following chronic D-amphetamine treatment. *Brain Res* 1984;309:283-292.
99. White FJ, Wolf ME. Psychomotor stimulants. In: Pratt JA, ed. *The biological basis of drug tolerance and dependence*. London: Academic, 1991;153-197.
100. Wise RA, Leeb K. Psychomotor-stimulant sensitization: a unitary phenomenon? *Behav Pharmacol* 1993;4:339-349.
101. Wolf ME, Jeziorski M. Coadministration of MK-801 with amphetamine, cocaine or morphine prevents rather than transiently masks the development of behavioral sensitization. *Brain Res* 1993;613:291-294.
102. Wolf ME, White FJ, Hu X-T. MK-801 prevents alterations in the

mesoaccumbens dopamine system associated with behavioral sensitization to amphetamine. *J Neurosci* 1994;14(3):1735-1745.
103. Yi S-J, Johnson KM. Chronic cocaine treatment impairs the regulation of synaptosomal ^{3}H-DA release by D_2 autoreceptors. *Pharmacol Biochem Behav* 1990;36:457-461.

Depression and Mania: From Neurobiology to Treatment: edited by G. Gessa, W. Fratta, L. Pani, and G. Serra. Raven Press, New York © 1995.

Manipulation of Inositol-Linked Second Messenger Systems as a Therapeutic Strategy in Psychiatry

R.H. Belmaker, Y. Bersudsky, J. Benjamin, G. Agam, J. Levine, O. Kofman

Ministry of Health Mental Health Center, Faculty of Health Sciences, Ben Gurion University of the Negev, PO Box 4600, Beersheva, Israel

Allison and Stewart (3) first reported that lithium (Li) reduces brain levels of inositol. Hallcher and Sherman (21) showed that this reduction is due to inhibition of inositol monophosphatase, the enzyme synthesizing inositol in brain. Hallcher and Sherman (21) showed that the K_i of Li to inhibit the enzyme (20) was within the therapeutic range (K_i = 0.86 mM) and that *in vivo* physiological effects of this inhibition were apparent since rats treated chronically with Li show declines in brain inositol levels and build-up of 20-40 fold in the substrate, inositol monophosphate (42). Berridge et al. (12) appreciated the role of inositol phosphates as a new second messenger system for numerous neurotransmitters. Berridge et al. (12) showed that several neurotransmitters cause breakdown of a membrane phospholipid, phosphatidylinositol-P_2 (PIP_2) into two second messengers, inositol triphosphate (IP_3) and diacylglycerol (DAG), by activation of the enzyme phospholipase C. Berridge et al. (11) noted the possible psychiatric implications of Li inhibition of inositol monophosphatase, as they described the widespread role of the phosphatidylinositol (PI) cycle as a second messenger system. Berridge et al. (11, 12) suggested that Li inhibits PI-derived second messengers of activated systems only, without interfering with basal function. This hypothesis was based on the fact that inositol, derived from inositol phosphate breakdown, is essential for the resynthesis of phosphatidylinositol (18). Overactive systems or over-stimulated receptors would be dampened by Li's depletion of the inositol pool available for resynthesis of the parent compound phosphatidylinositol, while stable systems would be unaffected.

This provides a possible explanation of Li's paucity of behavioral effects in normals and its powerful effects in mania and depression.

Based on Berridge's theory, several groups have used inositol reversal as a technique to study the role of Li on the PI system (25). It seemed critical to us to apply the technique of inositol reversal to behavioral effects of Li, since Li clearly has multiple biochemical effects and not all of them need be related to the therapeutic mechanism in mania and depression. However, inositol has been shown to cross the blood-brain barrier poorly (44). We thus compared intracerebroventricular (icv) injections of 10 mg inositol in Li-treated and saline-treated rats (27).

The rats were anesthetized with Nembutal (50 mg/kg) and implanted with guide cannulae (Plastic Products) into the dorsal part of the third ventricle using standard stereotaxic procedures. Coordinates for the cannula were 4.3 mm posterior to bregma, and 4.5 mm ventral to dura, on the midline. At least 7 days recovery were allowed following surgery. Rats were observed to behave normally with the chronic indwelling icv cannula. Rats were injected intracranially with either 10 mg myo-inositol (250 μg/μl in a volume of 40 μl) or 40 μl artificial CSF (vehicle) over a period of 3 min using a Koehln 100 μl microsyringe, via an injection cannula that protruded 0.5 mm below the guide cannula.

Li-induced suppression of rearing is a well described behavioral effect of Li in rats. Rats received LiCl or NaCl (5 meq/kg, ip) and then activity was measured 24 hours later after inositol or vehicle given icv. Rats that received an acute injection of Li showed less rearing than rats treated with saline. Administration of icv inositol dramatically reversed the Li effect. This was the first finding suggesting that inositol could reverse a behavioral effect of Li (26).

INOSITOL REVERSES LI-PILOCARPINE SEIZURES IN RATS

While suppression of exploratory rearing has some face value as an animal model of mania, this behavior has a large variance and is not always replicable. In order to study the dose-response and time course of behavioural effects of inositol on Li-treated rats, we sought a behaviour that would give us a robust and consistent Li effect, which could then be modified by icv inositol. Following Tricklebank et al. (45), we examined the effect of inositol on limbic seizures induced by Li-pilocarpine, as first described by Honchar et al. (23). Initial experiments on this model tested the ability of icv inositol to postpone and prevent Li-pilocarpine seizures. We first used the standard doses of Li pretreatment (3 meq/kg) 24 hours prior to pilocarpine (30 mg/kg). Twenty eight male Sprague-Dawley rats were implanted with guide cannulae in the lateral ventricle and were randomly divided into three groups and injected icv with 10 mg inositol (N=10), control solution (N=9) or the stereoisomer of inositol, 10 mg L-chiro-inositol (N=9), which is not known to possess biological activity, 24 hr and 30 min before pilocarpine.

The animals were rated for the progression of limbic seizures once every five minutes for 75 minutes (27). The scoring was as follows: 0 = no response; 1 = gustatory movements and/or fictive scratching; 2 = tremor; 3 = head-bobbing; 4 = forelimb clonus; 5 = rearing, clonus and falling. In addition, the latency to attain forelimb clonus (a score of 4) was recorded for each rat. The inositol treated group had a significantly longer latency to clonus than either of the two control groups. Their seizure score was also significantly lower at 20, and 30-45 min.

In order to determine if inositol could prevent, and not just delay, the occurrence of limbic seizures, we repeated the experiment using a lower dose of pilocarpine (20 mg/kg). Again, inositol significantly increased the latency to exhibit clonus and lowered the seizure score. Eight of 16 rats treated with inositol did not have limbic seizures at all, whereas only one of the 14 vehicle-treated rats did not exhibit clonus. All the rats treated with L-chiro-inositol had limbic seizures. The ability of inositol to prevent seizures was highly significant ($X^2 = 6.53$, $p < 0.01$ for myo-inositol vs vehicle). Inositol has no effect on seizures induced by very high-doses of pilocarpine alone, and thus the inhibition is specific to the Li effect.

The specificity of the inositol interaction with Li in this behavior was challenged by testing another well-documented hypothesis of Li action. Since Li inhibits agonist-induced stimulation of cyclic AMP (9, 37), the Li-pilocarpine seizures were challenged by icv forskolin. Fourteen rats with cannulae in the lateral ventricle were injected with 3 meq/kg LiCl 20 hours before pilocarpine (20 mg/kg). One hour before administration of pilocarpine, rats were injected icv with forskolin (100 mg/5μl) or vehicle. There was no difference in the number of rats showing Li-pilocarpine seizures (7/7 forskolin-treated and 5/7 control rats) and no difference in the latency to onset of clonus (mean ± SD = 36.71 ± 12.8 min for forskolin and 32.7 ± 8 min for control rats, t = 0.69). Thus reversal of Li inhibition of adenylate cyclase by forskolin does not reverse Li-pilocarpine seizures. Indeed the biochemical finding that Li inhibits cyclic AMP accumulation has no known behavioral correlate (8).

TABLE 1. *Lack of effect of icv inositol on lethality following 14 meq/kg Li*

Treatment	N	% dead
Vehicle	9	66
myo-inositol	9	77
L-chiro-inositol	10	100

modified from (15)

LITHIUM TOXICITY AND LETHALITY

A major problem with Li treatment in humans is its narrow therapeutic window. Li toxicity involves the central nervous system, sometimes accompanied by seizures, but always by sedation and coma. It would be of great theoretical importance and also of great practical value if inositol could reverse Li toxicity or lethality (15).

We thus attempted to prevent Li overdose death with icv inositol (15). Twenty-eight male Sprague-Dawley rats weighing 300-400 gm were implanted with guide cannulae in the lateral ventricle as described above. Rats were injected icv with either control CSF solution, myo-inositol (10 mg) or L-chiro-inositol (10 mg) and 90 min later with LiCl (14 meq/kg, ip). There was no difference in the number of rats dying among the treatment conditions. Six of the nine CSF, all ten L-chiro-inositol rats and seven of nine inositol rats died (Table 1). Icv inositol did not alleviate Li lethality, nor did it reverse inhibition of activity following toxic doses of Li. Thus, Li toxicity and lethality apparently have a different biochemical basis than the other behavioral and biochemical effects of Li described above. This would not be surprising for an ion with so many biological effects.

DIFFICULTIES WITH THE INOSITOL THEORY OF LI ACTION

However, one problem with the inositol theory of Li action is that the dose of Li injected ip necessary to reduce rat brain inositol by 30% is 10 mEq/kg, leading to a peak plasma level of 7.5 mM, far above therapeutic levels (41). Injection of 3 mEq/kg LiCl, leading to plasma levels which are therapeutic in humans, reduces rat brain inositol by less than 10%. Perhaps more importantly, chronic administration of 40 mM LiCl/kg food to rats, leading to therapeutic levels of 0.3-0.6 mM in cortex, lowered brain inositol by a variable percentage not more marked than the effect of a single ip dose of 3 mM/kg LiCl. It thus seemed important to study whether Li treatment in humans reduces cerebrospinal fluid (CSF) inositol levels. If inositol monophosphatase is the therapeutic site of Li action, measurement of the hypothesized CSF inositol level reduction could predict response to Li in patients. We studied schizophrenic patients with willingness to participate in a trial of Li supplementation to ongoing neuroleptic therapy (2). None had previously participated in studies of inositol treatment of schizophrenia. All gave written informed consent. The protocol was approved by the hospital Helsinki Committee and the Ministry of Health.

Li treatment was given at 1200 mg per day for three days to 7 patients. All were males, mean age 42.7 (range 32-55), meeting DSM-IIIR criteria for schizophrenia. Lumbar puncture was performed by an experienced neurosurgeon on the morning before starting Li treatment and then on the morning of the fourth day, after a total of 3600 mg of Li and twelve hours after the last Li dose. Two additional male patients, age 42 and 39, were treated with Li at 1200

TABLE 2. *Human CSF inositol levels before and after Li treatment*

Patient	Inositol (μg/ml)		Li (mmol/L)	
Nº	before Li	after Li	CSF	Plasma
86	22.5	24.2	0.1	0.4
87	39.2	34.7	0.4	0.7
88	22.7	34.7	0.1	0.3
89	30.5	37.1	0.3	0.7
90	22.7	33.6	0.3	0.6
91	30.0	19.3	0.1	0.6
92	20.7	28.6	0.2	0.7
95	21.1	21.0	0.3	0.5
96	22.2	27.5	0.2	0.4
x ± SD	25.7 ± 6.2	27.7 ± 6.3	0.2 ± 0.1	0.5 ±0.2

reprinted from (2) with permission

mg per day for 7 days and lumbar puncture was performed on the morning of the eighth day. Table 2 presents the results. Li treatment did not reduce CSF inositol levels in seven patients treated for three days, or in two additional patients treated for 7 days.

The lack of effect of Li treatment upon CSF inositol levels appears at first surprising and attributable to methodological reasons, such as the short period of Li treatment and the relatively low Li levels achieved in the serum and the CSF. However, in rat studies an acute large single dose of Li rapidly reduces brain inositol levels as much as chronic treatment (40). In the present study, the mean serum Li level in the patients is 0.5 ± 0.2 mM, within the Li prophylactic therapeutic range, and CSF levels are usually about half to one third of these levels, as expected.

It is possible that Li did not reduce CSF inositol levels in the present study because CSF inositol derives mainly from the plasma via the choroid plexus (44), and Li raises, rather than lowers, plasma inositol (3, 43). Moreover, brain inositol levels are more than 10 times CSF inositol levels (44). Thus brain cells must highly concentrate inositol, and lowering brain inositol concentrations might well not be reflected in CSF levels. Another explanation of the above results is that more than one pool of brain inositol appears to exist (13, 39) and CSF inositol may equilibrate with the osmolyte-relevant brain pool and not with the neurochemically relevant phosphatidylinositol (PI) cycle related pool which is more likely to be lowered by Li inhibition of inositol monophosphatase.

We were able to directly study the question of the existence of two pools of cellular inositol, using behavioral techniques (13). Hyponatremia can lower brain inositol and hypernatremia can raise brain inositol. We found that induction of low brain inositol by hyponatremia followed by pilocarpine did not cause limbic seizures. Induction of high brain inositol using hypernatremia followed by Li-pilocarpine administration did not reverse limbic seizures. These data support the concept that inositol available for PI synthesis and inositol for osmotic function are sequestered in different cellular pools.

Li-pilocarpine seizures are a dramatic, easily quantifiable behavioral effect of Li in rats that can be clearly ascribed to Li inhibition of inositol monophosphatase. Sherman (41) raised the question of whether it occurred in other species such as mice as well as rats. Oppenheim et al. (38) gave physostigmine to Li-treated patients and did not observe Li-potentiation of the physostigmine effect. Recently, Hokin's group (28) has studied effects of cholinergic agonists on PI metabolism in cortical slices from several species, including monkeys, rats and guinea pigs. They concluded that Li-pilocarpine interactions occur only in species with low basal brain inositol levels, such as rats, and do not occur in monkeys or guinea pigs. *In vitro* the phenomenon can be elicited whenever cellular inositol levels are depleted in a low inositol medium.

To test Hokin's hypothesis *in vivo*, we attempted to elicit Li-pilocarpine seizures in a wide variety of species (14). Rats (Sprague-Dawley, ≈ 300 gm), mice (ICR ≈ 25 gm), guinea pigs (≈ 250 gm), rabbits (≈ 500 gm), chicks (≈ 70 gm) and goldfish (≈ 30 gm) were used. Animals were administered Li chloride (Li) i.p. before the s.c. injection of pilocarpine (Pi) and were observed for the 2 h following pilocarpine administration. Control groups were administered low-dose pilocarpine alone, after preliminary experiments determined pilocarpine doses necessary to elicit seizures without Li.

Rats, mice and goldfish show a standard limbic seizure syndrome after Li-pilocarpine and not with pilocarpine alone, with rhythmic contraction, loss of consciousness, fluctuating improvement and eventual death. One guinea pig of 9 with pilocarpine alone and one with Li^+-pilocarpine seized in a tonic-clonic manner and died immediately. One of two rabbits treated with Li-pilocarpine died without seizures, but neither had a Li-pilocarpine syndrome. Chicks show pilocarpine effects such as salivation, head bobbing and beak movements but there was no difference between pilocarpine alone versus Li^+-pilocarpine; there was no loss of consciousness or rhythmic muscle contraction. Frogs showed no pilocarpine (1 gm/kg) or carbachol (100 mg/kg) response up to very high dose, and no response to Li^+-pilocarpine or carbachol.

The present results suggest that Li-pilocarpine seizures are unique to rats, mice and goldfish, do not occur in other mammals or birds, or even in guinea pigs. This supports the concept of Hokin (28) that Li-pilocarpine interactions are dependent on the low baseline inositol present in rat brain. The fact that goldfish show Li-pilocarpine interactions and guinea pigs do not suggests that the property is not restricted to a specific evolutionary branch of brain development, but is potentially present since at least teleost development (goldfish) but is dependent on specific aspects of brain physiology.

It is interesting to speculate on the importance of the above finding for the use of Li-pilocarpine seizures as a model for the testing of Berridge's inositol depletion theory of Li action. Contraction of guinea pig ileum was a key model for the study of serotonin receptors, even though guinea pig ileum is uniquely suited for these experiments. The underlying biochemical principles were generalizable to other species and other serotonin receptors, including brain. Li-pilocarpine seizures may be such a model with no face validity but useful for mechanistic study.

Since inositol reverses Li effects on a cholinergic behavior, we searched for other behavioral effects of Li to test for inositol reversal (24). Two behavioural syndromes elicited by serotonergic agonists are differentially modified by chronic Li in rats. Li enhances the 5-HT_{1A} - linked serotonin syndrome, characterized by flat posture, hind limb abduction, tremor, forepaw treading and head-weaving. In contrast, wet-dog shakes, which have been attributed to stimulation of 5-HT_2 receptors, are attenuated by Li. To determine if inositol reverses the effect of Li on the serotonin syndrome, inositol was injected intracerebroventricularly (icv) in rats treated with either chronic dietary Li or control diet prior to administration of 5 methoxy N, N, dimethyltryptamine. The severity of each component of the behavioural score was reduced by inositol in Li-treated, but not control rats. There was a near-significant interaction between Li and inositol ($F_{1,39} = 3.23$, $p < 0.08$) for the total serotonin syndrome score, suggesting that inositol reverses the effects of Li to enhance the serotonin syndrome. Wet dog shakes following 5-hydroxytryptophan were counted in rats treated with chronic Li or control diets. Although Li significantly attenuated wet-dog shakes, inositol did not interact with Li and had no effect on control rats. These findings suggest that some, but not all of lithium's interactions with serotonin may be due to its effects on the phosphatidylinositol cellular signaling system.

Perhaps the most serious problem in the inositol depletion hypothesis of Li action was recently suggested by Jope (R Jope, personal communication) who reported that epi-inositol as well as myo-inositol reverses Li-pilocarpine seizures. Following Jope, we gave 7 rats icv myo-inositol, 6 control solution and 7 rats epi-inositol icv (all 10 mg/40 μl), 90 min before pilocarpine. None of the epi-inositol rats seized, one of the myo-inositol treated rats seized, and 4 of the control rats seized. Thus epi-inositol, a biologically inactive isomer of myo-inositol, is behaviorally active in the Li-pilocarpine model. The scientific meaning of an absence of effect of one stereoisomer, chiro-inositol, and positive effect of two others, myo and epi, is not clear. There is no evidence to suggest that epi-inositol epimerizes to myo-inositol *in vivo*. It is possible that epi-inositol can replace myo-inositol in osmolyte function, and "push" myo-inositol into the pool for PI synthesis. Tricklebank et al. (45) reported that scyllo-inositol is inactive against Li-pilocarpine seizures, and thus chiro-inositol is not the only inactive enantiomer.

PHARMACODYNAMICS OF INOSITOL EFFECTS

The dramatic antagonism of limbic seizures by icv inositol is a useful paradigm to study the time-course and dose-response function of behavioural effects of inositol. This information is essential for further studies of effects of inositol on behavior. We conducted a series of experiments in which we injected rats with 3 meq/kg of Li chloride, as described above, and 10 mg of inositol icv at different time intervals (0, 1, 4, 8, 12 and 24 hr) before the subcutaneous injection of pilocarpine (20 mg/kg). Latency to onset of forearm clonus and number of rats that displayed seizures in each group were recorded by an observer blind to the treatment. Inositol was effective at 1, 4 and 8 hours before pilocarpine, preventing seizures in 8/10, 9/10 and 9/10 rats, respectively. When injected immediately before or 24 hr before pilocarpine, inositol did not prevent seizures in any rat, and when injected 12 hours before pilocarpine 5/10 rats seized. The results of the time-course of inositol's prevention of limbic seizures are summarized in Table 3. This time-course suggests that inositol must have time to distribute within brain and to enter cells, and that it is extruded from brain or metabolized within 8-24 hrs after injection (16).

To obtain a dose-response curve for inositol effects, 35 Li-treated rats were injected icv one hour before pilocarpine (20 mg/kg) with either 40 μl vehicle (N=13), 5 mg inositol (N=16) 10 mg inositol (N=6). The number of rats attaining forelimb clonus in each group is presented in Table 3. The prevention of seizures by 5 mg inositol icv is almost significantly different from vehicle treated rats, (X^2=3.77, p=0.052), but the moderate effect of this dose of inositol is significantly less than the dramatic effect of 10 mg inositol, icv

TABLE 3. *Dose response relationship of icv inositol prevention of limbic seizures*

Dose of inositol icv (mg/rat)	N° of rats	Time (h)					
		0	1	4	8	12	24
0	seized		17		8		8
	no seizure		1		1		0
5	seized		12				
	no seizure		4				
10	seized	7	1	1	1	4	8
	no seizure	0	20	9	9	4	0

modified from (16) with permission

(X^2=6.14, $p<0.01$; 5 mg vs 10 mg). When we compare the latency to onset of clonus between those rats that did attain Stage 4 in the control vs 5 mg group, we find a significant protective effect of the lower dose of inositol. Mean latency to clonus was 28.3 ± 6.4 min for the CSF group and 37.9 ± 11.8 min for the 5 mg inositol group (two-tailed t = 2.57, $p < 0.02$). These data suggest that there is a dose response for attenuation of behavioural effects of Li. Brain concentrations of inositol are very high, about 10 mM (43). Total inositol content of a rat brain can be estimated at close to 5 mg. The 10 mg dose is necessary for optimal prevention of limbic seizures, which cause drastic reductions in inositol; however, lower doses may prove to be sufficient for more subtle behavioural effects of Li. Considering the poor penetration of inositol into cells, 10-30 mM concentrations, several times intracellular physiological levels, are usually required for *in vitro* studies of inositol reversal of biological effects of Li (19).

Inositol enters the brain poorly. However, high doses of inositol may penetrate the blood-brain barrier sufficiently to influence behaviour. We injected (1) male rats with LiCl ip (3 meq/kg), followed 18 hr later by 12 gm/kg inositol ip (10% in isotonic saline) or an equal volume of glucose. Six hours after the peripheral inositol injection, rats were injected sc with pilocarpine, and rated for limbic seizures as described above. Peripheral high-dose inositol significantly reduced Li-pilocarpine seizures. Cortical inositol levels were measured in rats treated with ip glucose or inositol. Inositol-treated rats had a 35% increase in cortical inositol.

In a human study, 12 gm daily of inositol was shown to raise CSF inositol levels by 70% (34). Subjects were 8 chronic inpatients at Abarbanel Mental Health Center meeting DSM-IIIR criteria for chronic schizophrenia, age 20-55, physically healthy, who were able and willing to consent in writing to a clinical trial of 12 gm of inositol daily for 7 days with lumbar puncture before and after the course of treatment.

Inositol was given in powder twice daily, 6 gm each time, dissolved in juice. Lumbar punctures were performed between 8-10 am, fasting. The last dose of inositol was given at 8 pm on the evening before the second lumbar puncture.

CSF samples were stored for 10 days at -20 °C and 30 days at -70 °C. Free myo-inositol in CSF aliquots was analyzed as trimethylsilyl (TMS) derivatives by gas-liquid chromatography, as previously described (7) with minor modification. 75 μl of each CSF sample were lyophilized (3 hr Speed Vac SC 110); silylation of the dried sample was carried out with 100 μl of a mixture of pyridine: bis (trimethylsilyl) trifluoroacetamide: chlorotrimethylsilan 10:2:1 (v/v/v) for 24 hr at room temperature. 3 μl aliquots were chromatographed on a 6-ft column packed with 3% SE-30 on 80/100 mesh gas chrome Q (Supelco), using a Carbo Erba SCU 600 gas chromatograph with a hydrogen flame ionization detector. The oven temperature was isothermal at 220 °C and the carrier gas was nitrogen with a flow of 120 ml/min. The TMS derivatives of myo-inositol had a retention time of 11 min. Under these conditions quantitation

TABLE 4. *Human CSF inositol levels before and after oral inositol treatment*

Patient	Inositol (μg/ml)	
	Before	After
1	13.2	42.0
2	21.1	37.0
3	20.7	21.1
4	21.1	35.7
5	9.4	18.9
6	22.2	45.7
7	23.6	19.7
8	30.1	56.6
x ± SD	20.2 ± 6.3	34.6 ± 13 *(p = 0.011)

modified from (34) with permission

was performed with the use of TMS derivatives of standard myo-inositol under the same conditions. Standard curves were run daily and linearity was verified at the beginning and periodically during the processing of the samples.

All samples were assayed in a balanced manner so that samples before and after inositol treatment were run in the same batch, randomly ordered, with the biochemical assay performed blind as to the identity of the samples. Results presented are the average of duplicates for every case.

Table 4 presents CSF inositol levels before and after oral inositol treatment. Mean levels increase almost 70%. CSF inositol levels increased from a mean of 20.2 ± 6.3, to a mean of 34.6 ± 13, $p = 0.011$ (paired t-test).

These data suggest that peripherally administered inositol at high enough doses can enter brain and affect behavior in rats (1) and enter CSF in humans (34). The icv dose response and time curves suggest that twice daily administration of inositol may be sufficient for behavioral effects but that the dose-response curve is steep and thus the highest possible doses may be necessary to affect behavior.

CLINICAL TRIALS OF INOSITOL

Barkai et al. (7) reported that CSF levels of inositol were lower in depressed patients than in normal subjects. In Europe, over-the-counter inositol has long been used as a folk remedy for anxiety and depression. We hypothesized that inositol may be deficient in some brain systems in depression. This does not contradict the concept that Li reduces inositol levels and that Li is an antidepressant, since the PI cycle serves as a second messenger for several balancing and mutually interactive neurotransmitters. Li could alleviate depression by reducing inositol and a primary hyperactivity of one hypothetical brain system; low inositol levels in another system could cause second messenger dysfunction and thereby depression. Exogenous inositol could hypothetically alleviate inositol deficiency in one system without increasing inositol above normal levels in another.

After an encouraging open trail of 6 gm daily inositol in treatment resistent depression (32), we performed a double-blind controlled trial of 12 gm daily of inositol in 28 depressed patients for four weeks (30). Significant overall benefit for inositol compared to placebo was found at week 4 but not at week 2 on the Hamilton Depression Scale (HDS). Item analysis of the HDS found significant effects of inositol compared with placebo on mood, insomnia, anxiety, agitation, diurnal variation and hopelessness. No changes were noted in hematology, kidney or liver function. One patient in the placebo group developed a mania after week 2, but none in the inositol group did so.

Since many antidepressant compounds are also effective in panic disorder, we performed a trial of inositol in panic (10). Twenty-one patients with panic disorder with or without agoraphobia completed a double-blind, random assignment crossover treatment trial of inositol 12 grams per day versus placebo, with four weeks in each treatment phase. Frequency of panic attacks and severity of panic disorder and of agoraphobia declined significantly more on inositol than on placebo; the effect was comparable to that of imipramine in previous studies. Side-effects were minimal. Figures 1 and 2 show the clinical response of panic disorder patients to 4 weeks of treatment with inositol or placebo.

Since drugs effective in panic and depression could be nonspecific anxiolytics, we examined the effect of inositol 12 g single dose (33), on cognitive processes and mood of 11 healthy volunteers. There were 3 males, 8 females, mean age 42.0 $\pm$ 9 (23-56), mean years of education 17 $\pm$ 3 (13-24). Five subjects were given inositol (single dose) first and placebo 7 days after and the other 6 patients were given placebo first and inositol 7 days after. Inositol or placebo was given in a single dose dissolved in juice. Cognitive tests included digit repetition, picture recall test, story repetition and categorization. For picture recall and story repetition, 3 different versions were used. Digit span is thought to measure concentration and immediate memory; story test measures short term verbal memory; picture recall measures short-term visual memory and categorization measures long term semantic memory. Subjective feeling was evaluated using the profile of mood states (POMS). The cognitive tests battery and POMS were administered 3 times for each drug: immediately before the drug was given, 1½ h later and 6 h later.

Cognitive test results show no difference between inositol and placebo. POMS results show a trend for depression, hostility, tension and fatigue to

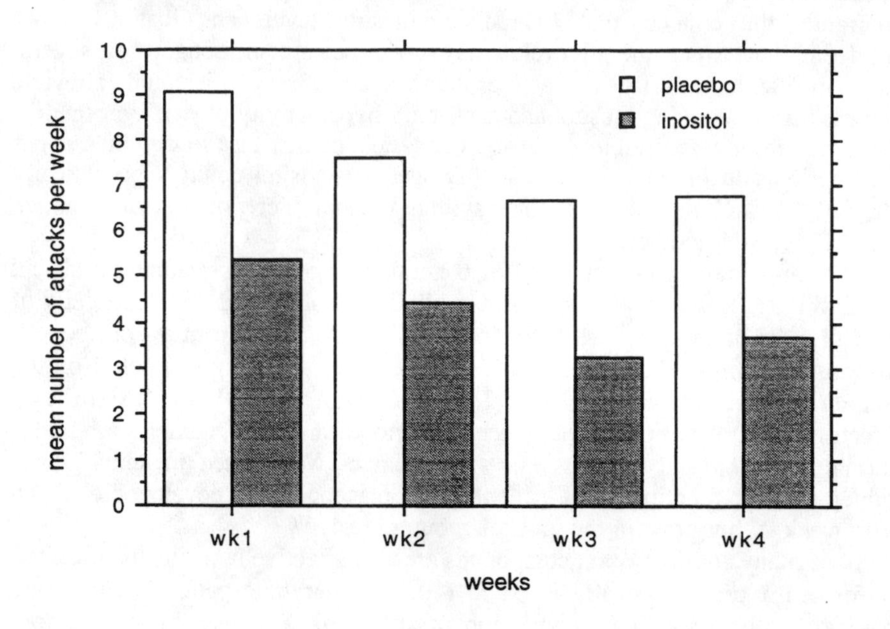

FIG. 1. Mean number of panic attacks during inositol or placebo

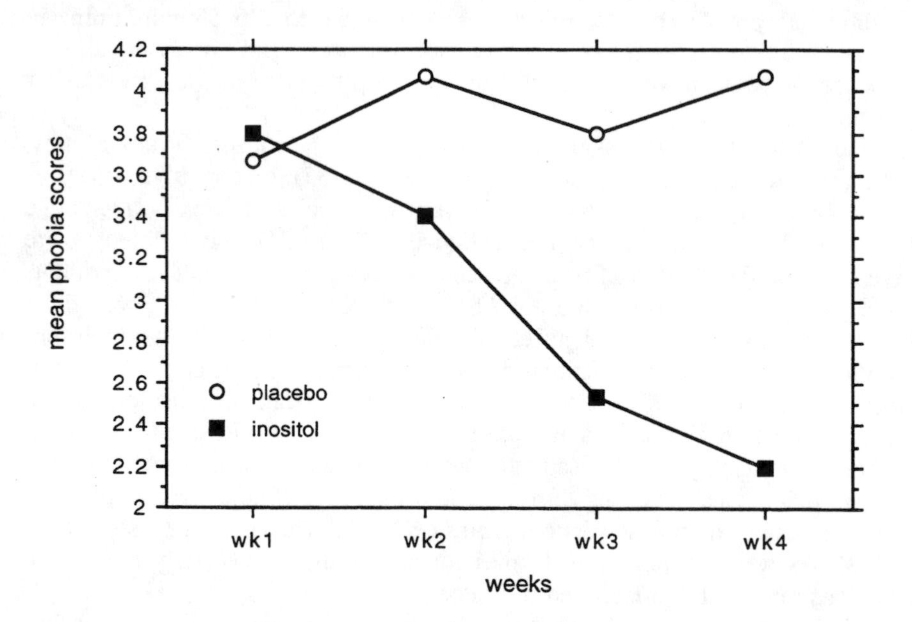

FIG. 2. Mean phobia scores during inositol or placebo treatment

improve more with inositol than placebo. Vigor also, declined less with inositol than placebo. These trends were entirely dependent on the subgroup of 4 subjects with initial POMS depression scores greater than 10. For instance, in the 4 subjects with baseline POMS depression scale above 10, inositol reduced depression from 14.5 to 8.5 and placebo increased depression from 6.5 to 11.5. These results in normals are consistent with an effect of inositol on mood. It is not clear if the inositol effect occurs in the manner of a stimulant on normal mood, or only in those subjects with pre-existing low mood.

Since muscarinic cholinergic processes have been implicated in Alzheimer's Disease (AD) and several muscarinic receptors use PI as a second messenger system, we did a double-blind controlled crossover trial of 6 gm daily in AD (6). The drug was given for one month at the lower dose of 6 gm for geriatric pharmacokinetic reasons. Eleven patients were studied for one month on inositol and one month on placebo. No significant clinical benefit was seen, but there was a trend in favor of inositol on cognitive tests and no side effects were seen. The trial should be repeated with a higher dose and longer time period, and more mildly ill patients.

We have completed 3 separate double-blind controlled trials of inositol in schizophrenia. Eleven patients were studied in the first psychiatric study of inositol, with 6 gm/day for 10 days (36). There were no clinical effects or side effects. A separate group of 10 schizophrenic patients were then studied with 6 gm daily for 30 days, in a controlled double-blind crossover trial, with no significant side effects and no clinical effects (32). Most recently 12 schizophrenic patients selected for anergia and negative signs were studied for one month on inositol 12 gm daily in a double-blind crossover controlled trial (31). No clinical effects or side effects were observed.

Since some antidepressants are useful in ADD-H, we studied 9 children mean age 8.3 years with 200 mg/kg inositol daily for one month in a double-blind controlled crossover trial. There was a strong trend for inositol to <u>worsen</u> hyperactivity but there were no side effects (29). We are therefore planning a trial of a diet with less than the normal 1 gm daily of inositol in ADDH. We also studied 10 children with childhood autism, age 3½-14, in a double-blind crossover trial of inositol 200 mg/kg for one month vs placebo. No improvement or side effects were seen (35).

A review of our safety data up to today shows that 107 patients have been treated with inositol. Of these, 61 have had full chemistry and hematology before and after inositol. Only two patients showed any changes in blood chemistry, both in the depression study. Both showed a mild increase in blood glucose that disappeared on repeat in one but continued in the other several weeks after discontinuation of inositol. Total side effects were flatus in four patients, nausea in one, sleepiness in two and insomnia in two.

Inositol has been given in diabetes for possible therapeutic effects on peripheral neuropathy, at doses of 20 gm per day with no side effects (4). Recently, newborns were treated with inositol 80 mg/kg with marked benefit in respiratory distress syndrome and no side effects were reported (22).

TABLE 5. *Clinical efficacy of inositol*

DEPRESSION:	(a) Open study, 11 resistant patients, 6 gm, 9 improved (b) Controlled study, 28 patients, 12 gm, $p<.05$ after 4 weeks
SCHIZOPHRENIA:	(a) Controlled crossover, 6 gm 10 days, no effect, no side effects (b) Controlled crossover, 6 gm one month, no effect, no side effects (c) Controlled crossover, 12 gm one month, negative symptoms patients, no effect, no worsening
PANIC DISORDER:	21 patients, controlled double-blind crossover, 12 gm for one month, $p = 0.02$ on panic attack severity/frequency
AUTISM:	10 children, age 3½-14, controlled double-blind crossover, 200 mg/kg for one month, no effect
ADDH:	9 children, mean age 8-3, controlled double-blind crossover 200 mg/kg for one month, worsening

The most serious theoretical side effect of inositol treatment could be reversal of therapeutic effects of Li or induction of mania in bipolar patients. So far, this has not been definitely seen in 4 bipolar depressed patients treated with full 12 gm daily inositol for depression (30) or in 18 Li-treated bipolar patients treated with low dose inositol for polyuria (17) or EEG abnormalities (5).

CONCLUSIONS

A number of different experimental approaches support the idea of behavioral effects of inositol. These include inositol reversal of various Li behavioral effects in a time-dependent and dose-dependent manner, the demonstration that pharmacological doses of peripheral inositol penetrate the blood brain barrier in animals and man, and inositol's clinical effects in depression and panic disorder. The activity of a biologically inactive enantiomer, epi-inositol, in one behavioral model of reversal of Li effects is a problem for this theory. So does the failure of long-term Li in therapeutic doses to lower inositol CSF levels. The pathophysiological relationship of inositol reversal of Li side effects and inositol therapeutic efficacy in depression and panic is not clear. The absence of toxicity warrants further studies using higher doses.

ACKNOWLEDGMENTS

This work was supported by grants from the Theodore and Vada Stanley Foundation, the German-Israel Foundation, grant No I-245-098.02/92 and the National Institute for Psychobiology in Israel.

REFERENCES

1. Agam G, Shapiro J, Bersudsky Y, Kofman O and Belmaker RH. Effect of high-dose peripheral inositol: brain inositol levels and prevention of behavioral changes due to inositol depletion. *Pharmacology, Biochemistry and Behavior* 1994; 49: 341-343.
2. Agam G, Shapiro J, Levine J, Stier S, Schields C, Bersudsky Y and Belmaker RH. Short-term lithium treatment does not reduce human CSF inositol levels. *Lithium* 1993; 4: 267-269.
3. Allison JH and Stewart MA. Reduced brain inositol in lithium-treated rats. *Nature New Biology* 1971; 233: 267-268.
4. Arendrup K, Gregersen G, Hawley J, Hawthorne JN. High-dose dietary myo-inositol supplementation does not alter the ischemia phenomenon in human diabetics. *Act Neuro Scand* 1989; 80: 99-102.
5. Barak Y, Levine J and Belmaker RH. The effect of inositol on lithium induced EEG abnormalities. *European Neuropsychopharmacology* 1994; 4: 419-420.
6. Barak Y, Levine J, Glasman A, Elizur A, Belmaker RH. Inositol treatment of Alzheimer's Disease. (Submitted, *International Psychogeriatrics*).
7. Barkai IA, Dunner DL, Gross HA, Mayo P, Fieve RR. Reduced myo-inositol levels in cerebrospinal fluid from patients with affective disorder. *Biol Psychiatry* 1978; 13: 65-72.
8. Belmaker RH, Benjamin J, Kaplan Z and Roitman G. A comparison of theories of lithium action based on phosphatidylinositol metabolism with theories based on cyclic AMP. In: Lerer B and Gershon S (eds) *New Directions in Affective Disorders*, Springer-Verlag, New York, 1989; 134-137.
9. Belmaker RH. Receptors, adenylate cyclase, depression and lithium. *Biol Psychiat* 1980; 16: 333-350.
10. Benjamin J, Levine J, Fux M, Aviv A, Levy D and Belmaker RH. Inositol treatment for panic disorder. (Under revision).
11. Berridge MJ, Downes CP and Hanley RR. Neural and developmental action of lithium: a unifying hypothesis. *Cell* 1989; 59: 411-419.
12. Berridge MJ, Downes CP, Hanley MR. Lithium amplifies agonist-dependent phosphatidyl-inositol responses in brain and salivary glands. *Biochem J* 1982; 206: 587-595.

13. Bersudsky Y, Shapiro J, Agam G, Kofman O and Belmaker RH. Behavioral evidence for the existence of two pools of cellular inositol. *European Neuropsychopharmacology* 1994; 4: 463-467.
14. Bersudsky Y, Mahler O, Kofman O and Belmaker RH. Species differences in susceptibility to Li-pilocarpine seizures. (In press, *European Neuropsychopharmacology*).
15. Bersudsky Y, Vinnitsky I, Ghelber D, Kofman O and Belmaker RH. Mechanism of lithium lethality in rats. *J Psychiat Res* 1993; 27: 415-422.
16. Bersudsky Y, Vinnitsky I, Grisaru N, Kofman O and Belmaker RH. Dose-response and time-curve of inositol prevention of Li-pilocarpine seizures. *European Neuropsychopharmacology* 1993; 2 (special issue): 428-429.
17. Bersudsky Y, Vinnitsky I, Grisaru N, Yaroslavsky U, Gheorghiu S, Ivgi D, Kofman O and Belmaker RH. The effect of inositol on lithium-induced polyuria-polydipsia in rats and humans. *Human Psychopharmacology* 1993; 7: 403-407.
18. Downes CP, Hawkins PT, Stephens L. Identification of the stimulated reaction in intact cells, its substrate supply and the metabolism of inositol phosphates. In: Michell RH, Drummond AH and Downes CP (eds) *Inositol Lipids in Cell Signalling*. Academic Press, London, San Diego, New York, Berkeley Boston, Sydney, Tokyo, Toronto, 1989; 3-38.
19. Downes CP, Stone MA. Lithium induced reduction in intracellular inositol supply in cholinergically stimulated parotid gland. *Biochem J* 1986; 234:199-204.
20. Gee NS, Ragan CI, Watling KJ, Aspley S, Jackson RG, Reid GG, Gani D and Shute JK. The purification and properties of myo-inositol monophosphatase from bovine brain. *Biochem J* 1988; 249: 883-889.
21. Hallcher LM and Sherman WR. The effect of lithium ion and other agents on the activity of myo-inositol-1-phosphatase from bovine brain. *J Biol Chem* 1990; 255: 10896-10901.
22. Hallman M, Bry K, Hoppu K, Lappi M and Pohjavouri M. Inositol supplementation in premature infants with respiratory distress syndrome. *New England J of Medicine* 1992; 326: 1233-1239.
23. Honchar MP, Ackerman KE, Sherman WR. Chronically administered lithium alters neither myo-inositol monophosphatase activity nor phosphoinositide levels in rat brain. *J Neurochem* 1989; 53: 590-594.
24. Kofman O and Levin U. Lithium's behavioural interactions with serotonin agonists in rats are differentially affected by intracerebroventricular myo-inositol. (In press, *Psychopharmacology*)
25. Kofman O and Belmaker RH. Biochemical, behavioral and clinical studies of the role of inositol in lithium treatment and depression. *Biological Psychiatry* 1993; 34: 839-852.
26. Kofman O, Belmaker RH. Intracerebroventricular myo-inositol antagonizes lithium-induced suppression of rearing behavior in rats. *Brain Res* 1990;

534: 345-347.

27. Kofman O, Sherman WR, Katz V and Belmaker RH. Restoration of brain myo-inositol levels in rats increases latency to lithium-pilocarpine seizures. *Psychopharmacology* 1993; 110: 229-234.
28. Lee CH, Dixon JF, Reichman M, Moummi C, Los G and Hokin LE. Li^+ increases accumulation of inositol 1,4,5-trisphosphate and inositol 1,3,4,5-tetrakisphosphate in cholinergically stimulated brain cortex slices in guinea pig, mouse and rat. *Biochem J* 1992; 282: 377-385.
29. Levine J, Aviram A, Ring A, Hollan D, Barak Y, Belmaker RH. Double-blind controlled crossover trial of inositol in childhood autism. (In preparation).
30. Levine J, Barak Y, Gonsalves M, Szor H, Elizur A, Kofman O and Belmaker RH. A double-blind controlled trial of inositol treatment of depression. (In press, *American Journal of Psychiatry*).
31. Levine J, Goldberger I, Rapaport A, Schwartz M, Schields C, Elizur A, Belmaker RH, Shapiro J, Agam G. CSF inositol in schizophrenia and high-dose inositol treatment of schizophrenia. *European Neuropsychopharmacology* 1994; 4: 487-490.
32. Levine J, Gonsalves M, Babur I, Stier S, Elizur A, Kofman O, Belmaker RH. Inositol 6 g daily may be effective in depression but not in schizophrenia. *Human Psychopharmacology* 1993; 8: 49-53.
33. Levine J, Pomerantz T, Belmaker RH. The effect of inositol on cognitive processes and mood states in normal volunteers. *European Neuropsychopharmacology* 1994; 4: 418-419.
34. Levine J, Rapaport A, Lev L, Bersudsky Y, Kofman O, Belmaker RH, Shapiro J and Agam G. Inositol treatment raises CSF inositol levels. *Brain Research* 1993; 627: 168-170.
35. Levine J, Ring A, Barak Y, Elizur A, Belmaker RH. Inositol in attention deficit disorder with hyperactivity. (In preparation).
36. Levine J, Umansky R, Ezrielev G, Belmaker RH. Lack of effect of inositol treatment in chronic schizophrenia. *Biological Psychiatry* 1993; 33: 673-675.
37. Newman M. and Belmaker RH. Effect of lithium in vitro and ex vivo on components of the adenylate cyclase system in rat cerebral cortex membrane. *Neuropharmacol* 1987; 26:211-217.
38. Oppenheim G, Ebstein RP and Belmaker RH. Effect of lithium on the physostigmine-induced behavioral syndrome and plasma cyclic GMP. *J Psychiat Res* 1979; 15: 133-138.
39. Shayman JA, Wu D. Myo-inositol does not modulate PI turnover in MDCK cells under hyperosmolar conditions. *Am J Physiol* 1990; 258: 1282-1287.
40. Sherman WR, Gish BG, Honchar MP, Munsell LY. Effects of lithium on phoshoinositide metabolism in vivo. *Fed Proc* 1986; 45: 2639-2646.
41. Sherman WR, Honchar MP, Munsell LY. Detection of receptor-linked

phophoinositide metabolism in brain of lithium treated rats. In: Bleasdale JE, Eichborg J, Hauser C (eds). *Inositol and Phosphoinositides: Metabolism and Regulation.* Humana Press, Clifton, NJ, 1985; 49-65.
42. Sherman WR, Leavitt AL, Honchar MP, Hallcher LM, Phillips BE. Evidence that lithium alters phosphoinositide metabolism: chronic administration elevates primarily D-myo-inositol-1-phosphate in cerbral cortex of the rat. *J Neurochem* 1981; 36: 1947-1951.
43. Sherman WR. Lithium and the phosphoinositide signalling system. In: Birch NJ (ed). *Lithium and the Cell.* Academic Press, London, 1991; Chapter 8, 121-157.
44. Spector R, Lorenzo AV. Myo-inositol transport in the central nervous system. *Am J Physiol* 1975; 288:1510-1518.
45. Tricklebank MD, Singh L, Oles RJ. Evidence that a proconvulsant action of lithium is mediated by inhibition of myo-inositol phosphatase in mouse brain. *Brain Res* 1991; 558: 145-148.

Depression and Mania: From Neurobiology to Treatment: edited by G. Gessa, W. Fratta, L. Pani, and G. Serra. Raven Press, New York © 1995.

Recent Developments in Genetics of Bipolar Illness

Elliot S. Gershon, M.D.

Clinical Neurogenetics Branch
National Institute of Mental Health
Bethesda, Maryland 20892 USA

Bipolar illness falls into the genetic classification of common diseases with complex inheritance, meaning that a single gene cannot account for all the cases of a disease, even within a single family. As in other members of this class of diseases, progress toward identifying specific susceptibility genes has become possible with the advances in DNA technology, and in analytic methodologies which are robust to this type of inheritance. Of particular importance is the emergence of a very dense and highly informative linkage map. To take advantage of these technological advances, a thorough knowledge is needed of the diagnostic epidemiology of the illness, and families must be identified and studied who can efficiently generate information on linkage or association of particular genes with illness.

GENETIC DIAGNOSTIC EPIDEMIOLOGY OF BIPOLAR (BP) ILLNESS

Coaggregation of BP and Related Diagnoses in Families

The twin, family, and adoption studies of bipolar illness have been extensively reviewed elsewhere (32,55), and these have led to a general consensus that there is a familial aggregation of major depression (unipolar mood disorder; UP) and schizoaffective disorder in families of BP patients, as compared with control rates.

Relatives of BP patients have more BP illness, but about the same UP illness, as relatives of UP patients. This is one of the findings that have led to the conclusion that there is an overlap of inherited susceptibility to BP and UP illness, although of course one is not assuming that there is only one inherited susceptibility to either disorder.

Schizoaffective disorder, it is generally agreed, is associated with BP illness in many families. The identical twins of schizoaffective patients tend to have the same disorder, but the first-degree relatives have a considerable frequency of affective disorder, both unipolar and bipolar, and also small but consistent increases in schizoaffective disorder and schizophrenia, as compared with controls. The problem is that schizoaffective disorder is also found in relatives of schizophrenics; the family data are reviewed elsewhere (10,14,55). The picture is further complicated by recent studies in which major depression is increased in relatives of schizophrenia (44,55).

There are differences of opinion over whether this and other evidence constitutes evidence for genetic overlap of BP and schizophrenia, or whether the Kraepelinian dichotomy is valid and these overlapping diagnoses have indeterminate origin (10,14). As a practical matter for genetic linkage and

TABLE 1. *Lifetime prevalence of psychotic and affective disorders in first-degree relatives of patients and controls*

Proband Dx	No. of relatives	SZ	SA-chronic	SA-acute	Other psychosis	BP (I & II)	UP
Schizophrenia	108	3.1	0	5.0	3.1	1.3	14.7
Schizoaffective (chronic psychosis)	129	1.7	2.5	0	6.7	8.8	9.3
Schizoaffective (acute psychosis)	69	4.9	1.6	5.8	3.2	11.7	16.4
BP (I&II)	738	0.3	0.1	1.6	0.6	7.2	14.9
Unipolar	165	0	0	0.7	4.4	2.9	16.7
Controls	380	0.6	0	0.6	1.2	0.3	6.7

Notes: prevalences are morbid risk (percent). DX = diagnosis. SZ= schizophrenia. SA = schizoaffective. BP = bipolar. UP = Unipolar. Psych. - psychosis. From Gershon et al., (25,29).

association studies, the investigator must balance the added statistical power of including schizoaffectives and unipolars as affected in bipolar families, against the risk that one is including, as affected, persons with a different genetic basis for their disease. It appears to us acceptable, in families with more than one bipolar person, to consider bipolar illness to be a core entity, with unipolar illness and schizoaffective disorder to be the outcome when additional non-shared genetic or environmental features are present.

Cohort effect

People born in the decades starting approximately in 1940 have a higher lifetime prevalence of affective disorders than people born earlier, as reviewed elsewhere (55). In our own data on relatives of BP and SA patients, the age at onset for bipolar and schizoaffective disorders has become earlier and the total lifetime prevalence appears likely to be much higher in the cohorts born since 1940 (30).

In our original description of this finding, we interpreted it as a gene-environmental interaction, since the increased rates were far higher in relatives of patients than in population data, and it did not appear that genetic change could occur so rapidly (from one generation to the next).

Recently, a new form of genetic change which occurs rapidly within predisposed families has been described. Expansion of *DNA trinucleotide repeat sequences* can occur as germ cells are formed and in early stages of embryonic development. This has been found to be the disease mutation in several CNS-related diseases, including Huntington's disease and Fragile-X mental retardation. A clinical feature of these diseases is *anticipation*, which refers to an increase in disease severity and/or earlier age of onset in successive generations. It has recently been argued (45) that anticipation occurs in Bipolar illness, and that trinucleotide repeat expansion may thus prove to be the basis of the genetic predisposition. The argument on anticipation is not compelling, since in family data it would appear to be impossible *not* to confound anticipation with a birth-cohort effect from another cause.

Other interpretations have also been offered. It has been argued that the entire finding is an artifact of recollection (65); this argument would not be valid for studies of contemporaneously collected data on BP illness, such as that of Angst (1).

DETECTION OF SUSCEPTIBILITY GENES THROUGH LINKAGE

Segregation Analysis

The inheritance patterns of BP in families do not fit simple Mendelian transmission (they do not segregate in families as simple recessives or dominants). Complex segregation analyses (that is, analyses with variable penetrance, presence of multifactorial inheritance, etc.) have not, so far, yielded a uniquely supported set of genetic transmission parameters (penetrance and allele frequencies), in the sense that there is significant rejection of all but one set of parameter values in a particular set of nested genetic models, as reviewed elsewhere (55). More recent analyses give similar outcomes. Curtis et al (16) recently did segregation analysis on five selected Icelandic pedigrees. It is not clear whether the pedigrees were selected because they appeared to have dominant transmission. Dominant inheritance gave equally likely fit to the mixed model, when bipolar [only] was considered affected. The mixed model fit better when unipolar illness was included as affected.

Risch (61) has demonstrated that some conclusions on inheritance can be drawn, even though segregation analyses are not conclusive about an illness. When a single gene or multilocus additive genes causes illness susceptibility, the risk ratio (risk to relatives vs. population risk; λ) progressively decreases, according to a fixed ratio, as one examines more distantly related relatives. For example, the observed value of the expression λ-1 should be twice as high in monozygotic twins as in dizygotic twins. In schizophrenia, the risk to monozygotic twins is too much greater than the risk to siblings to fit these types of inheritance. Although Risch does not discuss bipolar illness, the same conclusions would apply. One would look for oligogenic inheritance with interactions between susceptibility loci. These may prove to be detectable through linkage analysis methods which do not require that genetic transmission parameters be specified, such as the affected-sib-pair method (ASP; ref. 68), or the affected-pedigree-member method (APM; ref. 69).

Results of Genomic Scanning Linkage Studies in Bipolar Illness

The strategy of systematic genomic scanning for a susceptibility locus to bipolar illness has not yet been widely applied. The first comprehensive map using DNA marker loci was reported by Donis-Keller et al in 1987 (20). Since then, the informativeness of DNA markers has greatly improved, particularly with the development of microsatellite markers, gaps have been filled, and the density of the map has increased. A recent map has 2,066 microsatellite markers, with only modest gaps (36).

Understandably, the number of bipolar pedigrees studied with many markers is modest; no group of investigators has yet reported that it has completed its scan of the entire genome. Preliminary results of genomic scans have been reported by several investigators. In the Old Order Amish, following the failure of replication of the reported linkage on chromosome 11p (40). Ginns et al (35) reported on 250 RFLP markers and Pakstis et al (56) reported on 185 markers, without linkage detection. Curtis et al (16) reported on regions of chromosome 11p, 11q, 8q, 5q, 9q and Xq in five Icelandic pedigrees, where linkage was not found. Coon et al (11) examined eight U.S. pedigrees at 328 marker loci. Again, linkage was not detected. A marker locus on the distal portion of 5q, a region containing several receptor genes, gave a slightly positive lod score, but examination in that region of the D1 receptor and a closely linked marker (CRI-L1200) gave very negative lod scores (39).

Straub et al (66) reporting on 47 U.S. and Israeli pedigrees, have applied up to 157 marker loci per pedigree. One family had a lod score of 3.4 at locus PFKL on chromosome 21q, under dominant inheritance, although the multipoint lod score in that region was negative. Analysis by the parameter-free APM method showed statistically significant evidence for linkage in the pedigree series as a whole. This implies a susceptibility gene with small effect, possibly as part of an oligogenic inheritance system.

My colleagues and I have been studying a series of 22 U.S. pedigrees (7). Including a manuscript submitted for publication (Berrettini et al, submitted) 537 loci have been studied (6,18,19,22,23). The locus reported by Straub et al (66) is not linked to illness in our series (S. Detera-Wadleigh, unpublished data).

In one region on chromosome 18, Berrettini et al (5) observed lod scores >1 for several pedigrees in this series, with different pedigrees having these scores under dominant and under recessive inheritance. The highest lod score for one pedigree was 2.3 under recessive inheritance. Analysis was performed by parameter free methods. ASP was strongly suggestive at one locus, and multipoint APM showed statistically significant evidence for linkage (Table 2). As with the locus described by Straub et al this appears to be a susceptibility gene which is part of a complex, possibly oligogenic inheritance.

To be established as a linkage, of course, replication is required. This is not necessarily to be expected in every data set, however. In pedigrees simulated under additive oligogenic inheritance with six loci, where any combination greater than a threshold number of "susceptibility" alleles at these six loci can lead to a trait, Suarez et al (67) have demonstrated that a much smaller sample is needed to initially detect linkage to one of the trait loci than to replicate linkage to that locus. This result is intuitively reasonable, since any of the six loci can be the first to be detected, but in any given sample that same locus may or may not be playing enough of a role to be detectable.

Linkage Studies of Candidate Genes

This strategy may appear more appealing than genomic scanning in common diseases until one asks, in bipolar illness, on what basis is any gene a candidate. As reviewed elsewhere (55), the pathophysiology of illness is not well enough

TABLE 2. *Multilocus affected pedigree member analysis chromosome 18 markers in bipolar pedigrees*

Map region: D18S62-.20-D18S37-.026-D18S53-.024-D18S40

	Statistic	p-value	Empirical p-value
f(p)=1	1.48	.0692	.0670
f(p)=1/√p	1.74	.0404	.0438
f(p)=1/p	0.99	.1598	.1492

Map region: D18S40-.03-D18S45-.035-D18S44-.086-D18S66-.033-D18S56

	Statistic	p-value	Empirical p-value
f(p)=1	3.66	.00013	< .0001
f(p)=1/√p	3.41	.00033	.0007
f(p)=1/p	1.71	.04335	.0550

From Berrettini et al., (5)

elucidated to give promising candidate genes. However, based on the neuropharmacology of treatment agents for depression and for psychosis, dopamine and serotonin receptor genes and transporter genes have been appealing to many psychiatric geneticists.

Other candidate genes have been based on reported linkage findings and segregation analyses. It must be noted that some candidates have taken on a life of their own, even when the initial findings that generated the candidates have lapsed. This is true for the tip of the short arm of chromosome 11 (11p15). The genes in that small region include structural genes for insulin, tyrosine hydroxylase, the dopamine D4 structural gene (DRD4), and HRAS-1. It is generally agreed that linkage to bipolar illness in that region is not detectable, following the failure of replication of the linkage finding within the Old Order Amish pedigree where it was originally reported (40), and the lack of other confirmatory reports. Linkage studies of the DRD4 and of the enzyme tyrosine hydroxylase (or of the region spanning them) have continued to be reported (9,16,17,21,41,42,48,51,53,57,64); none have detected linkage.

Other dopamine receptor genes have been studied in bipolar illness, with linkage not detected to DRD1 (11,39,50,54), DRD2 (16,17,21,41,50,54), and DRD3 (52,60,63).

Multiple candidates have been tested in large scale genomic mapping scans of bipolar illness. Curtis et al (15,16) report exclusion of linkage to genes for 5HT1a receptor, proenkephalin, and dopamine-beta-hydroxylase. In my colleagues and my genomic scans and specific linkage studies of putative candidate genes, we have observed no linkage to these receptors: cannabinoid, α2-adrenergic (2 separate genes), α1-adrenergic, β1 and β2 adrenergic, DRD2, and human glucocorticoid receptor (reviewed in ref. 46).

By and large, these exclusions of candidate genes are based on lod score computations, based on "reasonable" single locus models of bipolar illness. The validity of the exclusion depends on the model used. Since non-model-based analytic methods may be required for detection of linkage in very complex inheritance disorders, one must consider all these exclusions to be tentative.

X-Linkage

Linkage of bipolar illness to the color blindness genes (which are in tandem on the X-chromosome (Xq28)) was reported by Reich et al in two families in 1969 (59), and corroborated by multiple pedigree reports of Mendlewicz and Fleiss (46,47), and Baron et al (3). However, controversy arose. The original investigators were never able to find a pedigree which replicated the findings, the work of Mendlewicz and Fleiss had mapping inconsistencies (reviewed in Gershon et al, ref. 28), and the report of Baron et al (3) was not replicated in follow-up of the same pedigrees (2,27). Other reports on this region were negative (see review in Gershon et al., ref. 28). Bocchetta et al (8) recently reported association of a G6PD allele with bipolar illness in Sardinia, but this also has been disputed (4,26).

In a more proximal region of the X-chromosome (Xq27), centering on the locus for blood clotting factor IX (FIX), there have been several independent reports of linkage (24,49,58), and interesting reports of disease association/linkage in two families with a FIX disease (Christmas disease) (13,33) and one with Fragile-X syndrome (38). Other reports have been negative (22).

With the recent positive reports, linkage to FIX appears to be a more supported hypothesis than the earlier data on Xq28. It should be noted that the FIX locus is far enough from the color blindness locus so that a disease in tight linkage with one would be unlinked to the other.

ASSOCIATION

Association exists when there is an allele which is more frequent in a series of unrelated patients as compared with population frequencies. Association may occur as follows: over the course of many generations, numerous recombinations occur on mutation-bearing chromosomes. These recombinations occur randomly along the chromosome, so even over many generations they are unlikely to occur within a specifiable very small region, such as the DNA sequences within 200 kb of an illness mutation. This region with no recombination over many generations is a region of linkage disequilibrium; if it contains polymorphic restriction enzyme recognition sites, an RFLP will be associated with the illness.

The chromosomal region scanned by an association test is usually much smaller than the region scanned by testing for linkage in pedigrees. Within a pedigree, which extends over only a few generations, there is a relatively large region around a disease mutation in which recombination does not occur during these few generations, or occurs infrequently. Thus, a marker at some distance will be co-inherited (linked) with an illness gene in a family, but may not be associated with it in a large population.

Association is often a more powerful strategy statistically than linkage (31,62). This is generally true for association to a true disease mutation, even when the gene is playing only a modest role in illness susceptibility. For polymorphisms within a linkage region, association due to linkage disequilibrium may be detectable or not, depending on the number of ancestral disease mutations and other factors.

When there is no prior hypothesis that a particular allele is associated with illness, the statistical problem of multiple hypothesis testing develops. This is especially the case for the current generation of highly polymorphic markers, because each of many alleles can be separately tested for association. Additionally, for dinucleotide repeat markers, rapid mutation of the dinucleotide sequence may obscure associations. It has been suggested that use of multiple diallelic sequence polymorphisms in a small non-conserved genomic region of a gene may prove to be the best strategy for detecting associations.

Some allelic associations have been reported with tyrosine hydroxylase, possibly stimulated initially by the report of linkage to an adjacent marker (insulin) on chromosome 11p15, which is discussed above. Following an initial positive association report (43) of bipolar illness with tyrosine hydroxylase, a series of negative studies was reported (34), and there has been an additional recent negative report (37).

Associations have also been sought at the end of the long arm of the X-chromosome, as well, again because of linkage reports. The gene responsible for the Fragile-X condition, FMR1, which has been hypothesized to lead also to affective disorder, has been studied but no abnormality was detected in bipolar illness (12).

DISCUSSION

With the improvements in the informativeness and density of the genetic linkage map, and the important increases in the number of pedigrees being collected and the number of laboratories doing molecular studies in this illness, one can be optimistic about progress in the genetics of bipolar illness. Discovery of reproducible linkages to susceptibility genes appears to be assured, providing the susceptibility genes exist and enough "brute force" is applied. At this time, promising new linkage findings have been reported on chromosomes 18 and 21, which are awaiting replication studies. Several independent reports of linkage to FIX on the X-chromosome are also promising.

Once linkage is demonstrated, the next goal is to identify the susceptibility gene and its mutations within the linkage region. A general methodology for doing this in common disease with complex inheritance has not yet been developed. The problem is that one cannot use individual recombinants (persons who do not fit the linkage) even if they have illness, to rule out chromosomal regions from containing the susceptibility gene, when there is a substantial probability of phenocopies. In the case of chromosome 18, in addition, the region within which linkage is detectable is large (tens of centimorgans), too large to attempt to clone every gene within that region.

Thus, successes in detecting linkage will lead to new challenges, which may be equally difficult to overcome. Nonetheless, I expect that within the next decade there will be mutations identified in susceptibility genes, and that this will in turn lead to advances in diagnosis and treatment of this devastating disorder.

REFERENCES

1. Angst J. Switch from depression to mania: A record study over decades between 1920 and 1982. *Psychopathology* 1985;18:140-154.
2. Baron M, Freimer NF, Risch N, et al. Diminished support for linkage between manic depressive illness and X-chromosome markers in three Israeli pedigrees. *Nature Genet* 1993;3:49-55.
3. Baron M, Risch N, Hamberger R, et al. Genetic linkage between X-chromosome markers and bipolar affective illness. *Nature* 987;326:289-292.
4. Baron M, Straub RE, Lehner T. et al. Correspondence: Bipolar disorder and linkage to Xq28. *Nature Genet* 1994;7:461.
5. Berrettini WH, Ferraro TN, Goldin LR, et al. Chromosome 18 DNA markers and manic-depressive illness: Evidence for a susceptibility gene. *Proc Natl Acad Sci USA* 1994;91:5918-5921.
6. Berrettini WH, Goldin LR, Gelernter J, et al. X-chromosome markers and manic-depressive illness: Rejection of linkage of Xq28 in nine bipolar pedigrees. *Arch Gen Psychiatry* 1990;47:366-373.

7. Berrettini WH, Goldin LR, Martinez MM, et al. A bipolar pedigree series for genomic mapping of disease genes: Diagnostic and analytic considerations. *Psychiatr Genet* 1991;2:125-160.
8. Bocchetta A, Piccardi MP, Del Zompo M. Is bipolar disorder linked to Xq28? *Nature Genet* 1994;6:224.
9. Byerley W, Plaetke R, Hoff M, et al. Tyrosine hydroxylase gene not linked to manic-depression in seven of eight pedigrees. *Hum Hered* 1992;42:259-263.
10. Cloninger CR. Tests of alternative models of the relationship of schizophrenic and affective psychoses. In: Gershon ES, Cloninger CR, eds. *Genetic Approaches to Mental Disorders: American Psychopathological Association Series*. Washington, DC: American Psychiatric Press; 1994;149-162.
11. Coon H, Jensen S, Hoff M, et al. A genome-wide search for genes predisposing to manic-depression, assuming autosomal dominant inheritance. *Am J Hum Genet* 1993;52:1234-1249.
12. Craddock N, Daniels J, McGuffin P, Owen M. Variation at the fragile X locus does not influence susceptibility to bipolar disorder. *Am J Med Genet* 1994;54:141-143.
13. Craddock N, Owen M. Christmas disease and major affective disorder. *Br J Psychiatry* 1992;160:715.
14. Crow TJ. The demise of the Kraepelinian binary system as a prelude to genetic advance. In: Gershon ES, Cloninger CR, eds. *Genetic Approaches to Mental Disorders: American Psychopathological Association Series*. Washington, DC: American Psychiatric Press, Washington, 1994;163-202.
15. Curtis D, Brynjolfsson J, Petursson H, et al. Segregation and linkage analysis in five manic depression pedigrees excludes the 5HT1a receptor gene (HTR1A). *Ann Hum Genet* 1993;57:27-39.
16. Curtis D, Sherrington R, Brett P, et awl. Genetic linkage analysis of manic depression in Iceland. *J R Soc Med* 1993;86:506-510.
17. De bruyn A, Mendelbaum K, Sandkuijl LA, et al. Nonlinkage of bipolar illness to tyrosine hydroxylase, tyrosinase, and D2 and D4 dopamine receptor genes on chromosome 11. *Am J Psychiatry* 1994;151:102-106.
18. Detera-Wadleigh SD, Berrettini WH, Goldin LR, et al. A systematic search for a bipolar predisposing locus on chromosome 5. *Neuropsychopharmacology* 1992;6:219-229.
19. Detera-Wadleigh SD, Hsieh WT, Berrettini WH, et al. Genetic linkage mapping for a susceptibility locus to bipolar illness: Chromosomes 2,3,4,7,9,10p,11p,22, and Xpter. *Am J Med Genet (Neuropsychiatr Genet)* 1994;54:206-218.
20. Donis-Keller H, Green P, Helms C, et al. A genetic linkage map of the human genome. *Cell* 1987;51:319-337.

21. Ewald H, Mors O, Friedrich U, Flint T, Kruse T. Exclusion of linkage between manic depressive illness and tyrosine hydroxylase and dopamine D2 receptor genes. *Psychiatr Genet* 1994;4:13-22.
22. Gejman PV, Detera-Wadleigh SD, Martinez MM, et al. Manic depressive illness not linked to factor IX region in an independent series of pedigrees. *Genomics* 1990;8:648-655.
23. Gejman PV, Martinez M, Cao Q, et al. Linkage analysis of fifty-seven microsatellite loci to bipolar disorder. *Neuropsychopharmacology* 1993;9:31-40.
24. Geller B, Fox LW, Clark KA. Rate and predictors of prepubertal bipolarity during follow-up of 6- to 12-year-old depressed children. *J Am Acad Child Adolesc Psychiatry* 1994;33:461-468.
25. Gershon ES, DeLisi LE, Hamovit J, et al. A controlled family study of chronic psychoses: Schizophrenia and schizoaffective disorder. *Arch Gen Psychiatry* 1988;45:328-336.
26. Gershon ES, Goldin LR. Bipolar disorder and linkage to Xq28. *Nature Genet* 1994;7:461-462.
27. Gershon ES, Goldin LR. Replication of genetic linkage by follow-up of previously studied pedigrees. *Am J Hum Genet* 1994;54:715-718.
28. Gershon ES, Goldin LR, Martinez MM, Hoehe MR. Detecting discrete genes for susceptibility to bipolar disorder or schizophrenia. In: Gershon ES, Cloninger CR, eds. *Genetic Approaches to Mental Disorders: American Psychopathological Association Series*. Washington, DC: American Psychiatric Press; 1994;205-230.
29. Gershon ES, Hamovit J, Guroff JJ, et al. A family study of schizoaffective, bipolar I, bipolar II, unipolar, and normal control probands. *Arch Gen Psychiatry* 1982;39:1157-1167.
30. Gershon ES, Hamovit JR, Guroff JJ, Nurnberger JI Jr. Birth-cohort changes in manic and depressive disorders in relatives of bipolar and schizoaffective patients. *Arch Gen Psychiatry* 1987;44:314-319.
31. Gershon ES, Martinez MM, Goldin LR, Gelernter J, Silver J. Detection of marker associations with a dominant disease gene in genetically complex and heterogeneous diseases. *Am J Hum Genet* 1989;45:578-585.
32. Gershon ES, Nurnberger JI Jr. Bipolar illness. In: Oldham JM, ed. *Review of Psychiatry, Vol. 14*. Washington, DC: American Psychiatric Press; 1995;(in press).
33. Gill M, Castle D, Duggan C. Cosegregation of Christmas disease and major affective disorder in a pedigree. *Br J Psychiatry* 1992;160:112-114.
34. Gill M, Castle D, Hunt N, et al. Tyrosine hydroxylase polymorphisms and bipolar affective disorder. *J Psychiatr Res* 1991;25:179-184.
35. Ginns EI, Egeland JA, Allen CR, et al. Update on the search for DNA markers linked to manic-depressive illness in the Old Order Amish. *J Psychiatr Res* 1992;26:305-308.

36. Gyapay G, Morissette J, Vignal A, et al. The 1993-94 Genethon human genetic linkage map. *Nature Genet* 1994;7:246-339.
37. Inayama Y, Yoneda H, Sakai T, et al. Lack of association between bipolar affective disorder and tyrosine hydroxylase DNA marker. *Am J Med Genet* 1993;48:87-89.
38. Jeffries FM, Reiss AL, Brown WT, et al. Bipolar spectrum disorder and fragile X syndrome: A family study. *Biol Psychiatry* 1993;33:213-216.
39. Jensen S, Plaetke R, Holik J, et al. Linkage analysis of the D1 dopamine receptor gene and manic depression in six families. *Hum Hered* 1992;42:269-275.
40. Kelsoe JR, Ginns EI, Egeland JA, et al. Re-evaluation of the linkage relationship between chromosome 11p loci and the gene for bipolar affective disorder in the Old Order Amish. *Nature* 1989;342:238-243.
41. Kelsoe JR, Kristbjanarson H, Bergesch P, et al. A genetic linkage study of bipolar disorder and 13 markers on chromosome 11 including the D2 dopamine receptor. *Neuropsychopharmacology* 1993;9:293-301.
42. Law A, Richard CW, Cottingham RW Jr, et al. Genetic linkage analysis of bipolar affective disorder in an Old Order Amish pedigree. *Hum Genet* 1992;88:562-568.
43. Leboyer M, Malafosse A, Boularand S, et al. Tyrosine hydroxylase polymorphisms associated with manic-depressive illness. *Lancet* 1990;335:1219.
44. Maier W, Lichtermann D, Minges J, et al. Continuity and discontinuity of affective disorders and schizophrenia. Results of a controlled family study. *Arch Gen Psychiatry* 1993;50:871-883.
45. McInnis MG, McMahon FJ, Chase GA, et al. Anticipation in bipolar affective disorder. *Am J Hum Genet* 1993;53:385-390.
46. Mendlewicz J, Fleiss JL. Linkage studies with X-chromosome markers in bipolar (manic-depressive) illness. *Biol Psychiatry* 1974;9:261-294.
47. Mendlewicz J, Fleiss JL, Fieve RR. Evidence for X-linkage in the transmission of manic-depressive illness. *JAMA* 1972;222:1624-1627.
48. Mendlewicz J, Leboyer M, De bruyn A, et al. Absence of linkage between chromosome 11p15 markers and manic-depressive illness in a Belgian pedigree. *Am J Psychiatry* 1991;148:1683-1687.
49. Mendlewicz J, Simon P, Sevy S, et al. Polymorphic DNA marker on X chromosome and manic depression. *Lancet* 1987;1230-1232.
50. Mitchell P, Selbie L, Waters B, et al. Exclusion of close linkage of bipolar disorder to dopamine D1 and D2 receptor gene markers. *J Affect Disord* 1992;25:1-11.
51. Mitchell P, Waters B, Morrison N, et al. Close linkage of bipolar disorder to chromosome 11 markers is excluded in two large Australian pedigrees. *J Affect Disord* 1991;21:23-32.

52. Mitchell P, Waters B, Vivero C, et al. Exclusion of close linkage of bipolar disorder to the dopamine D3 receptor gene in nine Australian pedigrees. *J Affect Disord* 1993;27:213-224.
53. Nanko S, Kobayashi M, Gamou S, et al. Linkage analysis of affective disorder using DNA markers on chromosomes 11 and X. *Jpn J Psychiatry Neurol* 1991;45:53-56.
54. Nothen MM, Erdmann J, Korner J, et al. Lack of association between dopamine D1 and D2 receptor genes and bipolar affective disorder. *Am J Psychiatry* 1992;149:199-201.
55. Nurnberger JI Jr, Goldin LR, Gershon ES. Genetics of psychiatric disorders. In: Winokur G, Clayton PJ, eds. *The Medical Basis of Psychiatry*. Philadelphia: W.B. Saunders; 1994;459-492.
56. Pakstis AJ, Kidd JR, Castiglione CM, Kidd KK. Status of the search for a major genetic locus for affective disorder in the Old Order Amish. *Hum Genet* 1991;87:475-483.
57. Pauls DL, Gerhard DS, Lacy LG, et al. Linkage of bipolar affective disorders to markers on chromosome 11p is excluded in a second lateral extension of Amish pedigree 110. *Genomics* 1991;11:730-736.
58. Pekkarinen P, Bredbacka PE, Terwilliger J, et al. Evidence for a susceptibility locus for manic-depressive disorder in Xq26. *Am J Hum Genet* 1994;55:A133.
59. Reich T, Clayton PJ, Winokur G. Family history studies: The genetics of mania. *Am J Psychiatry* 1969;125:1358-1368.
60. Rietschel M, Nothen MM, Lannfelt L, et al. A serine to glycine substitution at position 9 in the extracellular N-terminal part of the dopamine D3 receptor protein: No role in the genetic predisposition to bipolar affective disorder. *Psychiatry Res* 1993;46:253-259.
61. Risch N. Linkage strategies for genetically complex traits. I. Multilocus models. *Am J Hum Genet* 1990;46:222-228.
62. Schaid DJ, Sommer SS. Genotype relative risks: Methods for design and analysis of candidate-gene association studies. *Am J Hum Genet* 1993;53:1114-1126.
63. Shaikh S, Ball D, Craddock N, et al. The dopamine D3 receptor gene: No association with bipolar affective disorder. *J Med Genet* 1993;30:308-309.
64. Sidenberg DG, King N, Kennedy JL. Analysis of new D4 dopamine receptor (DRD4) coding region variants and TH microsatellite in the Old Order Amish family (OOA110). *Psychiatr Genet* 1994;4:95-99.
65. Simon GE, VonKorff M. Reevaluation of secular trends in depression rates. *Am J Epidemiol* 1992;135:1411-1422.
66. Straub RE, Lehner T, Luo Y, et al. A possible vulnerability locus for bipolar affective disorder on chromosome 21q22.3. *Nature Genet* 1994;8:291-296.
67. Suarez BK, Hampe CL, Van Eerdewegh PV. Problems of replicating linkage claims in psychiatry. In: Gershon ES, Cloninger CR, eds. *Genetic*

Approaches to Mental Disorders: American Psychopathological Association Series. Washington, DC: American Psychiatric Press; 1994;23-46.
68. Suarez BK, Rice JP, Reich T. The generalized sib pair IBD distribution: Its use in the detection of linkage. *Ann Hum Genet* 1978;42:87-94.
69. Weeks DE, Lange K. The affected-pedigree-member method of linkage analysis. *Am J Hum Genet* 1988;42:315-326.

Depression and Mania: From Neurobiology to Treatment: edited by G. Gessa, W. Fratta, L. Pani, and G. Serra. Raven Press, New York © 1995.

Toward a Temperament-Based Approach to Depression: Implications for Neurobiologic Research

Hagop S. Akiskal, M.D.

Department of Psychiatry, University of California, San Diego
La Jolla, California 92093-0603

This chapter summarizes research conducted by the author and his collaborators during the past two decades in developing a temperament-based approach to understanding the origin of different affective subtypes. Description of the temperaments themselves and the theoretical underpinnings of this model, as well as their clinical implications have been documented in previous publications (1-5). The present contribution focuses on those elements of the approach which are of the greatest relevance to neurobiologic investigations.

THE NEED FOR AN INNOVATIVE CLASSIFICATION OF DEPRESSION

Depressive states have been by tradition classified on the basis of the acute clinical picture such as "retarded," "agitated," "anxious," "atypical," "hostile," etc (6). These constructs, in turn, were often dichotomized into overlapping, though not necessarily synonymous, contrasting terminology such as melancholic-neurasthenic, psychotic-neurotic, endogenous-reactive, and primary-secondary. Implicit in these dichotomies is biologic vs. psychological causation, the former due to genetic factors impinging on a more or less normal or "obessoid" personality, the latter arising from environmental adversity in the setting of an abnormal personality with "neurotic," "immature" or "psychopathic" traits. Except for the stability of the psychotic subtype across episodes (7), prospective observations have generally failed to support the longitudinal validity of these dualistic nosologic schemas.

The most damaging evidence against the foregoing schemas derives from prospective observations on the transformation of "neurotic depressions" into its antitheses (8,9). Despite these inconsistencies, elements of these dualistic concepts have survived within the general framework of the bipolar-unipolar dichotomy favored by the two official current classification systems of mental disorders (the DSM-IV and ICD-10). In both manuals, the larger and heterogeneous universe of unipolar major depressions receives further qualification, e.g.,"major depressive" vs "dysthymic" or "melancholic" vs "atypical." An important limitation of these manuals is that long-standing traits are not taken into consideration, leading to errors in affective subtyping. For instance, clinically depressed patients with subtle expressions of bipolarity at the temperamental level can be misclassified as unipolar. Such errors occur because "Dysthymia" and "cyclothymia" - believed to be the trait expressions, respectively, of major unipolar and bipolar disorders - often co-exist with these disorders in apparently conflicting ways, e.g. bipolar disorder (mania) arising from a dysthymic baseline or a major depressive episode developing on the ground of cyclothymic mood swings (3). The official diagnostic manuals in use today have no provisions for such situations.

The proposed temperament-based approach to depressive states (4,5) attempts to address these inconsistencies and inadequacies in our traditional as well as current nosologic schemas of mood disorders. This new classification builds on the trait (temperament)-state (affective episode) spectrum model inherent in the Kraepelinian and Kretschmerian systems. For instance dysthymia is considered a subaffective expression and/or precursor of major depressive episodes. The model further postulates temperamental dysregulation to be the fundamental pathology of mood disorders (3). This postulate envisions reversal of a temperament to its "opposite" affective state, e.g. dysthymia leading to a manic state. Temperamental instabilities in this model represent the proximal behavioral phenotypes of the genetic diathesis underlying recurrent mood disorders. Indeed, clinical and family studies - among affective probands and their biologic kin - have revealed an uninterrupted series of transitions between near-normal temperaments and fullblown affective illness (10-12). Behavioral phenotypes in most mental disorders today are considered quantitatively distributed with no hint of discontinuity (13). This is a fundamental fact with which modern molecular genetics will have to deal.

TEMPERAMENT IN THE PATHOGENESIS OF AFFECTIVE ILLNESS

Temperament refers to the individual's activity level, basal affective tone, moods, their intensity, reactivity, and variability. These expressions are hypothesized to be closest to the underlying biologic dysregulation. Personality - and personality disorder - represent more distal phenotypes, and refer primarily to interpersonal operations and their pathology. Affective episodes too are distal in the pathogenetic chain of mood disorders. What complicates the study of mood disorders is the "comorbidity" of affective episodes with their interpersonal and social problems. Temperaments offer the opportunity to study the affective illness in its more fundamental, relatively uncomplicated stage. In the model developed by the author (1), the affective temperaments are considered as intermediary processes between genetic predisposition, developmental factors, gender, and stressors on the one hand, and clinical episodes of depression on the other. It is submitted that genetic, developmental and gender-related factors lead to subaffective dysregulation at the temperamental level; these temperaments in turn create the life circumstances and biological stressors that precipitate fullblown clinical episodes. The life circumstances could include a turbulent love life as in cyclothymia (14), stimulant use as in hyperthymia (15), and job loss in dysthymia (16). There are obviously gender-specific stressors as well (e.g. postpartum episodes).

Our knowledge of temperaments is quite old (17), and comprises the sanguine, melancholic, choleric and phlegmatic types, the first three being still highly relevant to our current concepts of affective temperaments. In ancient medical treatise these temperaments were linked to humoral theory, and depicted as follows:

- the sanguine as a man who is very active, especially in the domain of amorous advances
- the melancholic as a sleeping person who looks feminine, and who is contrasted to her hard-working self between affective episodes
- the choleric, the most pathological of temperaments, in a flash of anger.

Today we consider the first to represent the hyperthymic temperament with its cheerful, upbeat and action-oriented disposition (15), and the second to represent the dysthymic temperament with its gloomy, contemplative and lethargic disposition (16); the third, also described as irritable, is a mixture of the two, being characterized by a combined dysphoric and restless disposition, a highly unstable mixture that manifests in such traits as habitual complaining, overcritical attitudes and angry outbursts (15). The cyclothymic, the type added by Kraepelin, combines elements of all three temperaments mentioned above, in that it alternates between 'up' and 'down' as well as exhibiting periods of irritability and explosive mood (14); mood lability then is an important characteristic of cyclothymia.

To recapitulate, these temperaments represent the formes frustes of major mood disorders, and are indicative of an inherent disposition to mood swings at a subaffective level (18). Accordingly, in individuals with these temperaments, the predisposition to major affective episodes is considered to be always subclinically active.

The relationship of these temperaments to mood disorders can be seen in a study of monozygotic twins (11), in which 58% were concordant for fullblown unipolar or bipolar disorder - defined as strict concordance where both co-twins were affectively ill. In 17% the co-twin was normal. In 25% the co-twin either had a severe "schizophreniform" psychotic illness, or was just 'moody' at the temperament level; this was considered broad concordance - i.e. discordant for the core or fullblown affective phenotypes, but concordant for a broad spectrum of affective psychopathology, thereby suggesting that the extreme psychotic phenotypes, the core affective phenotypes and the much milder (or subclinical) temperamental phenotypes are part of the same spectrum. The main point here is that these moody temperamental individuals, who had never been treated for a mood disorder, carried the same gene(s) as the core and more severe phenotypes, but had somehow escaped the fate of being clinically ill. This study is strongly supportive of the Kraepelinian position, which has recently received further major endorsement from Goodwin and Jamison (19), whose monograph defines manic depressive illness as a recurrent dysregulation that may manifest at different levels of intensity, from mild to severe, from non-psychotic to extreme psychotic, from unipolar to bipolar.

DEFINING AFFECTIVE TEMPERAMENTS

The clinic established in Memphis 20 years ago (8) - when the author was at the University of Tennessee - provided the opportunity to examine patients and their families between episodes. Even today, most biological psychiatrists work in hospital research units or laboratories and rarely see the patients' relatives, on many of whom Kraepelin made his observations of temperament; as for the patients, once discharged, they are usually followed up elsewhere. By contrast, an outpatient mood clinic provides ample opportunity to see the entire family, and patients can be observed not only during episodes but also between them (5). In this setting one can learn a great deal about affective patients as people - about their temperaments, their rhythms, their hopes and fears, their interpersonal crises and conflicts, their marital adjustment, their vocations, aspirations and ambitions: a rich body of information that psychiatry has yet to integrate systematically into the pathogenesis of mood disorders (3). Such attributes and events all seem to hinge on the patients' temperament, their biography being virtually written as a function of its intensity, its reactions, its variability over time, and the reactions which it provokes in others. Current evidence suggests that Kraepelin (10) and Kretschmer (20) were justified in suggesting that the affective temperaments were characterized by social liabilities and instabilities as well as by assets which, in gifted individuals, could translate into leadership and creativity (21).

The criteria for the temperaments which we have developed and operationalized are founded on classical descriptions (10,20,22), on our own observations (23) and, more recently, on collaboration with Professor Cassano's group (24) and that of Dr. Koukopoulos (25). The salient features of the two basic affective temperaments are highlighted next:

- The depressive or dysthymic temperament (16) is characterized by low energy, low spirits and negative cognitions. Being gloomy represents a "negative" trait, but brooding is not necessarily so; Aristotle, for instance, thought that it was related to creativity and eminence in intellectual domains (17). Most dysthymics, however, are preoccupied with inadequacy, and are sluggish, introverted and humorless, traits often considered as liabilities. However, they can invest all their energy in one line of work which they perform with relative constancy and in which they may excel, having no time for leisure. They may be "passive", yet may also be self-sacrificing and devoted, which are virtues. Kretschmer (20) observed that these people do all the "boring", supportive jobs for society, those that require painstaking attention to minutiae. They can be self-critical, skeptical, and hypercritical, which can serve as important virtues in science.

- The hyperthymic temperament (15) is defined largely of desirable traits - cheerful, self-assured, indefatigable and versatile. These individuals are also warm, extroverted, articulate, overtalkative, even meddlesome; the latter trait is often tolerated because of the foregoing interpersonal assets. Their liabilities relate in part to their enormous appetite for pleasures such as good food, cocaine and sex; indeed, such people may become involved in scandal. Being stimulus-seeking and risk-taking, they can endanger their family's financial assets, but can rapidly climb the ladder of success. Being short-sleepers, they can devote more time and energy to productivity and achievement.

TABLE 1. *The manifestations of cyclothymia**

Behavioral

1. Hypersomnia vs decreased need for sleep
2. Introverted self-absorption vs uninhibited people-seeking
3. Taciturn vs talkative
4. Unexplained tearfulness vs buoyant jocularity
5. Psychomotor inertia vs restless pursuit of activities

Subjective

6. Lethargy and somatic discomfort vs eutonia
7. Dulling of senses vs keen perceptions
8. Slow-witted vs sharpened thinking
9. Shaky self-esteem (alternating between low self-confidence and overconfidence)
10. Pessimistic brooding vs optimism and carefree attitudes

*Summarized from Akiskal et al. (14 and 23).

TABLE 2. *The Irritable Temperament**

1. Moodiness dominated by irritable-angry periods
2. Intense emotionality such that even normally pleasurable activities are often unendurable
3. Driven by inner tension and dysphoric restlessness
4. Dissatisfied, complaining and bitter disposition
5. Hypercritical attitudes towards others
6. Ill-humored, often biting humor
7. Obtrusive and importunate

*Modified from Akiskal (15)

The hyperthymic and dysthymic represent, in a sense, "opposite" temperaments. The dysregulation underlying these temperaments creates two types of instabilities: The cyclothymic (Table 1), which alternates between the hyperthymic and dysthymic poles, and the irritable (Table 2), a mixed form of the two.

PREVALENCE AND LONGITUDINAL COURSE

If the temperaments are the anlagé of affective episodes, they should be prevalent and must precede major affective episodes. Our first report (14) of 10% prevalence of cyclothymic and related temperaments in a mental health clinic was greeted with skepticism. Community and outpatient studies (26-30) both in the USA and Europe (Table 3) have shown that 4-6% of people display these temperamental styles, so that 10% reported in a clinical population is not unexpected. All of these studies pertain to temperaments with hypomanic, irritable, or labile traits. Two of these community cohorts (27,30) have been followed prospectively, showing - in comparison with controls - a significant excess of affective episodes and/or substance abuse, suicide attempts, and serious interpersonal altercations.

The prevalence of dysthymia in the community - a rough estimate of the depressive temperament - has been reported to be 3% in the US (31) and in Europe (32). Again, in comparison with controls, it has been shown that a significantly greater proportion of dysthymics in the community develop major depressive episodes when observed prospectively (33).

Similar studies have been conducted in clinical populations. For instance, the Memphis study (23) of cyclothymia (n=50) referred to above, showed that - prospectively examined - 25% developed major depressive breakdowns and 6% manic breakdowns. Furthermore, our study (12) of the offspring or juvenile kin of 68 individuals with recurrent mood disorders showed that 10 had prepubertal onsets; of these, eight exhibited temperamental dysregulation only - dysthymic, hyperthymic, or cyclothymic - while three had major affective episodes. Thus, of 10 children, eight had a diagnosable temperamental disturbance prepubertally; after three years' prospective follow-up, four of the eight temperaments evolved into major affective episodes. In a longer prospective follow-up of dysthymic children by Kovacs et al. (34), the majority developed major depressive episodes, of which one-third became bipolar; in other words, in a substantial minority of cases the depressive temperament "switched" into mania, i.e. a reversal of temperament to the opposite episode.

There is therefore evidence from three prospective studies - one in a familially defined high-risk population and the other two naturalistic follow-up of dysthymic and cyclothymic individuals without regard to family history - showing that affective temperaments precede clinically diagnosed major affective episodes. This is a fundamental requirement if the model proposed here is to be considered relevant to clinical depression.

Finally, in a retrospective study in collaboration with the Pisa Group (35), we examined temperament, family history in relation to age at onset of major depression. We found that temperament and family history are correlated with early age of onset of major depression. Depressions arising from temperamental dysregulation are thus both familial and have an earlier age of onset, a finding to be expected if the proposed model is valid.

TABLE 3. *Prevalence of cyclothymic and related temperaments.*

Authors (year)	Population	Rates(%)
Akiskal et al. (1977)	Chronic mental health clinic patients	10
Weissman and Myers (1978)	Community	6
Depue et al. (1981)	College students	6
Casey and Tyrer (1986)	Community	6
Wicki and Angst (1991)*	Community	4

*This study measured subsyndromal hypomania and showed it to be highly recurrent over a one year period.

TEMPERAMENTS AND AFFECTIVE EPISODES

The Depressive vs Hyperthymic Temperaments

Comparison of major depressive patients, with and without antecedent depressive temperament, shows that the depressive temperament predisposes to very young age of onset of depression, with more recurrent episodes, more suicide attempts, more severe depression and, remarkably, is associated with high rates of family history of mood disorders (35). This means that having both the temperament and the depression together ("double depression", 36) represents a more "genetic" form of major depressive illness. Major depression is a heterogeneous disorder, but adding the depressive temperament gives a purer group. This is extremely important for both clinicians and researchers: for clinicians because it predicts course, for researchers because this is the group in which one should logically explore genetic markers.

In collaboration with the Pisa group (37), we have shown that the depressive temperament accounts for slightly under 40% of a large consecutive series of major depressives in the Pisa-Memphis collaborative study; the hyperthymic temperament accounted for 13%, based on a conservative threshold of at least five hyperthymic items. Using four or more items - which is still associated significantly with bipolar family history - the proportion of major depressives with hyperthymic temperament jumps to nearly 20% (unpublished data). Furthermore, in major depression with hyperthymic temperament, the age at onset is older than in major depression with the depressive temperament. Patients with major depression but no temperament at all have the oldest age of onset, suggesting that one way to be protected against depression is not to have temperament at all! Overall, these data indicate that the natural tendency to gloom in the depressive temperament translates into earlier onset of depressive illness, whereas the more active, up-beat, hyperthymic temperament could protect, to some extent, against depressive breakdowns. The tendency to brooding and being excessively perturbed by life stressors - utilizing the so-called "ruminative" style - is more prevalent in women (24,38) which could explain their greater likelihood of succumbing to aversive life events and, ultimately, their higher rates of depression (39). The reverse appears to be the case with men, who tend to have a more "active" style for coping with negative events (38) and who are therefore protected, to some extent, against depressive illness. However, hyperthymic men tend to engage in substance (especially stimulant) abuse, which appears to predispose them to depression via a different mechanism (15).

Does "unipolar" major depression with hyperthymic temperament have anything to do with bipolar illness? The evidence (summarized in Cassano et al., 37) is that if one compares bipolar family history in bipolar I (defined by mania), bipolar II/III (defined by either spontaneous or pharmacologically-induced hypomania), and hyperthymic unipolars (U-HT), one observes a gradient in family history from 22% to 11% and 9% respectively, dropping sharply to a low of 2% in strict unipolars. This kind of data, compatible with a spectrum concept of bipolar illness (for B-I, B-II/III and U-HT), suggests that hyperthymic unipolars are actually "pseudo-unipolar" and represent a bridge between soft bipolar (II and III) and strict unipolar depression (40).

The study by Perugi et al. (24) revealed gender differences in temperaments, the hyperthymic being more common in men and the dysthymic in women. As pointed out, this is analogous to other findings (38) that men cope more actively with their depressions, and women engage in greater introversion and soul-searching. The profile for hyperthymia, developed by Possl and von Zerssen (41), consists of the following: vivid, active, verbally aggressive, self-assured, strong-willed, self-employed, risk-taking, sensation-seeking, breaking social norms, generous and spendthrift. Obviously cultural factors and upbringing play some role in shaping constitutional dispositions towards the depressive or hyperthymic pole. Given that by early adult life these temperamental styles are crystallized differently in the two genders, they could explain, in part, what Angst (42) reported 15 years ago - that males have more manic episodes and females more depressive episodes than men.

The Cyclothymic Temperament

In the late 1970s we prospectively demonstrated that patients with cyclothymic temperament were more predisposed to depressive episodes than to mania (14), i.e. were more likely to switch into depression than into mania. If a tricyclic antidepressant is given to such patients they switch very rapidly to hypomania: tricyclic antidepressants actually double the rate of hypomania in cyclothymic patients. These findings preceded the concept of rapid cycling subsequently developed by Wehr and Goodwin (43) and Koukopoulos et al (44).

Temperament and Mixed States

Another interesting perspective on temperaments and affective episodes is provided by ongoing studies on mixed states, suggesting that the latter arise when temperament and polarity of episodes are in "opposite" direction (45). Comparison of individuals with pure mania and mixed states (so-called dysphoric manics) shows that pure manics have less of a depressive than a hyperthymic temperament, and that patients with mixed states have a significantly higher rate of depressive temperament and are significantly less likely to be hyperthymic (Perugi et al., unpublished data). In other words, a manic patient with a temperament opposite to mania is more likely to develop a mixed state; if the temperament is concordant with mania, then the patient is less likely to develop a mixed state. These do not represent state-dependent findings. Obviously, a depressive temperament that develops mania cannot be showing a state-dependent variable, but a hyperthymic patient with mania could be, though there are reasons to believe that this is not so (24). When inquiring about them, often with the entire family present, we phrase our question as follows: "Was your relative like this ten, 15, 20, 30 years ago?" Reliability is very high with this approach (37). Such observations suggest that affective episodes are not mere linear exaggerations of temperaments, and that the basic affective dysregulation can swing in opposite directions.

The Irritable Temperament

The choleric temperament has not been systematically studied because these individuals can be unpleasant and hostile; in the USA they might be called 'borderline' but their core feature is nonetheless irritability (15). Followed up over time, they develop major depressions as well as hypomanic and mixed episodes, and have a high suicide rate (46). They may also resemble patients with brief recurrent depression (47), with angry suicide attempts (48). The sleep of borderline patients (49) is very much like that of the affectively ill, a finding now replicated in six sleep laboratories worldwide. This is a remarkable finding in biological psychiatry, where replication is very rare, especially given an unreliable entity like borderline personality. This unreliability, or basic instability, seems to be the very characteristic of the affective dysregulation that underlies borderline pathology. The affective instability is the pathology - which explains such a consistent biological finding!

In a more general vein, and as discussed in greater detail elsewhere (3), the very intensity and variability of the temperaments under consideration often create situations that could precipitate affective episodes (e.g. falling in and out of love, transmeridian travel, substance abuse, sleep deprivation). Finally, individuals with affective temperamental dysregulation tend to react more intensely - both positively and negatively - to events that for the average person are relatively neutral (25). Thus, in a literal sense, they create exciting, stormy or negative life situations around themselves, in the context of which their recurrent moods and episodes fluctuate.

CONCLUDING REMARKS

Space considerations do not permit discussion of putative anxious temperaments which have been described by other investigators (50,51) as being relevant to both anxious, anxious-depressive and major depressive episodes. This, too, represents a large universe of human suffering which has benefitted from longitudinal prospective research, demonstrating the relevance of specified anxious temperamental types in the origin of clinical depression and related anxiety states There are good reasons to believe that this spectrum of anxious temperaments, just like those described in the present communication, run in families. This is their main relevance to genetic and neurobiologic research in general (52).

I submit that research studies are more likely to discover specific genetic, neurochemical or neurophysiologic abnormalities if their methodology would focus on familially- and temperamentally-defined affective subtypes. This would reduce the heterogeneity of major depressive disorders as defined by the so-called research diagnostic criteria (RDC). Most importantly, in an era when high-tech sophistication has permeated neurobiology, clinical diagnoses of depression too should be made with the requisite sophistication. We have developed, in collaboration with Dr. Perugi, a semi-structured instrument for the precise quantification of the temperamental dysregulation underlying depressive disorders (unpublished at this writing). It is now being used in several French, Italian and North American studies. It is beyond the scope of this chapter to discuss the predictive use of the proposed temperament-based approach in the psychopharmacology and clinical management of depressive disorders. This has been covered in great detail in previous contributions (53,54). For neurobiologic investigations, the exciting news is that prospective long-term research extending over more than a decade is beginning to show the predictive value of labile or cyclothymic temperamental traits in the switch process from depression to hypomania (55). Such data re-inforce the intimate connection between temperamental instability and the dysregulation underlying major affective disorders. It is hard to envision fundamental research on affective disorder that can afford to ignore such considerations in the design of studies.

REFERENCES

1. Akiskal, HS. Personality as a mediating variable in the pathogenesis of mood disorders: Implications for theory, research and prevention. In:Helgason T, Daly RD *Depressive Illness: Prediction of Course and Outcome*. Berlin: Springer-Verlag; 1988:131-146.
2. Akiskal, HS. Validating affective personality types. In:Robins L, Barrett J,*The validity of psychiatric diagnosis*, New York: Raven Press; 1989:215-235.
3. Akiskal HS & Akiskal K. Cyclothymic, hyperthymic and depressive temperaments as subaffective variants of mood disorders. In:Tasman A Riba MB, *American Psychiatric Association Review*, Washington, DC: American Psychiatric Press; 1992:43-62.
4. Akiskal HS. Le deprimé avant la dépression. *Encéphale* 1992;18:485-9.
5. Akiskal HS. Temperament, personality, and depression. In:Hippius H & Stefanis C, *Research in Mood Disorders: An Update*, Gottingen: Hogrefe

& Huber Publishers; 1994:45-57.

6. Akiskal HS. Diagnosis and classification of affective disorders: new insights from clinical and laboratory approaches. *Psychiatric Developments*, 1983;1:123-60
7. Coryell W, Winokur G, Shea T, et al. The long-term stability of depressive subtypes. *Am J Psychiatry*, 1994;151:199-204.
8. Akiskal HS, Bitar AH, Puzantian VR et al. The nosological status of neurotic depression: a prospective three- to four-year follow-up examination in light of the primary-secondary and unipolar-bipolar dichotomies. *Arch Gen Psychiatry*,1978;35:756-66.
9. Bronisch T, Wittchen HU, Krieg C et al. Depressive neurosis. A long-term prospective and retrospective follow-up study of former inpatients. *Acta Psychiatr Scand* 1985;71:237-48.
10. Kraepelin E. *Manic-Depressive Insanity and paranoia*. Edinburgh: ES Livingstone; 1921.
11. Bertelsen A, Harvald B and Hauge M. A Danish twin study of manic-depressive disorders. *Br J Psychiatry* 1977;130:330-51.
12. Akiskal HS, Downs J, Jordan P et al., Affective disorders in referred children and younger siblings of manic-depressives: Mode of onset and prospective course. *Arch Gen Psychiatry* 1985;42:996-1003.
13. McClearn GE, Plomin R, Gora-Maslak G et al. The gene chase in behavioral science. *Psychology Sci* 1991;2:222-9.
14. Akiskal HS, Djenderejian AM, Rosenthal RH et al., Cyclothymic disorder: validating criteria for inclusion in the bipolar affective group. *Am J Psychiatry* 1977;134:1227-33.
15. Akiskal HS. Delineating irritable and hyperthymic variants of the cyclothymic temperament. *J Pers Dis* 1992;6:326-42.
16. Akiskal HS. Proposal for a depressive personality (temperament). In:Tyrer P & Stein G. *Personality Disorder Reviewed*. London:Gaskell; 1993:165-80.
17. Klibansky R, Panofsky E and Saxl F. *Saturn and Melancholy*, Liechtenstein: Nedeln, Kraus Reprint, 1979.
18. Akiskal HS. Subaffective disorders: dysthymic, cyclothymic and bipolar II disorders in the "borderline" realm. *Psychiatric Clinics of North America*, 1981;4:25-46.
19. Goodwin FK & Jamison KR. *Manic-Depressive Illness* New York: Oxford University Press, 1990.
20. Kretschmer E. *Physique and Character*. Trans. Miller, E. London: Kegan Paul, Trench, Trubner and Co. Ltd.; 1936.
21. Akiskal HS and Akiskal K. Re-assessing the prevalence of bipolar disorders: Clinical significance and artistic creativity. *Psychiatr Psychobiol* 1988;3:29S-36S.
22. Schneider K. *Psychopathic Personalities*. Trans. Hamilton MW. Springfield, Illinois; Charles C. Thomas; 1958.

23. Akiskal HS, Khani MK and Scott-Strauss A Cyclothymic temperamental disorders *Psychiatr Clin North Am* 1979;2:527-54.
24. Perugi G, Musetti L, Simonini E, et al. Gender-mediated clinical features of depressive illness: The importance of temperamental differences. *Br J Psychiatry* 1990;157:835-41.
25. Koukopoulos A, Tundo A, Floris GF et al. Changes in life habits that may influence the course of affective disorders. In:Stefanis et al.*Psychiatry - A World Perspective*. Amsterdam:Elsevier; 1990:478-88.
26. Weissman MM & Myers JK. Rates and risks of depressive symptoms in a United States urban community. *Acta Psychiatr Scand* 1978;57:219-31.
27. Depue RA, Slater JF, Wolfstetter-Kausch H et al. A behavioral paradigm for identifying persons at risk for bipolar depressive disorder: a conceptual framework and five validation studies. *J Abnorm Psychol* 1981;90:381-437.
28. Casey PR and Tyrer PJ. Personality, functioning and symptomatology. *J Psychiatr Res* 1986;20:363-374.
29. Akiskal HS & Mallya G. Criteria for the 'soft' bipolar spectrum:treatment implications. *Psychopharmacol Bull* 1987;23:68-73.
30. Wicki W and Angst J. The Zurich Study. X. Hypomania in a 28- to 30-year-old cohort. *Eur Arch Psychiatry Clin Neurosci* 1991;240:339-48.
31. Weissman MM, Leaf PJ, Bruce ML, Florio L. The epidemiology of dysthymia in five communities: rates, risks, comorbidity, and treatment. *Am J Psychiatry* 1988;145:815-819.
32. Angst J, Wicki W. The Zurich Study. XI. Is dysthymia a separate form of depression? Results of the Zurich Cohort Study. *Eur Arch Psychiatry Clin Neurosci* 1991;240:349-54.
33. Horwath E, Johnson J, Klerman G et al. Depressive symptoms as relative and attributable risk factors for first-onset major depression. *Arch Gen Psychiatry* 1992;49:817-23.
34. Kovacs M, Akiskal HS, Gatsonis C, et al. Childhood-onset dysthymic disorder. Clinical features and prospective naturalistic outcome. *Archives of Gen Psychiatry*, 1994;51:365-74.
35. Musetti L, Perugi G, Soriani A et al., Depression before and after the age of 65. A re-examination. *Br J Psychiatry* 1989;155:330-36.
36. Keller MB, Lavori PW, Endicott J et al. "Double depression": two-year follow-up. *Am J Psychiatry* 1983;140:694-8.
37. Cassano GB, Akiskal HS, Savino M et al. Proposed subtypes of bipolar II and related disorders: with hypomanic episodes (or cyclothymia) and with hyperthymic temperament *J Affect Dis* 1992;26:127-40.
38. Nolen-Hoeksema S, Morrow J and Fredrickson BL. Response styles nd the duration of episodes of depressed mood. *J Abnorm Psycholog* 1993;102:20-8.
39. Boyd JH & Weissman MM Epidemiology of affective disorders. A re-examination and future directions *Arch Gen Psychiatry* 1981;38:1039-46.

40. Akiskal HS. The bipolar spectrum: New concepts in classification and diagnosis. In:Grinspoon L, *Psychiatry Update: The American Psychiatric Association Annual Review*. Washington, DC:American Psychiatric Press; 1983:271-92.
41. Possl J and von Zerssen D. A case history analysis of the 'manic type' and the 'melancholic type' of premorbid personality in affectively ill patients. *Eur Arch Psychiatry Neurol Sci* 1990;239:347-55.
42. Angst J. The course of affective disorders. II. Typology of bipolar manic-depressive illness. *Arch Psychiatr Nervenkrank* 1978;226:65-73.
43. Wehr TA and Goodwin FK. Rapid cycling in manic-depressives induced by tricyclic antidepressants. *Arch Gen Psychiatry* 1979;36:555-59.
44. Koukopoulos A, Reginaldi D, Laddomada P et al. Course of the manic-depressive cycle and changes caused by treatment. *Pharmakopsychiatr Neuropsychopharmakol* 1980;13:156-67.
45. Akiskal HS. The distinctive mixed states of bipolar I, II, and III. *Clin Neuropharmacol* 1992;15:632A-633A.
46. Akiskal HS, Chen SE, Davis GC et al. Borderline: an adjective in search of a noun. *J Clin Psychiatry* 1985;46:41-48.
47. Angst J, Merikangas K, Scheidegger P. et al. Recurrent brief depression: a new subtype of affective disorder. *J Affect Dis* 1990;19:87-98.
48. Montgomery SA. The psychopharmacology of borderline personality disorders. *Acta Psychiatr Belg* 1987;87:260-6.
49. Akiskal HS, Yerevanian BI, Davis GC et al. The nosologic status of borderline personality: Clinical and polysomnographic study *Am J Psychiatry* 1985;142:192-198.
50. Nyström S, Lindegaard B. Predisposition for mental syndromes: A study comparing predisposition for depression, neurasthenia and anxiety state. *Acta Psychiatr Scand* 1975;51:69-76.
51. Kagan J, Reznick JS and Snidman N. Biological bases of childhood shyness. *Science* 1988;240:167-71.
52. Cassano GB, Akiskal HS, Perugi G et al., The importance of measures of affective temperaments in genetic studies of mood disorders. *J Psychiatr Res* 1992;26:257-68.
53. Akiskal HS. Psychopharmacologic and psychotherapeutic strategies in intermittent and chronic affective conditions. In:Montgomery SA, Rouillon F, *Long-Term Treatment of Depression*, Chichester: John Wiley & Sons; 1992:43-62.
54. Akiskal HS. Dysthymic and cyclothymic depressions: Therapeutic implications. *J Clin Psychiatr* 1994;55:Suppl.4:46-52.
55. Akiskal HS, Maser JD, Zeller P et al., Switching from "unipolar" to bipolar II: An 11-year prospective study of clinical and temperamental predictors in 559 patients. *Arch Gen Psychiatr* (February 1995, in press).

Depression and Mania: From Neurobiology to Treatment: edited by G. Gessa, W. Fratta, L. Pani, and G. Serra. Raven Press, New York © 1995.

Pharmacological Treatment of Depression and Comorbid Anxiety Disorders

Giovanni B. Cassano, Stefano Michelini

Institute of Psychiatry, School of Medicine, University of Pisa, Pisa, Italy.

Cross-sectional and longitudinal analysis remain powerful diagnostic tools of modern descriptive psychiatry; in this perspective, soft mood signs, temperamental features and comorbidity become strong and consistent specifiers of depression (1,17,19,20) and are crucial in the selection of medication (31). Recent data have shown, that in severely depressed patients, temperament predicted nearly 50% of the variance in treatment outcome (31). Comorbidity among mental disorders affects the course and treatment of depression; in particular, when depression is comorbid with anxiety disorders it has been associated with greater severity (5), poorer prognosis (29,68), higher rates of chronicity (61), decreased patient compliance and responsiveness to treatment (2,16,45,46,65), poorer psychosocial functioning (14,52), and higher family loading for depression and alcoholism (22). Recent data have also shown significantly elevated odd-ratios for suicide attempts in patients affected by both major depression and lifetime-anxiety disorders (15,34,36).

Several possible explanations have been raised for the observed relationship between depression and anxiety (55,42). The unitary view considered the two disorders as a single entity expressing both sets of symptoms concurrently or over time separately. Alternatively, depression and anxiety disorders may occur together by chance alone, both occurring at high frequency in the general population. A third explanation still conceives the independent origin of the two disorders but the presence of one disorder makes the occurrence of the other more likely.

Far from being only a theoretical problem, physicians often face a complex array of depression-anxiety co-occurring syndromes, which cannot be fully understood using only dimensional systems of classification. This minimization of the clinical importance of comorbidity leads to prototypical descriptions of patients with specific disorders, which are often oversimplifications of multifaceted clinical profiles.

Intra-episodic comorbidity with full-blown anxiety disorders may be easily detectable in depressed patients, and thought of as a more severe clinical condition; however, even the presence of a few symptoms of other anxiety syndromes may induce significant impairment in the patient's social functioning, and may modify the phenomenology of the depressive episode, thereby delaying and misleading the diagnosis. Furthermore, this occurrence may lead to hyperinclusive diagnoses such as "neurotic-atypical" depression and borderline personality or to the oversimplified diagnosis of a depressive episode accompanied by an Axis II disorder. However, detailed cross-sectional and longitudinal evaluation of these patients, often reveals temperamental dysregulations accompanied by panic or social phobic features and/or obsessive compulsive symptoms. Early recognition of these specific comorbid symptoms leads to more appropriate treatment strategy.

Depressive disorders have the potential to co-exist with other disorders more often than any other psychiatric illness (44,66). It is beyond the scope of this chapter to discuss the many different patterns of comorbidity, and we will narrow our clinical observations to the diagnosis and treatment of depression with symptoms of concomitant anxiety. We also stress that physicians should acquire a more flexible key to the interpretation of depressive illness, one that is based on detection of all forms of comorbidity and/or symptom co-occurrence.

SYNDROME AND SYMPTOM CO-OCCURRENCE

Anxiety and depressive disorders are not randomly distributed in the population, but have a higher probability of occurring in the same subjects (15,21,40,59). Boyd et al. (12) showed that depressed patients have an average of 14 times the odds of having an additional anxiety disorder compared with non-depressed patients. In the ECA study (53) it was estimated that, during a 6-month period, anxiety occurred in 33% of adults with a depressive disorder, and depression was present in 21% of those with an anxiety disorder.

Angst et al. (6) have shown, in a longitudinal study, that primarily anxious patients were more likely to develop comorbid depression at follow up than vice versa. Further, both pure disorder groups were about just as likely to switch to the pure form of the other disorder.

An additional perspective for the clinical evaluation of concomitant anxiety and depression comes from the assessment of co-occurring symptoms that cut across different diagnostic categories, giving a more defined psychopathological characterization to the patients. Clayton has in fact estimated that nearly two thirds of depressed patients have other anxiety symptoms such as obsessive compulsive features, hypochondriasis, and feelings of depersonalization (22).

Syndrome and symptom co-occurrence have also been detected in the context of child and adolescent depression (35). In a review of epidemiological studies using DSM-III and DSM-III-R criteria, comorbid anxiety disorders were found to range from 30% to 75% (4). The greater variability found in the rates of symptoms of anxiety (11-70%) probably reflects heterogeneous sampling and assessment (35).

In the elderly, the comorbidity of anxiety and depression has received relatively little attention (30,41,48). Ben Harie et al. (9) have found in depressed patients a 26.3% rate of comorbid generalized anxiety disorder and 5.3% of comorbid panic attacks. Recent data have shown that the rate of co-occurring generalized anxiety disorder in old age is similar to that found in younger patients (26); in contrast to younger adults, the depressed elderly have only mildly increased rate of panic disorder (26).

Kendler et al. (33) have recently reported that the frequency of comorbidity between panic disorder and depression was much greater than that found with social phobia or simple phobia. However, the distribution of discrete comorbid anxiety disorders has not been investigated thoroughly. Comorbidity between depression and panic, generalized anxiety and obsessive compulsive disorder has been investigated more extensively than with post-traumatic stress disorder, social and simple phobia. In the following paragraphs we will review the most relevant data concerning the rates of comorbidity with specific anxiety disorders and then we will discuss the drug treatment of patients affected by these complexities.

Panic Disorder

Comorbidity of depression with panic disorder is frequent and may be tricky to detect, especially when soft signs of the panic disorder are hidden by the depressive phenomenology or diluted in the patient's past. A typical example is that of a depressed grieving patient unable to overcome the loss of a loved one. In our clinical experience, we have often observed that an abnormal grief reaction mirrored the presence of underlying features of the panic-separation spectrum, which also is synonymous of extremely intense and tight social bonding. In such a case, the psychiatrist should verify the presence of the "panic profile", scanning throughout the life of the patient for the presence of limited-symptom panic attacks, and/or other symptoms of the panic spectrum (18).

Many clinical reports have found a high rate of comorbidity of depression with panic disorder, ranging from 30% to 90% (11,14,19,46,62,63). Boyd et al. (12) have estimated that the risk, in terms of odd-ratio, of a patient affected by major depression, of having panic disorder is 18.8 times greater than one without depression.

Di Nardo and Barlow (25) and Clancy et al. (21) have shown a consistent rate of co-primary diagnoses (27% and 29%, respectively), while a longitudinal diagnostic overlapping was found to occur in a lower rate (11%) by Angst et al. (6).

Comorbidity between panic disorder and bipolar spectrum has been explored by Savino et al. (58), who found a co-occurrence of 2.1% with mania; 5% with hypomania; 6.4 % with cyclothymia; 34% with hyperthymic temperament; the same authors have also shown that panic disorder was diagnosable in 22.9% of melancholic depression. Depressive disorders were also found to occur in 18% of a group of 86 patients suffering from panic with agoraphobia (25).

Percentages ranging from 15% to 33% of depressed patients were found to experience recurrent panic attacks during their major depressive episode (22). Patients whose depression was accompanied by panic disorder have reported to be similar to patients without comorbidity for age, sex, marital status and age of onset. However, the coexistence of the two disorders was associated with more severe symptoms of panic, higher rate of hospitalization and suicide attempts, and higher probability of showing social phobia and generalized anxiety disorder (52).

Obsessive Compulsive Disorder

Obsessions and compulsions are common in depressive illnesses ranging consistently from 20 to 38%. (10,21,27,32,39); the course of the obsessions and compulsions parallels the swing of the primary illness, diminishing as the patient improves and vice versa.

On the other hand, depression frequently complicates obsessive compulsive disorder (10); in a community survey, Boyd et al. have estimated that patients with obsessive compulsive disorder were 10.8 times more likely to experience depression (12). Rasmussen and Tsuang (51) have estimated that 75% patients with obsessive compulsive disorder have a lifetime diagnosis of depression, contrasting with the 34% rate found by Rosenberg (54) and 14% by Di Nardo and Barlow (25) in clinical studies.

Generalized Anxiety Disorder

Several studies have found that a frequent association exists between depression and generalized anxiety disorders (7,24,25,57). In a small number of 74 patients with generalized anxiety disorder, comorbidity with depression was found to range from 6% to 59%. Brawman-Minter et al. (13) using a larger group of 109 patients, have shown a 42% rate of lifetime comorbidity with depressive disorders.

Di Nardo and Barlow (25), and Clancy et al. (21) have shown that the most commonly assigned additional diagnosis to depression was generalized anxiety disorder (45% and 37%, respectively). Generalized anxiety disorder has also been diagnosed in 33% of dysthymic patients (25).

Social Phobia

An extremely high rate of comorbidity has been found between social phobia and depression (38%) (21) and between social phobia and dysthymia (44%) (25). Interestingly, dysthymia was the most frequent additional diagnosis (23%) of a sample of 48 social phobic patients (25), suggesting a close link between these two disorders. A 9% rate of comorbidity was found in clinical studies by Di Nardo and Barlow (25). Mood disorder was found to be the most common additional diagnosis (82.5%) in a sample of 57 social phobic patients by Van Ameringen et al. (64). A lower rate of comorbidity (35%) has been shown by Stein et al. (63) in their clinical samples.

Simple Phobia

In a community survey, Boyd et al. (12) have estimated that the odds of a person diagnosed with an episode of major depression having simple phobia is 9 times that of someone without depression. Consistent results have been reported in some clinical studies on the rate of comorbidity of depression with simple phobia (9%) (21,25). Dysthymia has been found to complicate simple phobia in 8% of a group of 24 patients.

Post-Traumatic Stress Disorder

Limited data are available concerning comorbidity between depression and post-traumatic stress disorder. Two studies have shown a consistent high rate (72-77%) of lifetime comorbidity between the two disorders (28,60).

DRUG SELECTION CRITERIA

Despite the documented extent and significance of comorbidity between depression and anxiety, official taxonomic systems still do not provide clinicians and researchers with any indications for specific treatments. Confirming this negative informational trend, also the guidelines for the therapy of depression and bipolar disorders have given relatively little attention to the clinical importance of comorbidity for treatment strategies and outcome (3,56) .

In our opinion, defining the type of depression and delineating the features of comorbid conditions, are crucial issues in the selection of the most suitable pharmacotherapy. A good strategy to treat depression comorbid with clear-cut or subsyndromal mental disorders is to use drugs acting on both the depressive episode and the comorbid disorder. However, in some cases, the physician is forced to limit his pharmacological choice by the presence of concomitant physical disorders: for example, heart diseases, glaucoma, prostatic hypertrophy or cerebrovascular disease, impose the choice of administering drugs with minimal anticholinergic effects, such as selective serotonin reuptake inhibitors (SSRIs). In other cases, a low seizure threshold advises use of low doses of tricyclic antidepressants (TCAs) in combination with carbamazepine or valproic acid.

Regardless of the presence of comorbid disorders, the features of polarity of the depressive disorder and its location along the bipolar spectrum, are strong determinants of the drug selection and therapeutic strategy. It is also worth mentioning that even the anamnestic presence of mild signs of bipolarity, including hyperthymic temperament, should be carefully evaluated.

Once the physician has acquired the major clinical features of depressive episode and investigated the presence of concomitant physical disorders, then he can choose the most specific pharmacological treatment for the comorbid anxiety. Imipramine and clomipramine are first-choice drugs when unipolar depression is comorbid with panic disorder. In our clinical experience, these patients also respond well to paroxetine, an SSRI with antidepressive action. Monoamine oxidase inhibitors (MAOIs) have also been reported to be effective, especially when reversed vegetative symptoms, rejection sensitivity and fatigue are present (40,50).

It is worth remembering that, in some cases, the concomitance of the "panic-agoraphobic habitus" confers to the depressed patients a hypersensitivity reaction to TCAs, which can lead to an exacerbation of the attacks (40,69). In this respect even anamnestic symptoms of panic spectrum (18), should caution the physician to begin the treatment of depressive episodes with doses as low as 10 mg/day and reach the therapeutical dosage at a very slow rate.

In bipolar I or II patients, TCAs and MAOIs should be used only for short-term treatment of severe episodes and in combination with mood-stabilizing drugs. In these patients, the risk of inducing mixed states or the onset of rapid cycling has been extensively documented (8,36,38,47). However, even the presence of soft signs of bipolarity or hyperthymic temperament should warn the physician against the use of antidepressants without an adequate mood-stabilizing therapy; a pre-existing bipolar diathesis may in fact lead to mixed states, increasing the syndromic complexity and reducing therapeutic options. If such a complication occurs, a combination of SSRIs with mood-stabilizing drugs should be considered in the event of an attenuated mixed state. Electroconvulsive therapy would probably represent the first-line choice to treat violent and mixed psychotic states; however, in our experience, ECT may resolve the depressive episode, while exacerbating panic attacks.

The presence of obsessive-compulsive symptoms or comorbid obsessive-compulsive disorder favours the use of clomipramine or other drugs with a selective action on the serotoninergic system, such as fluoxetine and fluvoxamine. Obsessive and panic symptoms have been reported to co-occur with bipolar spectrum disorders (43,58); such a multiple comorbidity often results in troubled lives, leading the physician to formulate the diagnosis of borderline personality disorder (1). Interestingly, borderline personality disorder has been found to respond to carbamazepine, probably revealing its bipolar nature (23).

SSRIs and MAOIs have been found to be more effective than TCAs for treating depression accompanied by social phobia or social phobic traits (reviewed by Liebowitz, 40). The efficacy of reversible MAOIs remains to be demonstrated reliably.

CONCLUDING REMARKS

Evidence for comorbidity of anxiety and affective disorders has been derived from several sources, including epidemiological, pharmacological, clinical and genetic studies (reviewed by Maser et al. 42). Despite this broad body of evidence, we agree with Maser, when he says that DSM approach "treats comorbid disorders and co-occurring symptoms as noise, interference with the primary task of matching symptoms to the DSM-III-R's diagnostic criteria." (42).

Although psychopathology involves a complex degree of overlap among diagnostic categories, specific patterns of comorbidity appear to be stable; and, when distinct clinical syndromes are erroneously interpreted as a single entity, it is not believed that different neurobiological substrates are involved. This approximation leads to another order of mistakes; a diagnostic one, creating "atypical" or "borderline" syndromes which banishes the patient in a kind of "psychiatric no man's land". A second mistake involves therapeutic strategy; though it is true that TCAs and SSRIs treat both depressive and anxiety disorders, comorbid syndromes often require different acute, continuation and maintenance doses and a distinct timing of administration and suspension of the treatment. It is not too speculative to imagine that the drug targets in brain are different in a patient with a pure depressive episode compared to a patient with depression and comorbid panic and/or obsessive-compulsive disorders.

A third mistake is "beyond the patient" and concerns clinical trials, which are conducted on patients whose depressive symptomatology fits a particular diagnosis coded by standardized criteria. Other disorders (including Axis II and III) are often ignored when characterizing the sample. On the contrary, the presence of co-occurring symptoms is systematically overlooked, and for example, a depressed patient, who just misses one panic attack to be a "real" panic patient, is included in the trials as well as a patient who has never experienced panic-fear during his life. The presence of such an heterogeneous sample, for example, may dilute the differences between the active drug and placebo or some alternative treatment. The results obtained from clinical trials designed in such an inaccurate fashion, must be interpreted with caution; not only, but when these results are applied to the complex reality of comorbid disorders, prediction of treatment outcome can have little reliability. The resulting incomplete knowledge of the spectrum of action of the available antidepressants may, in some cases, be the cause of a poor response to treatment and, in other cases, of unusual outcomes of depressive episodes co-occurring with anxiety disorders or symptoms; for example, we have often observed the exacerbation of the concomitant symptomatology, after suspension of the drug utilized to treat both conditions.

In this way, physicians face the impact of comorbidity in their daily clinical practice. Many treatment failures are due to neglect of this crucial aspect of psychopathology; psychiatrists usually do not screen the syndrome comorbidity (especially the lifetime comorbidity) and symptom co-occurrence, with the same attention devoted, for example, to the screening and evaluation of cognitive impairment. Thus, we could not agree more with Phillips and Nieremberg (49), who suggest that "physicians need to be detectives when looking for "secret" comorbid disorders".

Developing a treatment strategy for depression entails two major steps: i) diagnosing the discrete subtypes of depression, including comorbidity and symptom co-occurrence; ii) choosing the proper pharmacotherapy for acute, continuation and maintenance phases.

Since new antidepressants still lack specificity, the diagnostic effort still represents the key to a therapeutic strategy and it should combine descriptive, categorical and dimensional approaches; indeed, beyond the codes, the diagnosis must also include the cross-sectional and longitudinal evaluation of symptomatology, soft bipolar indicators, comorbidity, premorbid temperament, subclinical depressive episodes, frequency of recurrences, and pattern of cyclicity. Within this conceptual frame, mood disorders can be better approached pharmacologically; further, some traditional "black holes" of clinical psychiatry, such as the chronic forms and so-called refractory depression, will be hopefully enlightened.

ACKNOWLEDGMENTS

The authors appreciate the detailed comments provided by Jack D. Maser, Ph.D., Chief, Anxiety and Somatoform Disorders Program. National Institute of Mental Health-National Institutes of Health.

REFERENCES

1. Akiskal HS, Maser JD, Zeller PJ, Endicott J, Coryell W, Keller M et al. Switching from "unipolar" to bipolar II: an 11 year prospective study of clinical and temperamental predictors in 559 patients. *Archives of General Psychiatry* (in press).
2. Albus M, Sheibe G. Outcome of panic disorder with and without concomitant depression: a 2-year prospective follow-up study. *The American Journal of Psychiatry* 1993;150:1878-1880.
3. American Psychiatric Association. Practice guideline for the treatment of patients with bipolar disorder. *The American Journal of Psychiatry* 1994; Suppl 151(N° 12):1-36.
4. Angold A, Costello EJ. Depressive comorbidity in children and adolescents: empirical, theoretical and methodological issues. *The American Journal of Psychiatry* 1993;150:1779-1791.
5. Angst J, Dobler-Mikola A. The Zurich study, VI: a continuum from depression to anxiety disorders? *Eur Arch Psychiatr Neurol Sci* 1985;235:178-186.
6. Angst J, Vollrath M, Merikangas KR, Ernst C. Comorbidity of anxiety and depression in the Zurich cohort study of young adults. In: Maser J, Cloninger R, eds. *Comorbidity of mood and anxiety disorders*. American Psychiatric Press, 1990;7:123-137.
7. Barlow DH, Di Nardo PA, Vermilyea BB, Vermilyea JA, Blanchard EB. Comorbidity and depression among anxiety disorders: issues in diagnosis and classification. *J Nerv Ment Dis* 1986;174:63-72.
8. Bauer MS, Whybrow PC. Rapid cycling bipolar disorder, II: treatment of refractory rapid cycling with high-dose levothyroxine: a preliminary study. *Arch Gen Psychiatry* 1990;47:435-440.
9. Ben-Harie O, Swartz L, Dickman BJ. Depression in elderly living in the community: its presentation and features. *Br J of Psychiatry* 1987;150:169-174.
10. Black DW, Noyes R Jr. Comorbidity and obsessive compulsive disorder. In: Maser J, Cloninger R, eds. *Comorbidity of mood and anxiety disorders.* American Psychiatric Press, 1990;19:305-316.
11. Bowen RC, Kohout J. The relationship between agoraphobia and primary affective disorders. *Canadian Journal of Psychiatry* 1979;24:317-322.
12. Boyd JH, Burke JD, Gruenberg E, Holzer CE, Rae DS, George LK, Karno M et al. Exclusion criteria of DSM-III: a study of co-occurrence of hierarchy-free syndromes. *Archives of General Psychiatry* 1984;41:983-989.
13. Brawman-Mintzer O, Lydiard RB, Emmanuel N, Payeur R, Johnson M, Roberts J et al. Psychiatric comorbidity in patients with generalized anxiety disorder. *The American Journal of Psychiatry* 1993;150:1216-1218.
14. Breyer A, Charney DS, Heninger MD. Agoraphobia with panic attack:

development, diagnostic stability, and course of illness. *Archives of General Psychiatry* 1986;43:1029-1036.

15. Bronish T, Wittchen HU. Suicidal ideation and suicide attempts: comorbidity with depression, anxiety disorders, and substance abuse disorder. *Eur Arch Psychiatry Clin Neurosci* 1994;244(2):93-98.
16. Buller R, Maier W, Benkert O. Clinical subtypes in panic disorder: their descriptive and prospective validity. *J Affect Disord* 1986,11:105-114.
17. Cassano GB, Akiskal HS, Perugi G, Soriani A, Musetti L, Mignani W. Psychopathology, temperament, and past course in primary major depressions. 2. Toward a redefinition of bipolarity with a new semistructured interview for depression. *Psychopathology* 1986;22:278-288.
18. Cassano GB, Savino M. Symptomatology of panic disorder: an attempt to define the panic-agoraphobic spectrum phenomenology. In: Montgomery S, ed. *Psychopharmacology of panic*. Oxford Medical Publication, 1993:38-57.
19. Cassano GB, Musetti L, Perugi G, Akiskal HS. The nature of depressing presenting concomitantly with panic disorder. *Compreh Psych* 1989;30:1-10.
20. Cassano GB, Akiskal HS, Savino M, Musetti L, Perugi G, Soriani A. Proposed subtypes of bipolar II and related disorders: with hypomanic episodes and with hyperthymic temperament. *J Affect Disord* 1992;26:127-140.
21. Clancy J, Noyes R, Hoenk PR, Slymen DJ. Secondary depression in anxiety neurosis. *Journal of Nervous and Mental Disease* 1978;166:846-850.
22. Clayton PJ. The comorbidity factor: establishing the primary diagnosis in patients with mixed symptoms of anxiety and depression. *J Clin Psychiatry* 1990;51(Suppl 11):35-39.
23. Cowdry RW, Gardner DL. Pharmacotherapy of borderline personality disorder. Alprazolam, carbamazepine, trifluoperazine and tranylcypromine. *Arch Gen Psychiatry* 1988;45:119.
24. De Ruiter C, Rijken H, Garssen B. Comorbidity among the anxiety disorders. *The American Journal of Psychiatry* 1989;3:57-68.
25. Di Nardo PA, Barlow DH. Syndrome and symptom co-occurrence in the anxiety disorders. In: Maser J, Cloninger R, eds. *Comorbidity of mood and anxiety disorders*. American Psychiatric Press, 1990;12:205-230.
26. Flint AJ. Epidemiology and comorbidity of anxiety disorders in the elderly. *The American Journal of Psychiatry* 1994;151(N° 5):640-649.
27. Gittleson NL. The fate of obsessions in depressive psychosis. *Brit J of Psychiatry* 1966;112:705-708.
28. Green BL, Lindy JD, Grace MC. Post traumatic stress disorder: toward DSM-IV. *Journal of Nervous and Mental Disease* 1985;173:406-411.
29. Hecth H, Von Zerssen D, Krieg C et al. Anxiety and depression:

comorbidity, psychopathology, and social functioning. *Compr Psychiatry* 1989;30:420-433
30. Hyer L, Gouveia I, Harrison WR, Warsaw J, Coutsouridis D. Depression, anxiety paranoid reactions, hypochondriasis and cognitive decline of late-life inpatients. *J Gerontol* 1987;42:92-94.
31. Joyce PR, Mulder RT, Cloninger RT. Temperament predicts clomipramina and desipramine response in major depression. *Journal of Affective Disorder* 1994;30:35-46.
32. Kendell RE, Discipio WJ. Obsessional symptoms and obsessional personality trait in patients with depressive illness. *Psychological Medicine* 1970;1:65-72.
33. Kendler KS, Heath AC, Neale MC, Kessler RC, Eaves LJ. Alcoholism and major depression in women. A twin study of the causes of comorbidity. *Archives of General Psychiatry* 1993;50(9):690-698.
34. King MK, Schmaling KB, Cowley DS, Dunner DL. Suicide attempt history in depressed patients with and without a history of panic attacks. *Comprehensive Psychiatry* 1995;36(N° 1):25-30.
35. Kovacs M. Comorbid anxiety disorders in childhood-onset depressions. In: Maser J, Cloninger R, eds. *Comorbidity of mood and anxiety disorders.* American Psychiatric Press, 1990;16:271-281.
36. Kramer TL, Lindy JD, Green BL, Grace MC, Leonard AC. The comorbidity of post traumatic stress disorder and suicidality in Vietnam veterans *Suicide Life Theat Behav* 1994;24(1):58-67.
37. Koukopoulos A, Minnai A, Muller-Oelinngahauser B. Rapid cyclers, temperament, and antidepressants. *Compr Psychiatry* 1983;24:249-258.
38. Lerer B, Birmacher B, Ebstein RP et al. 48-hour depressive cycling induced by antidepressant. *Br J Psychiatry* 1980;137:183-185.
39. Lewis A. Problems of obsessional illness. *Proceedings of the Royal Society of Medicine* 1936;36:325-336.
40. Liebowitz MR. Depression with anxiety and atypical depression. *J Clin Psychiatry* 1993:54(Suppl 2):10-14.
41. Lindesay J, Briggs K, Murphy E. The Guy's/Age Concern Survey: prevalence rates of cognitive impairment, depression and anxiety in a urban elderly community. *Br J of Psychiatry* 1989;155:317-329.
42. Maser JD, Weise R, Gwirtsman H. Depression and its boundaries with selected axis I disorders: implications of comorbidity. In: Beckman EE, Weber WR, eds. *Handbook of depression* 2nd edition. New York: Guilford Publication Inc, 1994 (in press).
43. Mellman TA, Uhde TW. Obsessive-compulsive symptoms in panic disorder. *The American Journal of Psychiatry* 1987;144:1573-1576.
44. Mezzich JE, Ahn CW, Fabrega H Jr, Pilkonis PA. Evidence for comorbidity: treated samples and longitudinal studies. In: Maser J, Cloninger R, eds. *Comorbidity of mood and anxiety disorders.* American Psychiatric Press, 1990;16:271-281.

45. Noyes R Jr, Reich J, Suelzen M, Pfolhl B, Coryell WA. Outcome of panic disorder: relationship to diagnostic subtypes and comorbidity. *Arch Gen Psychiatry* 1990;47:809-818.
46. Noyes R Jr. The comorbidity and mortality of panic disorder. *Psychiatric Med* 1990;8:4166.
47. Oppenheim G. Drug-induced rapid cycling: possible outcomes and management. *The American Journal of Psychiatry* 1982;139:939-941.
48. Parmalee PA, Katz IR, Lawton MP. Anxiety and its association with depression among institutionalized elderly. *Am J Geriatric Psychiatry* 1993;1:46-58.
49. Phillips KA, Nieremberg AA. The assessment and treatment of refractory depression. *J Clin Psychiatry* 1994;55(Suppl 2):20-26.
50. Quitkin FM, McGrath PJ, Stewart JW et al. Atypical depression, panic attacks, and response to imipramine and phenelzine: a replication. *Arch Gen Psychiatry* 1990;47:935-941.
51. Rasmussen SA, Tsuang MT. Epidemiology and clinical features of obsessive compulsive disorder. In: Jenike MA, Baer L, Minichiello WE, Littleton MA, eds. *Obsessive Compulsive Disorders: a theory of management.* PSG Publishing, 1986;23-44.
52. Reich J, Warshaw M, Peterson M, White K, Keller M, Lavori P et al. Comorbidity of panic and major depressive disorder. *J Psychiatr Res* 1993;27(Suppl 1):23-33.
53. Reigier DA, Narrow WE, Rae DS. The epidemiology of anxiety disorders: the Epidemiologic Catchment Area (ECA) experience. *J Psychiatr Res* 1990;24(Suppl 2):3-14.
54. Rosenberg CM. Personality and obsessional neurosis. *Brit J of Psychiatry* 1967;113:471-477.
55. Roth M, Mountjoy C. The relationship between anxiety and depressive disorders. In: Kupfer DJ, ed. *Reflections on modern psychiatry*. APA Press, 1992;2:9-24.
56. Rush AJ, Golden WE, Hall GW, Herrera M, Houston A, Kathol R et al. *Depression in primary care: detection, diagnosis, and treatment.* U.S. Department of Health and Human Services, 1993;1:43-54.
57. Sanderson WC, Di Nardo PA, Rapee RM, Barlow DH. Syndrome comorbidity in patients diagnosed with a DSM-III-R anxiety disorder. *J Abnorm Psychol* 1990;99:308-312.
58. Savino M, Perugi G, Simonini E, Soriani A, Cassano GB, Akiskal HA. Affective comorbidity in panic disorder: is there a bipolar connection? *Journal of Affective Disorder* 1993;28:155-163.
59. Schatzberg AF, Samson JA, Rothschil AJ, et al. Depression secondary to anxiety: findings from the McLeasn Hospital Depression Research Facility. *Psychiatr Clin North Am* 1990;13:633-649.
60. Sierles FS, Chen JJ, McFarland RE, Taylor MA. Post-traumatic stress disorder and concurrent psychiatric illness: a preliminary report. *The*

American Journal of Psychiatry 1983;140:1177-1179.

61. Stavrakaky C, Vargo B. The relationships of anxiety and depression: a review of literature. *Br J Psychiatry* 1986;149:7-16.
62. Stein MB, Uhde TW. Panic disorder and major depression: a tale of two syndromes. *Psychiatric Clin N Am* 1988;11:441-461.
63. Stein MB, Tancer ME, Gelernter CS, Vittone BJ, Uhde TW. Major depression in patients with social phobia. *The American Journal of Psychiatry* 1990;147:637-639.
64. Van Ameringen M, Mancini C, Styan G, Donison D. Relationship of social phobia with other psychiatric illness. *J of Affect Disord* 1991;21:93-99.
65. Van Valkenburg C, Akiskal HS, Puzantian V, Rosenthal T. Anxious depression: clinical, family history and naturalistic outcome: comparison with panic and major depressive disorders. *J Affect Disord* 1984;6:67-82.
66. Wells KB, Rogers W, Burnam A, Greenfield S, Ware JE. How the medical comorbidity of depressed patients differs across health care settings: results from the Medical Outcomes Study. *The American Journal of Psychiatry* 1991;148:1688-1696.
67. Wittchen HU, Essau CA, Krieg JC. Anxiety disorders: similarities and differences of comorbidity in treated and untreated groups. *Br J Psychiatry* 1991,159(Suppl 12):23-33.
68. Wittchen HU, Essau CA. Natural course and spontaneous remission of untreated anxiety disorders. In: Hand I, Wittchen HU, eds. *Panic and Phobia.* Berlin: Springer-Verlag,1989.
69. Zitrin CM, Klein DF, Woerner MG et al. Treatment of agoraphobia with group exposure in vivo and imipramine. *Arch Gen Psychiatry* 1980;37:63-72.

Depression and Mania: From Neurobiology to Treatment: edited by G. Gessa, W. Fratta, L. Pani, and G. Serra. Raven Press, New York © 1995.

The Long Term Prophylaxis of Affective Disorders

Athanasio Koukopoulos, Daniela Reginaldi, Giampaolo Minnai *, Gino Serra §, Luca Pani #, F. Neil Johnson ¥

Centro "Lucio Bini" and Clinica Belvedere Montello, Rome, Italy.
** Dipartimento di Salute Mentale, Azienda USL 5, Distretto di Ghilarza, Italy.*
§ Institute of Biochemistry, School of Pharmacy, University of Sassari, Italy
 # "Bernard B. Brodie" Department of Neuroscience and Center for Neuropharmacology CNR, University of Cagliari, Italy.
¥ Reader in Neuropharmacology, Lancaster University, Lancaster, U.K.

The introduction of systematic prophylactic treatments in the management of affective disorders has advanced our knowledge and our methodology and has substantially improved the condition of a great number of patients. The prophylactic effectiveness of these treatments, however, has proven with years to be less effective and the toll in terms of side effects greater than hitherto believed.

Recent "naturalistic" studies cast doubt upon the extent of prophylactic effectiveness of lithium in clinical practice (1,13,21,39,41,49). Schou is critical of the methodological shortcomings of the "naturalistic" studies that use data from patients treated clinically under "real-life" conditions, rather than from controlled studies (45).

The fact remains, however, that therapies are applied under the less formal circumstances of everyday practice; one should not underestimate the strain of taking medications everyday for a long time. The assessments of effectiveness under such circumstances are therefore of relevance to the exigencies of therapy.

The observations about the consequences of drug discontinuation make the horizon of our prophylactic efforts even darker.

The fundamental question, however, is: what is the natural course of the disease we are trying to modify? All modern publications repeat that the natural course of the disease is a progressive one and the frequency of recurrences increases with time. The increase of frequency reported by Kraepelin is much smaller than what we see today (34). Rehm reports of a shortening of the free intervals only in 7% of periodic manias, 17% of periodic melancholias and 10% of bipolar cases (43).

Like in rapid cyclers, antidepressants and other stimulating agents may contribute to increased frequency of recurrences in other type of course (53).

Unfortunately the higher frequency of relapses is associated with poorer outcome of prophylactic treatments.

It is probably time to reconsider the whole problem of affective disorders and of their acute and prophylactic treatments.

The present study examines mainly the outcome of long term prophylactic treatments focusing particularly on the type of course of the cycles of manic depressive patients.

PATIENTS AND TREATMENTS

The data presented and discussed in this study concern 375 manic depressive patients who were treated by our group with prophylactic treatments for at least 5 years.

We have chosen arbitrarily a minimum of five years in order to better focus on the effects and outcome of long term prophylactic treatments. Exception was made for 8 cases that had a shorter time of treatment (see below).

Two-hundred thirty-two are women, and 143 are men. According to DSM-IV criteria, 221 were classified as Bipolar-I (20 of them were unipolar manias), 122 as Bipolar-II and 32 as Unipolar Depressives.

Table 1 presents the diagnostic groups according to sex and Table 2 the type of course of the bipolar patients.

Table 1: *diagnostic groups according to sex.*

	TOTAL	BP I	BP II	UP
MEN	143	101	34	8
WOMEN	232	120	88	24

Table 2: *type of course of the bipolar patients.*

MD	DM	RC	LC	IRR
188	63	53	22	15

Lithium salts, mainly carbonate, have been the main prophylactic treatment but many patients have received important adjunctive treatments including psychotherapy (22) (Table 3) or after lithium discontinuation have continued with other prophylactic treatments.

Table 3: *Adjunctive treatments to lithium*

Type of Therapy	N° of Patients
Anticonvulsant	80
Antidepressant	10
ECT	10
Benzodiazepines	15
Neuroleptics	39
Calcium Channel Blockers	7
Psychotherapy	20
Two or More Drugs	63

Only 152 patients had lithium monotherapy as prophylaxis. During relapses this group too had other medication or ECT.

The outcome data of this study therefore concern not only lithium long term treatment but rather combined prophylactic treatment as it has been given in the last 25 years in clinical practice. In the seventies this was lithium plus neuroleptics and benzodiazepines, in the eighties anticonvulsants were added (9) and in the nineties calcium channel blockers (14) and maintenance ECT was reapraised (25).

The prophylactic treatment lasted a mean of 12.2 years (range 5-24.6). The total observation time was of 13.5 years mean value (range 5.1- 33.5). The mean serum lithium concentration was 0.65 mmol/l (range 0.30-1.10) during the first year of treatment and 0.53 (range 0.20-0.97) during the last year of treatment.

The response to prophylactic treatment was classified as:

- **good**: absence or radical reduction of recurrences and hospitalizations and the patient's life was normalized.
- **partial**: substantial reduction of episodes and hospitalizations compared to the previous course of the disease. The severity of the episodes was often reduced.
- **poor**: no significant reduction of episodes and no improvement of patient's life as compared to the previous course.

OUTCOME

Given the extensive problems involved in the prophylaxis of affective disorders we have chosen to examine here only a few points.

Table 4 shows the comparison of episodes and hospitalizations per year before and during prophylactic treatment according to the type of response.

Table 4: *Frequency of episodes before and during prophylaxis.*

	BEFORE PROPHYLAXIS		DURING PROPHYLAXIS	
RESPONSE	EPISODES	HOSPITAL	EPISODES	HOSPITAL
GOOD	0.88	0.25	0.19	0.05
PARTIAL	0.79	0.19	0.39	0.09
POOR	0.79	0.19	0.93	0.30
ALL PATIENTS	0.85	0.22	0.45	0.13

There is a remarkable reduction of episodes and hospitalization in the groups of Good and Partial response, but in the Poor outcome group there is an increase of episodes by 18% and of hospitalizations by 36%. In many patients of this group a deterioration of their social and family life and of their working activity was seen through the years of prophylaxis.

This may be due to an intrinsic aggravation of the disease with ageing or to exogenous factors. But a deterioration due to discontinuations of treatments or reductions of the doses or other iatrogenic factors cannot be ruled out.

Table 5 shows the mean serum lithium levels (mmol/l) according to the outcome.

Table 5: *mean serum lithium levels (mmol/l) according to outcome*

RESPONSE	MEAN ± sd	Min	Max
GOOD	0.61±0.14	0.3	1.1
PARTIAL	0.67±0.15	0.3	1.1
POOR	0.67±0.13	0.2	1.0

BP-I BP-II UP

Table 6 shows the outcome according to the diagnostic groups. It is interesting to note the excellent response of the unipolar depressive group who also needed the lowest serum lithium level.

Table 6: *outcome according to diagnostic groups.*

	GOOD	PARTIAL	POOR	Total
BP-I	80 (36%)	63 (29%)	78 (35%)	221
BP-II	45 (37%)	32 (26%)	45 (37%)	122
UP	19 (59%)	7 (22%)	6 (18%)	32
Total	144 (39%)	102 (27%)	129 (34%)	375

We think that the good response of the unipolars is due to the hyperthymic temperament of 17 (53%) of them. This temperament is attenuated by lithium and thus depressions are prevented (29)

MDI - DMI

Table 7 reports the outcome according to the sequence of the manic depressive cycle.

Table 7: *outcome according to the sequence of the manic depressive cycle.*

	GOOD		PARTIAL		POOR	
	N°	%	N°	%	N°	%
MD	81	43	52	28	55	29
DM	18	29	19	30	26	41
RC	16	30	11	21	26	49
CC LC	4	18	9	41	9	41
IRR	6	40	3	20	6	40
UP	18	58	7	22	6	31
CHRONIC	0	0	2	67	1	33

The finding of better outcome of patients whose cycle follows the sequence of mania-depression-free interval than those with the sequence depression-mania-free interval is confirmed.

This finding has been reported and confirmed several times (30, 19, 20, 37, 15)

Rapid Cyclers

This group yields the poorest outcome despite suspension of antidepressants and use of anticonvulsants, neuroleptics and calcium channel blockers for many years. Rapid cyclers induced by antidepressants have, however, a higher good response than spontaneous rapid cyclers (33).

Among these rapid cyclers there are 11 that are no longer rapid cyclers but continue to recur in long cycles still resistant to stabilizing treatments of all kinds.

Also in Wehr's 51 cases (53) 8 rapid cyclers were transformed in slow cyclers still resistant to therapy. This should mean that, at least in these cases, the rapid cyclicity is not the cause of the resistance to prophylactic treatments but there may be another intrinsic factor determining both resistance and rapid cyclicity. Bauer and Whybrow (7) " raise the question of whether lack of response is simply a function of episode frequency or whether nonresponsiveness to lithium some way relates to the temporal pattern of affective episodes ".

We were impressed by the hypomanias of these cases: though very attenuated they remained resistant even to very intense antiexcitatory treatments. This hypomania usually consists of an early awakening, a mild hyperactivity and a lack of patience but its resistance is astonishing, thus determining, we think, the perpetuation of the cycling.

In recent years there have been several reports of good results in maintenance ECT of rapid cyclers (2,10,11,51) and three of our cases are doing well on ECT.

Continuous Circular With Long Cycles

These circular cases with less than two cycles per year also yield a scarce response: 18% good response and 41% of poor responses.

It is of interest to remember that in the 19th century it was a common opinion that circular cases had a worse prognosis than periodic ones i.e. cases with long intervals (17)

Fig 1: Sequence of episodes in Bipolar Cycles

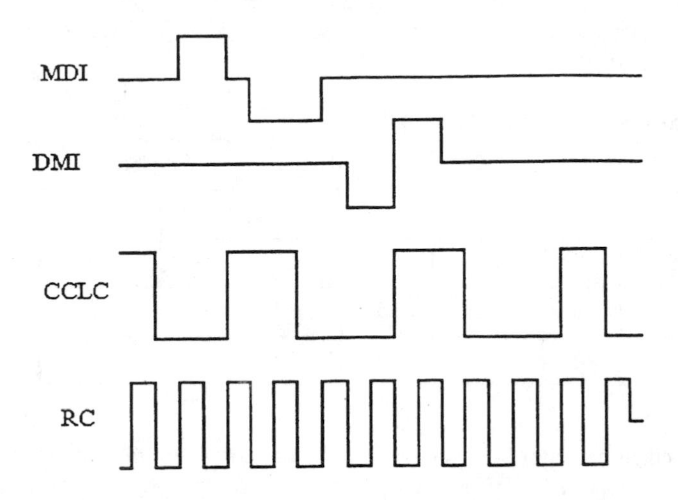

MDI= Mania (Hypomania)-Depression-Interval
DMI= Depression-Mania (Hypomania)- Interval
CCLC= Continuos Circular Courses with Long Cycles
RC= Rapid Cyclers

These three types of course (DMI, Rapid and Long Cyclers) of poor response have in common a rapid or slow switch without interval from depression to mania (Fig. 1).

Many years ago we thought that the bad response was due to the antidepressants given during the depression that accelerated the switch and rendered the emerging mania more resistant (27,31).

This is certainly true for many cases that responded well, after antidepressants were withdrawn. Other cases, however, remained poor responders even after suspension of antidepressants.

Insight

We have evaluated the insight of the patients into their morbid condition and

abnormal behaviour as a factor that may influence the outcome of affective disorders and the response to prophylactic treatments.
The evaluation was performed during the free intervals.

Insight was classified as complete, incomplete or lacking. As lacking insight were classified those patients who did not recognize their morbid condition and their behaviours or greatly minimized them and blamed a lot on others.

As can be seen in Table 8 the more complete is the insight and so much better the outcome of the patients.

Table 8: *Outcome according to the insight.*

	COMPLETE		INCOMPLETE		LACKING	
Outcome	N°	%	N°	%	N°	%
GOOD	118	82	17	12	9	6
PARTIAL	69	68	15	14	18	18
POOR	61	47	22	17	46	36

It is obvious that the better the insight and the more compliant the patient, the better the patient manages his life e.g. avoids coffee and other stimulants, takes better care of his sleep etc.

The relation insight-outcome may be more extensive and deeper than that. It certainly relates to the intelligence of the patient. We know of no studies on this subject but in the long and hard struggle that life is for a manic-depressive patient intelligence must be of importance both in the expression of the disease and in the outcome of it.

LITHIUM DISCONTINUATION

There is now little doubt that the discontinuation of lithium treatment is followed by early recurrences.

Schou's critique (44) is correct from a methodological point of view but numerous studies (46,54,35,26,38,47,48) and the clinical practice confirm the high risks of lithium discontinuation especially if abrupt (16).

Of the 375 patients presented in this study, 37 died during the observation period from natural causes: 18 during lithium treatment and 9 after lithium discontinuation, 4 committed suicide during lithium treatment and 6 after lithium discontinuation.

Fifty-six patients terminated lithium treatment: 24 because of kidney problems, 4 because of thyroid problems, 5 because of excessive weight gain, 1 because of psoriasis, 22 because of poor response.

One-hundred and ten patients discontinued lithium once or more because they felt well or because of expected pregnancy or because of minor side effects,and their further course is known to us; 21 of them did not have major recurrences for a long time (see below) and lithium was not reinstituted, 89 patients relapsed and lithium was reinstituted.

Lithium was discontinued by 89 patients 114 times when the patient was well. The wellbeing had lasted for more than one year in 92 cases and for more than 6 months in 22 cases.

Figure 2 shows the type of recurrences and the time interval between lithium discontinuation and recurrences. The majority of relapses in the first 3 months are manias, 56 mania vs. 4 depression; after 6 months of interval manic and depressive relapses are almost equally frequent, 15 mania vs. 14 depression.

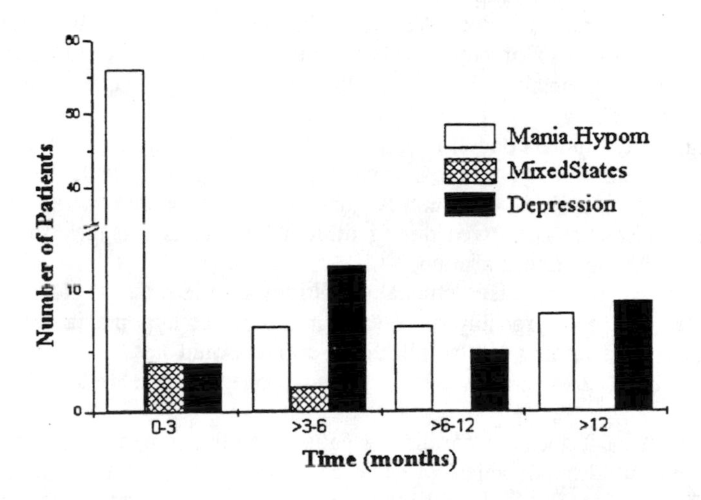

Fig 2: Time distribution of new recurrences after lithium discontinuation

This is almost a constant finding in lithium discontinuation studies; Suppes et al. (48) found that patients with Bipolar I disorder had over half of the instances of mania arising within the first 3 months following more-or-less abrupt lithium discontinuation, and a 50% recurrences of depression was not achieved by four-year follow-up.

This finding should be interpreted as a rebound phenomenon and it means that the main action of lithium is an antimanic activity. The depressive recurrences seem uninfluenced by lithium discontinuation; they spread out over several years. The finding that bipolar-I patients are most at risk from discontinuing lithium should be interpreted in the same way.

The discontinuation of a drug that had been assumed by a patient for a long time was easily accomplished by its replacement by another one of similar effect, even when the patient is not in stable wellbeing. We would like to report that in 8 Bipolar-I patients the discontinuation of lithium was performed under strict medical control (3 patients were hospitalized for this purpose) in a short time of 2 to 4 weeks. Lithium was gradually replaced by adequate dose of neuroleptics (4-10 mg of Haloperidol or 100-400 mg of Thioridazine) and/or anticonvulsants (600-1200 mg of CBZ or 600-1500 of valproate) and/or nimodipine (90 mg) and benzodiazepine. None of these patients had an early manic relapse.

It was more difficult to reduce the dose of a drug even very partially even in patients that have been steadily well for many years if the drug was not replaced by similar drugs. A 65 old BP-I woman after 10 years of stable well being was advised by us to reduce her lithium dose from 750 to 600 mg. After two weeks she complained of racing thoughts sensation of confusion, riemergencies of old memories, sleep reduction and muscular pains. We have observed reactions of this kind to minimal dose reduction also of anticonvulsants neuroleptics and benzodiazepines. Similar reaction to very small reduction of dose are not very frequent, but their significance is far reaching.

The fact that many bipolars do not relapse even after rapid lithium discontinuation may depend from the timing of the discontinuation. Bipolar patients have long tendentially depressive periods, like autumn and winter in patients with summer manias. These patterns are conserved during lithium treatments and they should be kept in mind in planning discontinuation.

The objection that in naturalistic clinical conditions a patient that decides to stop lithium or neglects it, may probably be already in a state of hypomania and under such circumstances the turning into a full blown mania would not be unexpected is certainly true, but it also means that a rebound phenomenon follows lithium withdrawal.

It also constitutes a further risk for bipolar patients: in the course of such patients there are short and mild hypomanias, often reactive or seasonal, that do not always progress into full manias. But if the patient is under pharmacological prophylaxis of any kind (lithium, neuroleptics, anticonvulsants) the suspension or reduction of the medication because of her/his hypomanic status becomes a powerful factor of provocation of a mania.

Three BP-II of our patients had a full blown mania after lithium discontinuation.

Tondo et al. (50) found that the risk of suicidal behaviour after lithium discontinuation was not only greater than during lithium but also greater than prior to lithium treatment.

Mueller-Oerlinghausen (40) reports that suicidal behaviour may increase after lithium discontinuation even in cases of poor response.
Of the 6 patients of our group who committed suicide after they had discontinued lithium, 2 were good responders but 4 were poor responders.

The risks of discontinuation of lithium maintenance treatment probably concern all other treatments with psychotropic drugs.
As Baldessarini et al. (6) point out, stopping maintenance treatment is not identical to not treating, but instead may carry additional iatrogenic pharmacologic risks. The implications for the treatment and for research results are evident.

LITHIUM DISCONTINUATION-INDUCED REFRACTORINESS

Robert Post published four cases who discontinued or tapered lithium after a substantial period of complete response. When a new episode emerged this failed to respond to lithium when the treatment was reinstituted. He named this event 'Lithium Discontinuation-Induced Refractoriness'. Since two of these cases did not show immediate relapses, Post comments that "these data suggest that it is not a lithium withdrawal syndrome itself that is associated with the refractoriness, but raise the possibility that it is the emergence of new episodes themselves that conveys the alteration of lithium responsiveness." (42).

Among our patients 13 showed loss of responsiveness under the same circumstances. Seven are women and 6 men. Their age at the beginning of the refractoriness ranged between 24 and 74, mean age 45. Lithium prophylactic treatment before discontinuation, had lasted for several years (Mean 8.8 years; range 4-18 years). They had been well (8 completely well and 5 substantially better with no hospitalizations) for a mean period of 7.8 years, range 1-11).
Seven patients relapsed within the first three months after lithium discontinuation and the others between 8 and 74 months.

Lithium was discontinued on the patient's decision in 5 cases, for desired pregnancy in 3 cases, and with the doctor's consent in 5 cases.

The period of refractoriness ranged from 2 to 7 years, mean 4.2 years. In 8 cases the refractoriness still continues. Other factors that could be associated with the refractoriness: none in 8 cases, hormonal treatments for fecondation in 2 cases and menopause, hepatitis and retirement in the other 3.

It should be said right away that the refractoriness does not concern only lithium treatment but all antimanic and antidepressive treatments including ECT to which the same patients had responded in former occasions. In support of this is the observation of 6 other patients who after a long lithium treatment (range 5-18 years, mean duration 10 years) stopped lithium for side effects (kidney, thyroid disfunction, weight gain) and showed refractoriness to all treatments.

The second observation of relevance is that all these patients had been continuously on lithium for more than 4 years (mean 8.8 years). Only one became refractory after the 3rd discontinuation after 24, 24, and 26 months of lithium treatment.

In Post cases it was 7 years in two cases, 15 years in one and in Dr. G.M. Goodwin's case ten years. In this last case there had been another lithium discontinuation after 2 years of treatment without loss of efficacy. The same happened with another of Post's cases.

It may well be that repeated discontinuations contribute to create this refractoriness but Post's cases and ours point also to another factor: the many years of constant lithium intake. In Bauer's case also lithium treatment had lasted twelve years before the discontinuation (8).

One could think that the presence of an element like lithium induced great adaptive changes in the Central Nervous System. These changes may be advantageous for the affective disorders (probably by lowering the nervous excitability), but as the years pass by, this adaptation becomes more definite, more permanent. When lithium is discontinued, the diminished homeostatic potentiality is shown by the great rate of relapses. The fact that in some patients this potentiality remains impaired for a long time or even forever should not be a cause of surprise.

In three of these patients the syndrome picture after lithium discontinuation changed (two became delusional and one obsessive) suggesting the possibility that deeper modifications caused by very long treatments and their discontinuations had taken place.

In this way of thinking refractoriness would be not the result of the emergence of new episodes but the result of previous treatments that were interrupted; adjunctive treatments may contribute also.

The question of the *discontinuation*-induced refractoriness should be viewed within the wider frame of the question of a possible *treatment*-induced refractoriness.

There are no systematic studies on this subject but some very common observations are relevant:

1) When a patient is treated for the first time with drugs his response is often striking.

2) ECT recoveries show today a much higher relapse rate (60%) than in the prepharmacologic era (12). To our knowledge there are no data on this, but there is little doubt about it. Max Fink (18) thinks there are changes in the practice of ECT (anaesthesia, low energy, short series of ECT) that could explain the difference.

One should not to neglect, however, the fact that today patients are referred for ECT only after more than one trial with antidepressants.

3) Chronicization of the course of affective disorders often is attributed to inadequate treatment but there are many cases that took a chronic course after many "adequate" treatments.

4) Rapid cycling is another malignant course that may be induced by treatments but here the pathogenesis is probably different: the activation of excitatory processes by antidepressants.

This line of thinking would cast doubts on the utility of both early and very prolonged treatments.

How frequent is this induced refractoriness?

Post found 7 patients (13.6%) that showed a pattern of lithium- discontinuation induced refractoriness among 66 patients that were referred to NIMH with lithium refractoriness.

Among our patients we know the outcome of the lithium discontinuation of 145 patients: 19 of them (13.1%) showed discontinuation-induced refractoriness (13 versus lithium and other treatments, 6 versus other treatments since lithium was not reinstituted). As the length of prophylactic treatment increases the proportion of cases with induced refractoriness may increase in the future.

The reason why this phenomenon has remained unknown so far depends probably from the fact that it needs a very long time to be produced. Another reason may be that the extreme variability of the course of affective disorders hides the effect of the drugs upon it. The first patient that took an IMAO became rapid cycler. It took almost three decades to recognize this phenomenon. Even today rapid ciclicity is often not recognized.

RESTORED HOMEOSTASIS

In contrast to these 19 patients who developed refractoriness after lithium discontinuation, there are 21 patients, 18 women and 3 men, 11 BP-I, 8 BP-II and 2 UP Depressive, that stayed well, or had only minor affective episodes, for a long time (Mean 10 years, range 3.5-22.5). The patients of this study have all had more than five years of prophylactic treatment. Because of their possible heuristic value, we have included also 8 cases that after a shorter period of lithium treatment (5 one year, 2 two year, 1 one year and half) stopped it and remained well for a long time. The other 13 patients had longer lithium treatments (mean 7 years, range 5-12.5 years). All suffered from severe manic depressive illness, 3 were rapid -cyclers.

The reason for terminating the lithium treatment were: complete well-being in 11 cases, pregnancy in 2 , side effects in 4 and poor response in 4.

Except for the cases of pregnancy or toxic effects the other patients terminated lithium on their own decision and often against strong medical advice.

It is worth mentioning that in these cases lithium was tapered very slowly over a period of many months and 5 patients were taking only 300 mg daily for more that one year.

We would like also to mention that in 8 cases better life conditions were associated with the good outcome of lithium discontinuation: work in 2 cases, happy marriage in 3, favourable change of partner in 3. In 2 BP-I cases the good outcome was associated with good insight that allowed them to control the emergence of mania with small doses of anticonvulsants and neuroleptics.

It is probably important to underline the fact that in 6 of these cases the duration of lithium treatment was rather short, 1-2 years, while in the Discontinuation Induced Refractoriness no case was less than 4 years.

It may be that the event of refractoriness can take place only in cases that had many years of lithium treatment.

These 19 patients indicate the possibility that, at least some cases, having overcome the acute episode and having been stable for some time (1-2 year) could very gradually suspend pharmacological prophylaxis. At this point the patient may have reached a stage very close to his previous homeostasis. If he is fully aware of his problems and has good insight into his disorder and he is well instructed about useful changes in his life habits, then he has a good chance of staying well for many years without pharmacological prophylaxis but only occasional use of sleeping and tranquilizing medications.

DEVELOPMENT OF LITHIUM TOLERANCE - CHANGE OF RESPONSE

When prophylactic treatments are effective, the next question which arises is whether efficacy is mantained over the long period of time for which treatment often has to be continued. It is usually assumed that no tolerance develops to lithium, since there is no documented need for doses to be increased progressively throughout lithium maintenance.

Against this however, Maj et al. (36) reported that among 49 patients with excellent response during the first two years of treatment, 25 suffered of new episodes in the following five years. Apparently lithium had lost its efficacy after few years of treatment in 51% of the patients. Also in Post's 66 cases of lithium refractoriness, 23 (35%) showed a pattern of tolerance development (42).

Among our patients, apart from the 13 cases of discontinuation induced refractoriness, 7 cases of good response and 4 cases of partial response became poor responders after an average of 10 and 15 years of lithium treatment respectively. Thus of the 129 patients with bad response 11(9%) reached it through the apparent development of tolerance.

One might think that the development of tolerance could be more important than our patients have shown but may have been compensated by adjunctive treatments, improved insight and diminished excitability with ageing. These factors may be more effective in patients who follow prophylactic treatments for many years like our group.

We would like to note, however, that a good and stable response to lithium usually allows reduction of the lithium dose and serum lithium concentration over the years in order to diminish toxic effects.The 144 patients of our group of full response had, during the first year, an average serum lithium concentration of 0.60 mmol/l. At the end of observation, i.e. after an aver age of 12 years had elapsed, they had maintained the full response but the average serum lithium level was reduced to 0.47 mmol/l. We are inclined to think that the worsening of the response to lithium is not due to the development of tolerance but is rather the expression of increasing severity of the illness and of concurrent factors like ageing, menopause, somatic and psychological stresses etc.etc..

We would like to present also the opposite phenomenon: improved response after many years of a poor one.

Twenty one patients after an average of 10 years of poor response showed an excellent and long lasting response (13 cases) or partial response (7 cases).

Factors associated: suspension of the use of antidepressants in 4 cases; psychotherapy in 3, improved insight in 5, suspension of alcohol intake in 1. Nothing known about the other 7 cases.

SIDE EFFECTS

The most frequent and troublesome side effects regarded:

1) Weight gain: 74 patients i.e. 20% of all patients showed 5 kg or more weight gain. Five of them discontinued lithium because of weight gain and one of them gained another 7 Kg on carbamazepine and discontinued it too.

2) Thyroid: 53 patients suffered of thyroid disfunction, 4 discontinued lithium because of it.

3) Kidneys: 71 patients (19%) suffered from poliuria, 24 h urine volume of more than 3 liters.Thirteen of them (3%) discontinued lithium because of intense poliuria, mean 24 h volume 5.7 l,sd 1.64 (range 3-8 l). Mean lithium treatment duration 8.3 years. Mean initial serum lithium level 0.72 mmol/l, final concentration 0.50. Mean age at the beginning of treatment 36 years. Serum creatinine concentration and creatinine clearance were within normal limits. After lithium discontinuation poliuria was only partially reduced.

Other 11 patients developed reduced creatinine clearance of 60 ml/min or less, 6 had high serum creatinine levels (1.90; 3.50; 2.13; 2.10; 4.5; 9.0). Mean lithium treatment duration 16.6 years. Mean age at lithium discontinuation 62.5 years. Initial serum lithium level 0.72 mmol/l,final concentration 0.50 mmol/l. One patient had kidney transplant. The long duration of lithium treatment in this group is of particular importance.

DISCUSSION

The aim of the present study is to estimate the outcome of long term prophylactic treatment on patients who suffer from affective disorders. It is a longitudinal study, not a follow up, on patients treated by our group. It carries all the methodological limitations of a "naturalistic" study. Controlled studies that cover such a long treatment periods would be anyway impossible.

Affective disorders tend to recur all life long and treatments may be needed all life long also. Longitudinal studies of a few year duration may not offer sufficient perspective to evaluate the real outcome. For this reason we have included patients with five years or more of prophylactic treatment, though we are aware that some poor prognosis patients may have abandoned systematic prophylactic treatment during the first five years.

The overall outcome of our patients, 39% good, 27% partial and 34% poor, may seem not very favourable, but patients that stay on prophylactic treatment for so many years have a particularly severe course.

Comparing the present results with those published by our group in 1980 (30), on 301 patients classified in the same way and including patients with 1 year or more of lithium treatment, one notices that the response of the earlier study was a better one: 46% good, 33% partial and 21% poor. This is in line with the data in the literature.

Schou attributes this change of response to the inadequate conditions of the recent "naturalistic studies (44)

Thase (49) advances the hypothesis that today there are more complex and more lithium resistant cases among the patients currently ill and currently studied. As a confirmation of this hypothesis could be regarded the group of unipolar depressives of our two studies. In both they show an excellent response: 58% but in the earlier study they represent 29% of the total group, while in the present study they are only 8.5%.

Patients and physicians are more aware today of the limitations of our prophylactic treatments and probably the patients that enter them in recent years are more severe than in the past. The lowering of lithium doses is also an important factor.

Looking at the outcome according to the type of course of the manic depressive cycle (Table 7) it is worth noting that the poor response increases with the increase of the cycle frequency. The poor response is 19% for unipolar depressives, 29% for Mania-Depression-Free Interval sequence, 41% for Continuous-Circular and Depression-Mania-Free Interval sequence (these patients are the more prone to become rapid cyclers) and 49% for Rapid Cyclers.

This confirms many previous observations that a high frequency of episodes and hospitalizations is negatively associated with a response. It is certainly a pity that prophylactic treatments are less effective where they are most needed.

In many patients, as in the majority of rapid cyclers, the high frequency of recurrences is induced by antidepressants. This acceleration of the course could be stopped timely by suspension of antidepressants and treating the depression with ECT and paying particular attention to the prevention-suppression of emerging hypomanias even if mild.

In 1973 we advanced the hypothesis, based on clinical observations, that the action of lithium was mainly an antimanic one and that prevented depressions by suppressing manias (32).

Neil Johnson (23) formulated a similar hypothesis on the basis of observations of the effects of lithium on stimulus processing. Moreover most of the biological effects of lithium on the CNS described so far are in line with the hypothesis of its antimanic activity (24).

This hypothesis finds an important support in the outcome of lithium discontinuation: the rapid emergence of manias, while the depressive recurrences follow a pattern similar to the natural course of the disorder, can be explained only as a rebound phenomenon, if mania is the result of the withdrawal of the drug, then the main action of the drug it must be an antiexcitatory one.

The drugs that preceded or followed lithium in the prophylactic treatment of bipolar patients in the last forty years (neuroleptics, carbamazepine, valproate, Ca-channel blockers) all have a clear antimanic action and many important side effects are due to sedation.

Yet the scientific community finds it difficult to recognize that the mechanism of action of the present prophylactic treatments is an antiexcitatory one. One reason for that may be that psychiatrists, alike patients, tend to underestimate mania or hypomania. In the fifties it was named " the disappearing disease". Another reason may be that mixed depressive syndromes (28) that have the clinical picture of major depression respond to lithium and/or anticonvulsants treatments and the clinical impression is that the treatment had an antidepressant effect.

We think that the recognition of the antiexcitatory mechanism of action of our present prophylactic treatments would be a step ahead for research and clinical practice.

PRIMARY PROPHYLAXIS

Withdraw Sensation and the System falls asleep.
William Cullen, 1770

Recent epidemiological findings show an increase of prevalence and an earlier age of onset of affective disorders. Frequency of recurrences and bipolarity seem also increased.

Angst (5) writes: "The hypothesis of an actual rise in the frequency of such disorders seem to be justified. Whether the increase is spontaneous or drug-induced remains an open question".

There are general factors able to trigger affective episodes for the first time in predisposed person or trigger new recurrences.

We would like to draw attention to important changes in life habits and life style that have taken place after the second world war, especially in western countries, which ultimately activate the nervous system.

The consumption of alcohol, coffee, tea and caffeine-containing beverages has much increased. The use among the population of marijuana, cocaine and other stimulating drugs has widespread as well as anorectic agents and steroid (29).

Habit changes have led to late hours for amusement or work, or to reduction of sleeping hours. Thomas Wehr has shown clearly the crucial importance of sleep reduction in the genesis of mania (52, see also Gessa et al. this volume).

Flying over different time zones may also have precipitating effects. The increase rhythm of life with frequent peaks of hectic activity constitutes a major activating factors able to trigger manic-depressive cycles in many people.

Many factors attract one another. The heat and the sun of summer combined with the excitement of travelling and amusements and often with late hours of an intense night life is an example.

Akiskal focused on the interaction between temperament and life events and life style. Hyperthymic temperaments create more activities and cyclothymics more emotionally charged situations (3,4). It is of interest that people with these temperaments are emotionally very reactive and that all our prophylactic drugs attenuate the responsiveness to stimuli (see also Akiskal, this volume)

It seems an ironical play on words that the endogenous factor of affective disorders is based, at least in part, on great reactivity of these persons.

It is not impossible to eliminate or to reduce these factors, especially their combination. Summer manias represent a paradigmatic opportunity for this type of intervention. By doing so the effectiveness of prophylactic treatment increases and doses can be reduced to a minimum. Young persons of clear predisposition to affective disorder (temperament and/or family history) should be fully informed about the importance of these activating factors and how to avoid them.

It should be tried, in this way, to prevent the onset of the first episode.

Given the present limitation of our drug treatments, these efforts of a primary prophylaxis should be more investigated and applied more extensively.

Cullen's striking intuition should be the inspiring principle of the strategy that we like to call primary prophylaxis.

REFERENCES

1. Aagaard J and Vestergaard, Predictors of outcome in prophylactic lithium treatment: a 2-year prospective study. *Journal of Affective Disorders*, 1990, 18: 259-266
2. Abrams R ECT as prophylactic treatment for bipolar disorde. *Am J Psychiatry* 1990; 147: 373
3. Akiskal HS, Djenderejian AM, Rosenthal RH et al., Cyclothymic disorder: validating criteria for inclusion in the bipolar affective group. *Am J Psychiatry* 1977;134:1227-33.
4. Akiskal HS. Delineating irritable and hyperthymic variants of the cyclothymic temperament. *J Pers Dis* 1992;6:326-42.
5. Angst J. Switch from depression to mania - a record study over decades between 1920 and 1982. *Psychopatology*, 1985, 18: 140-154
6. Baldessarini RJ, Faedda GL, Tondo L, Suppes T, Tohen M: Pharmacological Treatment of Bipolar Disorder Throghout the Life-Cycle. In: Shulman K, Tohen M, Kutcher SP, eds. John Wiley & Sons, Inc, New York NY, 1995, in press
7. Bauer ME, Whybrow PC: Rapid cycling bipolar affective. II. Treatment of refractory rapid-cycling with high-dose levothyrowine: A preliminary study. *Arch Gen Psychiatry* 1990; 47: 427-440
8. Bauer MS, Refractoriness induced by lithium discontinuation despite adequate serum lithium levels. *Am J Psychiatry* 1994; 151:1522
9. Bowden CL, Brugger AM, Swann AC, Calabrese JR, Janicak PG, Petty F, et al: Efficacy of divalproex vs. lithium and placebo in the treatment of mania.

JAMA 1994; 271: 918-924

10. Calabrese JR, Woyshville MJ: Diagnosis and treatment of rapid-cycling bipolar disorder. *Directions in Psychiatry* 1994; 14(16): 1- 8
11. Calabrese JR. Personal communication, January 1995
12. Devanaud DP, Sackeim HA, Prudic J.: Electroconvulsive therapy in the treatment-resistant patient. *Psychiatr. Clin. North Am.* 1991, 14(4): 905-923
13. Dickson WE, Kendell RE:Does maintenance lithium therapy prevent occurences of mania under ordinary clinical conditions? *Psychol Med* 1986; 16: 521-530
14. Dubovsky SL: Calcium antagonists in manic-depressive illness. *Neuropsychobiology* 1993; 27: 184-192
15. Faedda GL, Baldessarini RJ, Tohen M, Strakowsky SM, Waternaux C: Episode sequence in bipolar disorder and response to lithium treatment. *Am J Psychiatry* 1991; 148: 1237-1239
16. Faedda GL, Tondo L, Baldessarini RJ, Suppes T, Tohen M: Outcome after rapid vs gradual discontinuation of lithium treatment in bipolar mood disorders. *Arch Gen Psychiatry* 1993; 50: 448-455
17. Falret JP: Le cours Cliniques de Medecine Mentale. Premiere Partie. JB Bailliere, Paris, 1854
18. Fink M. Personal communication, December 1994
19. Grof E, Haag M, Grof P, Haag H: Lithium response and the sequence of episode priorities: preliminary report on a Hamilton sample. *Prog Neuropsychopharmacol Biol Psychiatry* 1987; 11: 199-203
20. Haag H, Heidron A, Haag M, Griel W: Sequence of affective polarity and lithium response: preliminary report on Munich sample. *Prog Neuropsychopharmacol Biol Psychiatry* 1987; 11: 205-208
21. Harrow M, Goldberg JF, Grossman LS, Meltzer HY: Outcome in manic disorders: a naturalistic follow-up study. Arch Gen Psychiatry 1990; 47: 665-671
22. Jamison KR. In: Goodwin FK, Jamison KR eds. *Manic-Depressive Illness.* 1990; New York: Oxford University press
23. Johnson FN. The psychopharmacology of lithium. London: The MacMillan Press LTD;1984
24. Jope RS and Williams MB. Lithium and Brain Signal Transduction System. *Biochem. Pharmacol.* 1994, 47: 429-441
25. Karliner W. Maintenance ECT.*J Psychiatric Treatment and evaluation* 1980; 2: 313-4
26. Klein HE, Broucek B, Greil W: Lithium withdrawal triggers psychotic states. *Br J Psychiatry* 1981; 139: 255-256
27. Kukopulos A, Caliari B., Tundo A et al. Rapid Cyclers, temperament and antidepressants. *Comprehens. Psych.* 1983, 14-249-258.
28. Koukopoulos A., Faedda G., Proietti R., D'Amico S., De Pisa E., Simonetto C. Un sindrome dèpressif mixte. *L'Encephale*, 1992; XVIII: 19-21
29. Koukopoulos A, Tundo A, Floris GF, Reginaldi D, Minnai GP, Tondo L.

Changes in life habits that may influence the course of affective disorders. In Stefanis CS et al. *A world of perspective, Vol 1.* Elsevier Science Publishers BV; 1990 478-483

30. Kukopulos A, Reginaldi D: Recurrences of manic-depressive episodes during lithium treatment. In: Johnson FN, ed. *Handbook of lithium therapy*. Lancaster: MTP, 1980: 109-117
31. Kukopulos A, Reginaldi D, Laddomada P, Floris G, Serra G, Tondo L: Course of the manic-depressive cycle and changes caused by treatments. *Neuropsychopharmakologie*. 1980; 13: 156-167
32. Kukopulos A, Reginaldi D. Does lithium prevent depression by suppressing manias? *Int.Pharmacopsychiat.* 1973; 8: 152-8
33. Koukopoulos A, Tondo L, Minnai G. Les cycles rapides. In: Olie JP, loo H, Poirier MF. *Les maladies depressives.* Paris: Edition flammarion; 1995
34. Kraepelin E. *Klinische Psichiatrie.* Dritter Band II Teil. Verlag von J.A.Bart. Leipzig; 1913:1325
35. Lapierre YD, Gagnon A, Kokkinidis L: Rapid recurrence of mania following lithium withdrawal. *Biol Psychiatry* 1980; 15: 859-864
36. Maj M, Priozzi R, Kemali D: Long-term outcome of lithium prophylaxis in patients initially classified as a complete responders. *Psychopharmacology* 1989; 98: 535-538
37. Maj M, Priozzi R, Starace F: Previous pattern of course of illness as a predictor of response to lithium prophylaxis in bipolar patients. *J Affect Disord* 1989; 17: 237-241
38. Mander AJ: Prediction of rapid relapse following lithium discontinuation. *Irish J Psychol Med* 1989; 6: 23-25
39. Markar HR, Mander AJ: Efficacy of lithium prophylaxis in clinical practice. *Br J Psychiatry* 1989; 155: 496-500
40. Muller-Oerlinghause B, Muser-Causemann B, Volk : Suicides and parasuicides in high-risk patient group on and off lithium long-term medication. *J Affective Disord* 1992; 25: 261-270
41. O'Connel RA, Mayo JA, Flatow L, Cuthbertson B, O'Brien BE: Outcome of bipolar disorder on long-term treatment with lithium. *Br J Psychiatry* 1991; 159: 123-129
42. Post R, Leverich GS, Pazzaglia PJ, Mikalauskas K, Denicoff K: Lithium tolerance and discontinuation as pathways to refractoriness. In: Birch NJ, Padgham C, Hughes MS, eds. *Lithium in medicine and biology*. Carnforth: Marius Press, 1993: 71.
43. Rehm O. *Manisch-Melancholische Irresein*. Berlin: Verlag von Julius Springer; 1919: 108
44. Schou M.: Is there a lithium withdrawal syndrome? An examination of the evidence. *Br. J. Psychiatry* 1993, 163: 514-518
45. Schou M.: Lithium Prophylaxis: About 'Naturalistic' or 'Clinical Pratice' studies. *Lithium*, 1993, 4: 77-81
46. Small JG, Small IF, Moore DF: Experimental withdrawal of lithium in

recovered manic-depressive patients: A report of five cases. *Am J Psychiatry* 1971; 127: 1555-1558
47. Suppes T, Baldessarini RJ,Faedda GL, Tondo L. Tohen M: Discontinuing maintenance treatment in bipolar manic-depression: Risks and implications. *Harvard Rev Psychiatry* 1993; 1: 131-144
48. Suppes T, Baldessarini RJ,Faedda GL, Tondo L. Tohen M: Risk of recurrence following discontinuation of lithium treatment in bipolar disorder. *Arch Gen Psychiatry* 1991; 48: 1082-1088
49. Thase M. What's become of this good-prognosis illness? *Bipolar Conference WPIC,* 1994
50. Tondo L, Baldessarini RJ, Silvetti F, Tohen M, Rudas N: Suicidal behavior in manic-depressive patients with and without lithium maintenance treatment 1995;(*submitted*)
51. Vanelle JM, Loo H, Galinowski A, et al. Maintenance ECT in intractable manic-depressive disorders. *Convulsive Ther* 1994; 10: 195-205
52. Wehr TA, Sacks D., Rosenthal NE, Sleep Reduction as a Final Common Pathway in the Genesis of Mania *Am. J. of Psychiatry*, 1987, 144:2 201-204.
53. Wehr TA, Sacks D., Rosenthal NE, Cowdry RW, Rapid Cycling affective disorders contributing factors and treatment responses in 51 patients. *Am. J. of Psychiatry*, 1988, 145, 179-184.
54. Wilkinson DG: Difficulty in stopping lithium prophylaxis? *Br Med J* 1979; 1: 235-236

Index